The German Problem Transformed

Social History, Popular Culture, and Politics in Germany
Geoff Eley, Series Editor

The German Problem Transformed

Institutions, Politics, and Foreign Policy, 1945–1995

THOMAS BANCHOFF

Ann Arbor

THE UNIVERSITY OF MICHIGAN PRESS

2002   2001   2000   1999   4   3   2   1

A CIP catalog record for this book is available from the British Library.

Library of Congress Cataloging-in-Publication Data

Banchoff, Thomas, 1964–
     The German problem transformed : institutions, politics, and
foreign policy, 1945–1995 / Thomas Banchoff.
          p.   cm. — (Social history, popular culture, and politics in
Germany)
     Includes bibliographical references (p.   ) and index.
     ISBN 0-472-11008-X (acid-free paper)
     1. Germany—Politics and government—1990– 2. Germany
(West)—Foreign relations—Europe, Eastern.   3. Europe,
Eastern—Foreign relations—Germany (West)   4. Germany—Foreign
relations—1945– 5. Germany—Foreign relations—1990–   .
I. Title.   II. Series.
DD290.29   .B34   1998
327.43—dc21   98-58102
                                                                      CIP

To Anja

Contents

Preface

This book addresses the complex relationship between history and foreign policy in Germany. No country has had to struggle with as terrible a historical legacy. And in very few countries has the past—and efforts to grapple with it—left so great a mark on politics and policies. Does the international position of the new Germany resemble that of its unified, pre-1945 predecessor? Or does it have more in common with that of the old Federal Republic? How has reflection on the German catastrophe of national socialism shaped the direction of German foreign policy, before and after reunification? These questions raise broader analytical issues about the interaction between history, memory, politics, and policy—questions that political scientists have only begun to explore.

In grappling with these issues and working on this book, I have benefited from the help of many institutions and individuals. A two-year grant from the German Academic Exchange Service (DAAD) made possible a master's degree at the University of Bonn. As a doctoral candidate at Princeton, I conducted two years of research in Germany, where I profited greatly from the resources and generous assistance of the German Society for Foreign Policy (DGAP), the Konrad-Adenauer Foundation, the Friedrich-Ebert Foundation, and the Hanns-Seidel Foundation. A Robert Bosch Fellowship at the American Institute for Contemporary German Studies in Washington, D.C., gave me the opportunity to begin revisions of the dissertation in the spring of 1994. As an assistant professor at Georgetown, I made further revisions with the help of a 1996 Mellon Summer Grant and a two-month stay at the DGAP. I completed the manuscript as a James Bryant Conant Fellow on leave from Georgetown at Harvard's Minda de Gunzburg Center for European Studies in 1997–98.

Over this period many teachers and colleagues provided invaluable support. Eberhard Schulz, my master's advisor at the University of Bonn, awakened an interest in links between history and foreign policy. My doctoral advisor at Princeton, Richard Ullman, provided generous guidance and encouragement. And the other members of my dissertation commit-tee—Nancy Bermeo, Robert Gilpin, and Kathleen Thelen—made helpful suggestions for revision. Since coming to Georgetown and its Center for German and European Studies, I have benefited from the comments and suggestions of many colleagues, including Samuel Barnes, Andrew Ben-nett, Victor Cha, Lily Gardner Feldman, Gregory Flynn, Robert Lieber, Joseph Lepgold, Eusebio Mujal-Leon, George Shambaugh, and Angela Stent. At Harvard Andrei Markovits was a particularly wonderful source of advice and encouragement. Other colleagues who have commented on parts of the manuscript include Thomas Berger, Beverly Crawford, Helmut Hubel, Peter Katzenstein, Friedrich Kratochwil, Carl Lankowski, Andrew Moravcsik, William Paterson, Simon Reich, Thomas Risse, Michael Ross, Mitchell Smith, Volker Rittberger, and William Wohlforth. I am particu-larly indebted to Roger Chickering, Gunther Hellmann, David Morris, and Martin Rickmann, who read and critiqued the entire text.

My greatest intellectual and professional debt is to A. James McAdams, now of the University of Notre Dame. From the beginning of my doctoral research, he has proved a terrific teacher, advisor, and friend, always ready to read yet another draft of the manuscript, to offer incisive comments, and to provide moral support.

My thanks, too, to series editor Geoff Eley, for his excellent critical sug-gestions, and to Susan Whitlock and the rest of the team at the University of Michigan Press, for shepherding the manuscript expertly to publication.

Most of all, I want to thank my family for their love and support. My parents, Tom and Lynore, have provided continuous encouragement before, during, and after my many years in school. My wife, Anja, and our three daughters, Emma, Luisa, and Sophie, have made the last several, very busy, years a thorough joy. This book is dedicated to Anja, my com-panion in life.

A tragedy overshadowed the final stage of this project. Jill Hopper, who contributed the index, died suddenly of a pulmonary embolism. Jill was a longtime research and teaching assistant, a great friend and collaborator. She was a deeply generous person, a dedicated teacher, and a creative scholar. Jill's death is a painful loss. Her life remains a powerful inspiration.

List of Abbreviations

CDU   Christian Democratic Union
DP   Germany Party
CFSP   Common Foreign and Security Policy
CSCE   Conference on Security and Cooperation in Europe
CSU   Christian-Social Union
EDC   European Defense Community
EC   European Community
ECSC   European Coal and Steel Community
EMU   European Monetary Union
EPC   European Political Cooperation
EU   European Union
FDP   Free Democratic Party
INF   Intermediate-Range Nuclear Forces
MBFR   Mutual and Balanced Force Reduction talks
MLF   Multilateral Force
NATO   North Atlantic Treaty Organization
NPD   National Democratic Party of Germany
NPT   Non-Proliferation Treaty
OSCE   Organization for Security and Cooperation in Europe
PDS   Party of Democratic Socialism
SALT   Strategic Arms Limitation Talks
SDI   Strategic Defense Initiative
SED   Socialist Unity Party
START   Strategic Arms Reduction Talks
SNF   Short-Range Nuclear Forces
SPD   Social Democratic Party of Germany
WEU   West European Union

CHAPTER 1

Introduction: The German Problem Transformed

The new German Problem, this book argues, is not akin to the old. Many observers have underscored the reemergence of Germany as Europe's central power. After four decades of division, they contend, Germany is once again fully sovereign and faced with a fluid European constellation. Without the strictures of bipolarity, its leaders are free to define and pursue national interests in East and West. From this perspective the reunified Federal Republic of Germany (FRG) faces challenges not unlike those of its unified predecessor a century earlier. German leaders may, like Otto von Bismarck, pursue national interests judiciously within the European balance of power and enhance stability on the continent. Or they might, like Bismarck's successors, embrace an aggressive course that leads to isolation and disaster. This view of the German Problem yields a third prospect: the new Germany, still traumatized by the catastrophe of national socialism, may fail to assume leadership in Europe commensurate with its power.

This book rejects this formulation of the German Problem. It acknowledges post-reunification challenges, but argues that postwar changes, not prewar analogies, best illuminate them. The decades after 1945 transformed the contours of the German Problem. As the Federal Republic grew increasingly powerful, its leaders anchored it within an ever thicker web of international institutions. At the same time, its multilateral, supranational foreign policy came to rest on a solid domestic political foundation. As a result of this transformation, the Germany that emerged after the collapse of the German Democratic Republic (GDR) is neither fully sovereign nor faced with a fluid balance of power abroad. And its basic foreign policy orientation—integration within the West and engagement in the East—is the object of a broad consensus at home. The new German Problem concerns not power and national interests, but rather difficult choices at the intersection of international institutions and domestic politics.

The enduring transformation of German foreign policy is most evident at its critical postwar turning points. Against a historical backdrop of dictatorship, war, and genocide, successive postwar chancellors secured domestic support for deeper ties with international institutions. During the cold war of the 1950s Konrad Adenauer integrated the Federal Republic into the North Atlantic Treaty Organization (NATO) and the European Community (EC). Amid the detente of the 1970s Willy Brandt negotiated the Eastern Treaties and made the FRG part of the Conference on Security and Cooperation in Europe (CSCE). During the new cold war and Intermediate-Range Nuclear Forces (INF) crisis of the early 1980s Helmut Kohl strengthened German ties with NATO while preserving institutional links with the East. And during the post–cold war 1990s Kohl both embedded the new Germany within established European institutions and pressed to strengthen those institutions further. Reunification and the collapse of the postwar European order did radically change the context of FRG foreign policy. But they did not alter its contours. German power remained constrained by institutions abroad, and a multilateral, supranational foreign policy remained an object of consensus at home. The postwar transformation of the German Problem persisted.

The book's core argument underscores the twofold significance of history as a backdrop for post-reunification foreign policy. First, it illustrates the effects of path dependence. Over the past decade political scientists have explored the importance of critical historical junctures in shaping subsequent policy trajectories. Once in place, institutions often have the capacity to maintain political support and shape policy outcomes, outlasting the circumstances of their creation. Scholarship on the staying power of institutions—a core theme of "historical institutionalism" in political science—has focused almost exclusively on their domestic policy effects through time. The German case provides an important example of foreign policy path dependence. International institutions linking the Federal Republic with its neighbors, originally an object of political controversy, gradually secured broad domestic support. Together, interlocking institutions and political consensus sustained German foreign policy continuity across the 1990 divide.[1]

---

1. On historical institutionalism, see Sven Steinmo, Kathleen Thelen, and Frank Longstreth, eds., *Structuring Politics: Historical Institutionalism in Comparative Analysis* (Cambridge: Cambridge University Press, 1992). For an overview of the literature on path dependence, see Paul Pierson, "Path Dependence, Increasing Returns, and the Study of Politics," *Center for European Studies Working Paper Series,* 7.7 (1997). An exceptional treat-

The book's argument underscores the importance not only of history, but also of historical memory. Political scientists have explored the effects of memory almost exclusively in the context of historical analogies and decision making.[2] In the German case, reflection on the past and its implications has had broader political and policy implications. Cumulative post-1945 institutional changes constrained FRG policy as much as they did only in combination with a dominant historical narrative—one that contrasted prewar disasters and postwar achievements. Had they been determined, German leaders might have embarked on a more independent foreign policy after 1990. Instead, they construed multilateralism and supranationalism as breaks with a catastrophic prewar past and as necessary foundations for the post–cold war future. This post-reunification consensus narrative, itself contested over the postwar decades, reinforced the institutional constraints on the foreign policy of the new Germany. Whether or not Germany remains as committed to a multilateral, supranational orientation in the future will depend on unpredictable international and domestic political developments. But it will also depend on the evolution of German views of the past and its lessons.

Return of the Old German Problem?

The collapse of the Soviet bloc, reunification, and the receding U.S. presence in Europe sparked a revival of traditional formulations of the German Problem after 1990. While some observers evoked the specter of a "Fourth Reich," most intellectuals and academics drew less explosive parallels with the past.[3] Peter Glotz, for example, referred to Germany's precarious central position [*Mittellage*] and noted that the country might once

ment of critical junctures in international relations is G. John Ikenberry, "Constitutional Politics in International Relations," *European Journal of International Relations* 4, no. 2 (June 1998): 147–77.

2. A recent important exception is Andrei S. Markovits and Simon Reich, *The German Predicament: Memory and Power in the New Europe* (Ithaca: Cornell University Press, 1997). On analogies, see Yuen Foong Khong, *Analogies at War: Korea, Munich, Dien Bien Phu, and the Vietnam Decisions of 1965* (Princeton: Princeton University Press, 1992). The recent historical literature on the relationship between memory and politics is extensive. See, for example, Yael Zerubavel, *Recovered Roots: Collective Memory and the Making of Israeli National Tradition* (Chicago: University of Chicago Press, 1995); Herbert Hirsch, *Genocide and the Politics of Memory: Studying Death to Preserve Life* (Chapel Hill: University of North Carolina Press, 1995); John R. Gillis, ed., *Commemorations: The Politics of National Identity* (Princeton: Princeton University Press, 1994).

3. See, for example, Brian Reading, *The Fourth Reich* (London: Weidenfeld and Nicolson, 1995); Martin Walker, "Overstretching Teutonia: Making the Best of the Fourth Reich," *World Policy Journal* 12, no. 1 (spring 1995): 1–18; Walter Russell Mead, "The Once and Future Reich," *World Policy Journal* 7, no. 4 (autumn 1990): 593–638.

again prove "too weak to lead Europe, and too unwieldy to be integrated within it." Hans-Peter Schwarz wrote of the persistence of old "German Dilemmas" rooted in the country's power and geography. Arnulf Baring went even further, situating German leaders "back in precisely that central European position which, to say the least, they did not handle very successfully in the decades between 1871 and the end of the Third Reich." Timothy Garton Ash, wary of such direct parallels, nevertheless considered the new Federal Republic "closer to the challenges of the nineteenth-century *Mittellage* than the old Federal Republic had been."[4]

These and other authors evoked parallels with the dilemmas facing Germany and Europe between the founding of a unified German state in 1871 and its destruction in 1945.[5] In the years before World War I, German foreign policy lurched from judicious but assertive diplomacy under Bismarck to Wilhelm II's aggressive bluster and diplomatic isolation. In the years before World War II, Gustav Stresemann's careful efforts to rehabilitate Germany in both East and West gave way to Adolf Hitler's policy of aggressive expansionism. Against this historical backdrop Wilhelm Röpke defined the German Problem in 1945 as "the protection of Europe against Germany and of Germany against herself." A. J. P. Taylor, writing around the same time, posed the question: "How can the peoples of Europe be secured against repeated bouts of German aggression?"[6] Over the postwar decades, superpower dominance and Germany's division gradually defused concerns about German power, nationalism, and

---

4. Peter Glotz, *Die falsche Normalisierung: Die unmerkliche Verwandlung der Deutschen 1989 bis 1994* (Frankfurt am Main: Suhrkamp, 1994), 12; Hans-Peter Schwarz, "Das Deutsche Dilemma," in *Deutschlands neue Außenpolitik*, ed. Karl Kaiser and Hanns W. Maull (Munich: R. Oldenbourg, 1994), 1:81–97; Arnulf Baring, ed., *Germany's New Position in Europe: Problems and Perspectives* (Oxford: Berg, 1994), 9; Timothy Garton Ash, *In Europe's Name: Germany and the Divided Continent* (New York: Random House, 1993), 384.

5. See also Hans-Peter Schwarz, *Die Zentralmacht Europas. Deutschlands Rückkehr auf die Weltbühne* (Berlin: Siedler, 1994); Michael Stürmer, *Die Grenzen der Macht: Begegnung der Deutschen mit der Geschichte* (Berlin: Siedler, 1992); Gregor Schöllgen, *Die Macht in der Mitte Europas: Stationen deutscher Außenpolitik von Friedrich dem Großen bis zur Gegenwart* (Munich: Beck, 1992); Christian Hacke, *Weltmacht wider Willen: Die Außenpolitik der Bundesrepublik Deutschland* (Frankfurt am Main: Ullstein, 1993); Heinz Brill, *Geopolitik Heute. Deutschlands Chance?* (Frankfurt am Main: Ullstein, 1994). For an account that places less emphasis on continuity across the 1989–90 divide, see David Schoenbaum and Elizabeth Pond, *The German Question and Other German Questions* (New York: St. Martin's Press, 1996).

6. Wilhelm Röpke, *The Solution of the German Problem* (New York: G. P. Putnam's Sons, 1947), xiv; A. J. P. Taylor, *The Course of German History* (London: Hamilton, 1945), 8. Other influential postwar assessments included Gerhard Ritter, *The German Problem: Basic Questions of German Political Life, Past and Present* (Columbus: Ohio State University Press, 1965); Ludwig Dehio, *Germany and World Politics in the Twentieth Century* (New York: Knopf, 1959).

seesaw policy [*Schaukelpolitik*] between East and West.[7] Detente between the FRG and the GDR in the early 1980s sparked some renewed controversy about German national identity and the problem of national unity.[8] Only with the collapse of the Soviet bloc and reunification, however, did traditional anxieties about Germany's place in Europe emerge with any force.

Historians and political scientists in the 1990s did not uncritically embrace old formulations of the German Problem. More often than not, they acknowledged important differences between the pre-1945 and post-1990 periods: a shift in the principal dimension of German power, from military to economic; the eradication of German militarism and the establishment of a stable democracy; and the emergence of international institutions such as NATO and the EC as a context for German foreign policy. Most observers concurred that Germany was no longer in a position to pursue military hegemony; that its stable democracy all but precluded an aggressive foreign policy; and that European institutions provided a framework for international cooperation. John Mearsheimer, an American political scientist, did suggest that the more powerful Germany might someday again pose a military threat to its neighbors. But for almost all of his colleagues on both sides of the Atlantic, reunification did not presage a return to the aggressive nationalism and pervasive instability of the past. As Schwarz put it, "The German Dilemma is of course less explosive today than during the history of the German Reich."[9]

Nevertheless, for many political scientists and historians, the old German Problem resembled the new in two key respects—the prominence of German power and of German national interests. Schwarz, for example, maintained that the reunified Germany, like its unified predecessor a century earlier, had become Europe's "central power." For Gregor Schöllgen the Federal Republic's pivotal position made it "the great power in the middle of Europe." According to Michael Stürmer, the new configuration placed Germany at the "geostrategic crux" [*Bruchzone*] of Europe and

7. For reassessments of the German Problem within the context of bipolarity, see David Calleo, *The German Problem Reconsidered: Germany and the World Order, 1870 to the Present* (Cambridge: Cambridge University Press, 1978); Renata Fritsch-Bournazel, *Confronting the German Question: Germans on the East-West Divide* (Oxford: Berg, 1988).

8. See, for example, Andreas Hillgruber, *Die Last der Nation: Fünf Beiträge über Deutschland und die Deutschen* (Düsseldorf: Droste, 1984); Arno Klönne, *Zurück zur Nation? Kontroversen zu deutschen Fragen* (Cologne: Diedrichs, 1984); Eberhard Schulz and Peter Danylow, *Bewegung in der deutschen Frage? Die ausländischen Besorgnisse über die Entwicklung in den beiden deutschen Staaten* (Bonn: Europa Union Verlag, 1984).

9. Schwarz, "Das Deutsche Dilemma," 97; John J. Mearsheimer, "Back to the Future: Instability in Europe after the Cold War," *International Security* 15, no. 1 (summer 1990): 32–37.

confronted the country with "all the dangers that this situation always entailed, and always will entail." Baring, more explicit about the parallels between the post-1990 and pre-1945 constellations, evoked the heart of the old German Problem. The new Germany, he argued, remains "too weak and at the same time too strong; too weak to shape the continent and too strong to be easily accepted by its neighbors." And Kenneth Waltz suggested that "Germans may ultimately find that reunification and the renewed life of a great power are more invigorating than the struggles, complications, and compromises" of European integration.[10]

For these and other authors a focus on German power went hand in hand with an insistence on the renewed salience of "the nation" and "the national interest" for FRG foreign policy. After four decades of division Stürmer argued that Germany had again emerged as a normal, sovereign nation. For Schwarz the stream of German history had "left a very artificial system of canals" and "flowed once again into the river bed of the nation state proclaimed on January 18, 1871, in the Versailles Hall of Mirrors."[11] The reality of the nation, from this perspective, necessitated an embrace of the concept of the national interest. None of these authors pressed for a revival of nationalism. But they insisted that German leaders soberly assess the new power configuration and define and pursue objective German interests. Christian Hacke advocated the national interest as "the guiding principle" of FRG foreign policy. And for Stürmer "Germany's powerful position in the middle of Europe" implied "an obligation to embrace realism, clarity of goals, and predictability of means."[12]

The construal of the German Problem in terms of power and interests has roots in the "primacy of foreign policy" [*Primat der Außenpolitik*] tradition of German historiography and the realist tradition in the study of international relations. In the nineteenth and early twentieth centuries, leading German historians—Leopold von Ranke, Heinrich von Tre-

---

10. Schwarz, *Die Zentralmacht Europas;* Schöllgen, *Die Macht in der Mitte Europas,* 177; Stürmer, *Die Grenzen der Macht,* 247; Baring, *Germany's New Position in Europe,* 2; Kenneth N. Waltz, "The Emerging Structure of International Politics," *International Security* 18, no. 2 (autumn 1993): 71.

11. Michael Stürmer, "Deutsche Interessen," in Kaiser and Maull, *Deutschlands neue Außenpolitik,* 1:39–61; Schwarz, *Die Zentralmacht Europas,* 12–13. See also Gregor Schöllgen, "National Interest and International Responsibility: Germany's Role in World Affairs," in Baring, *Germany's New Position in Europe,* 35–49.

12. Christian Hacke, "Nationales Interesse als Handlungsmaxime für die Außenpolitik Deutschlands," in Kaiser and Maull, *Deutschlands neue Außenpolitik,* 3:3–13; Stürmer, "Deutsche Interessen," 40. On German interests, see also Arnulf Baring and Rupert Scholz, eds., *Eine neue deutsche Interessenlage? Koordinaten deutscher Politik jenseits von Nationalismus und Moralismus* (Cologne: Bachem, 1994); Wilfried von Bredow and Thomas Jäger, eds., *Neue deutsche Außenpolitik: Nationale Interessen in den internationalen Beziehungen* (Opladen: Leske and Budrich, 1993).

itschke and Friedrich Meinecke—examined Prussian and later German foreign policy in terms of power politics and state interests, *Machtpolitik* and *Staatsräson*.[13] They viewed states as legitimate political orders locked in a struggle for international power. And they considered leaders bound to pursue objective interests defined in terms of power—and to make foreign policy judgements shielded from domestic political pressures. This analytical approach survived both world wars and weathered a barrage of criticism during the 1960s and 1970s, continuing to inform much scholarship on the history of German foreign policy.[14] Over the same time, realist scholars of international relations, indebted to these scholars and to common intellectual progenitors—Thucydides, Hobbes, and Machiavelli—emerged as a dominant force within political science. After 1945 a German émigré, Hans Morgenthau, helped to establish realism as the leading approach to the study of international relations in the United States. Over the postwar decades a focus on power and interests informed much of the leading analysis of FRG foreign policy.[15]

The "primacy of foreign policy" and realist traditions, this book argues, obscure the enduring transformation of German foreign policy. A focus on Germany's reemergence as Europe's "central power" misses the continued prominence of institutions as a framework for post-reunification foreign policy. The new Germany remains embedded within an array of important multilateral and bilateral institutions, East and West—NATO, the EC, the Eastern Treaties, and the CSCE. These institutional constraints represent the cumulative effects of choices made at key postwar junctures. Membership in NATO and the EC, the upshot of Adenauer's policy of Western integration, served as a foundation for subsequent German foreign policy. The Eastern Treaties and the CSCE, cornerstones of Brandt's New Ostpolitik, added to that foundation. Kohl's strong align-

---

13. Writing between the wars, Friedrich Meinecke provided a comprehensive overview of this tradition. See Friedrich Meinecke, *Die Idee der Staatsräson in der neueren Geschichte* (Munich: R. Oldenbourg, 1957). Ludwig Dehio, a student of Meinecke, was an influential representative of this general approach after 1945. See Ludwig Dehio, *The Precarious Balance: Four Centuries of European Power Struggle* (New York: Knopf, 1962).

14. See, for example, Klaus Hildebrand, *Das vergangene Reich: Deutsche Außenpolitik von Bismarck bis Hitler 1871–1945* (Stuttgart: Deutsche Verlags-Anstalt, 1995); Andreas Hillgruber, *Deutsche Großmacht und Weltpolitik im 19. und 20. Jahrhundert* (Düsseldorf: Droste, 1977).

15. Hans J. Morgenthau, *Politics among Nations: The Struggle for Power and Peace* (New York: Knopf, 1948). For a "primacy of foreign policy" approach to the Federal Republic, see Wolfram F. Hanrieder, *Germany, America, Europe: Forty Years of German Foreign Policy* (New Haven: Yale University Press, 1989).

ment with the United States during the INF crisis strengthened the Atlantic Alliance as a context for German foreign policy in the 1980s. And reunification within European institutions, East and West, shaped the trajectory of German foreign policy in the years after 1990. Post-reunification foreign policy unfolded within a dense institutional configuration forged and maintained over the previous four decades—one that continued to limit the scope of German power and frame German foreign policy alternatives. The new Germany remained, in Peter Katzenstein's words, a "tamed power."[16]

This institutional constellation did not emerge unscathed from the European transformation of 1989–91: the dissolution of the Warsaw Pact and the disintegration of the Soviet Union. The collapse of the postwar bipolar order triggered significant changes in the external circumstances of German foreign policy. NATO and the EC embarked on internal reforms and expansion eastward, while the CSCE and the Eastern Treaties were reworked to accommodate the end of the East-West conflict. On balance, however, these changes signified a strengthening, not a weakening of the institutional configuration. The 1992 Treaty on European Union (EU), for example, committed European leaders to a common currency by the end of the decade and the creation of a Common Foreign and Security Policy (CFSP). By 1995, moreover, NATO had not only survived the collapse of the Soviet threat, but had also emerged as the core of a new all-European security architecture. Germany was not once again fully sovereign and confronted with a fluid balance of power. With the end of the GDR and reunification, Germans did gain full sovereignty over their internal affairs. But the new FRG, like the old, remained constrained by multilateral, supranational institutions in the exercise of its foreign policy.[17]

The continued salience of European institutions did not negate the reality of greater German power. With reunification, the addition of East German population and economic potential increased FRG capabilities compared with those of France and Britain. More important, the collapse of one superpower and retrenchment of another left Germany the single most influential country in Europe. Nevertheless, the characterization of

---

16. On institutions as a continuing framework for German foreign policy, see Peter J. Katzenstein, "United Germany in an Integrating Europe," in *Tamed Power: Germany in Europe,* ed. Peter J. Katzenstein (Ithaca: Cornell University Press, 1997), 1–48; Jeffrey J. Anderson and John B. Goodman, "Mars or Minerva? A United Germany in a Post–Cold War Europe," in *After the Cold War: International Institutions and State Strategies in Europe, 1989–1991,* ed. Robert O. Keohane, Joseph S. Nye, and Stanley Hoffmann (Cambridge: Harvard University Press, 1993), 23–62.

17. On institutional constraints on German sovereignty, see Helga Haftendorn, "Gulliver in der Mitte Europas. Internationale Verflechtung und nationale Handlungsmöglichkeiten," in Kaiser and Maull, *Deutschlands neue Außenpolitik,* 1:129–52.

Germany as Europe's "central power," evocative of earlier historical configurations, was misleading. Germany was not, as it had been before 1945, a sovereign state within a fluid international balance of power. By binding states to one another in qualitatively new ways, channeling conflict and encouraging cooperation, European institutions did more than provide a new context for the exercise of national power. They also helped to diffuse the effects of any national preponderance, enabling Germany to cooperate peacefully and productively with its neighbors on a variety of policy issues. After reunification, continued multilateralism within NATO and shared sovereignty within the EU underscored the break with the prewar period. German power continued to evoke concerns abroad, but not on a scale comparable to the earlier era.[18]

While realism's focus on power misses the prominence of international institutions for post-reunification foreign policy, its emphasis on interests obscures the centrality of domestic politics. The image evoked by the "primacy of foreign policy"—one of leaders dispassionately reflecting on and pursuing the national interest—does not capture the effects of politics, in the German case and others. The basic foreign policy orientation of the new Germany reflected a particular balance of domestic forces. The political consensus around a multilateral, supranational foreign policy, like the institutional constellation within which it developed, was the product of successive postwar critical junctures. Western integration was the object of a domestic political struggle, as was the New Ostpolitik and German policy amid the INF crisis. Each juncture pitted different leaders, parties, priorities, and historical perspectives against one another. On the eve of reunification these successive controversies had given way to a broad political consensus around the importance of a sharp break with the nationalism and militarism of the past—a consensus that persisted after 1990.[19]

Like international institutions, German domestic politics underwent significant changes after the end of the cold war. The East German revolution of 1989 and the rapid absorption of the GDR into the FRG the fol-

18. For a detailed discussion of post-reunification German power and perceptions of it across Europe, see Markovits and Reich, *German Predicament;* Gunther Hellmann, "The Sirens of Power and German Foreign Policy: Who Is Listening?" *German Politics* 6, no. 2 (August 1997): 29–57; Helmut Hubel and Bernhard May, *Ein "normales Deutschland"? Die souveräne Bundesrepublik in der ausländischen Wahrnehmung* (Bonn: Europa Union Verlag, 1995).

19. On domestic politics as a context for German foreign policy, see Jeffrey J. Anderson, "Hard Interests, Soft Power, and Germany's Changing Role in Europe, " in Katzenstein, *Tamed Power: Germany in Europe,* 80–107; Simon Bulmer, *The Domestic Structure of European Community Policy-Making in Germany* (New York: Garland, 1986); Gebhard Schweigler, *West German Foreign Policy: The Domestic Setting* (New York: Praeger, 1984).

lowing year altered the societal context of German politics. Through the mid-1990s, economic and social reconstruction in the GDR absorbed the political energies of the major German parties—the Christian Democrats (CDU/CSU), Social Democrats (SPD), Liberals (FDP), and the Greens. Reunification even added a new, small party to the German political spectrum, the former East German communists (PDS). In the context of the foreign policy debate, however, these domestic changes had little impact. The less influential parties, the Greens and the PDS, expressed some reservations about Western integration. Yet the ruling CDU/CSU-FDP coalition, as well as the SPD in opposition, continued to adhere to the broad consensus that had emerged by the late 1980s—around a German foreign policy both embedded in Western institutions and actively engaged in the East. While some differences persisted, no more national orientation or divisive domestic political debate ensued.[20]

The salience of domestic politics for German foreign policy does not render the concept of "interest" meaningless. The Federal Republic, like other states, pursued basic interests in security and prosperity—both before and after 1990. However, the concept "national interest," with its implication of an objective *raison d'état,* distorts the dynamics of post-reunification foreign policy. It obscures the fact that domestic political competition, more than dispassionate reflection, determined the direction of policy in the decades after 1945. All of foreign policy cannot be reduced to politics; the international context certainly shaped the struggle over German priorities within and across parties. But attention to politics illuminates the particular content of those priorities through time. Successive German leaders managed to secure domestic support for German participation in an increasingly intricate web of international institutions. Security and prosperity, so the emergent and enduring political consensus, were best pursued in close cooperation with Germany's neighbors. While reunification meant the reestablishment of a single German nation state, then, it did not mark the reemergence of an independent German national interest.[21]

20. On post-reunification developments, see Michael G. Huelshoff, Andrei S. Markovits, and Simon Reich, eds., *From Bundesrepublik to Deutschland: German Politics after Unification* (Ann Arbor: University of Michigan Press, 1993); Ralf Altenhof and Eckhard Jesse, eds., *Das wiedervereinigte Deutschland: Zwischenbilanz und Perspektiven* (Düsseldorf: Droste, 1995).

21. On this point, see Dieter Senghaas, "Was sind deutsche Interessen?" in *Politik ohne Projekt? Nachdenken über Deutschland,* ed. Siegfried Unseld (Frankfurt am Main: Suhrkamp, 1993), 463–91; "Deutschlands verflochtene Interessen," *Internationale Politik* 50, no. 8 (August 1995): 31–37.

Explaining the Transformation of the German Problem

For it to be persuasive, the book's overall argument about the interaction of institutions and politics in driving German foreign policy must not only trace but also *explain* its evolution since 1945. It must show how, at each postwar critical juncture, the existing institutional constellation actually constrained choices; how the political configuration reinforced those constraints; and how the choices made altered subsequent institutional and political constellations. Such a task, to be carried out effectively, requires attention to the broader contexts within which European institutions and German politics participated. The policy effects of institutions are only intelligible within a given international structure of states, power, and problems. And domestic contests over foreign policy are driven not only by the balance of contending forces, but also by the interplay of competing foreign policy ideas. Most foreign policy analysis focuses on some of these explanatory factors—structure, institutions, ideas, and politics—to the exclusion of others. In the German case, however, only a multidimensional explanatory strategy attentive to all four factors and their interaction can provide a persuasive account of each critical postwar juncture and establish the path-dependent effects of institutions and politics through time.

In keeping with this multidimensional strategy, each of the chapters begins with a sketch of German foreign policy at a particular juncture and then addresses four questions in turn: How did changes at the level of international structure generate new foreign policy challenges? How did international institutions frame policy alternatives? How did the foreign policy ideas articulated by leading politicians structure the foreign policy debate? How did the struggle for power within and among parties shape the course of foreign policy? One could, of course, organize the analysis around other explanatory factors: interest groups and the bureaucracy, for example, or the personalities of individual leaders. The rest of this chapter provides empirical and theoretical justification for a focus on structure, institutions, ideas, and politics, and shows how, taken together, they constitute an effective explanatory strategy.

Broad trends in international structure—the focus of the "primacy of foreign policy" and realist traditions—provide a starting point for the explanation of postwar German foreign policy.[22] Structure refers here to the international balance of economic and military power, the interests pur-

---

22. On structural approaches to international relations in the realist tradition, see Kenneth N. Waltz, *Theory of International Politics* (Reading, Mass.: Addison-Wesley, 1979); John J. Mearsheimer, "The False Promise of International Institutions," *International Security* 19, no. 3 (winter 1994–95): 5–49; Robert O. Keohane, ed., *Neorealism and Its Critics* (New York: Columbia University Press, 1986).

sued by other states, and the policy challenges generated by both in combination. From the outset, the Federal Republic was at the center of the
East-West conflict, and U.S.-Soviet rivalry in particular. An initial structural shift—the breakup of the Anti-Hitler Coalition and the onset of the
cold war—led to the division of Germany and the founding of two German states in 1949. Subsequent trends in East-West relations occasioned
critical junctures in postwar German foreign policy: the intensification of
the cold war in the 1950s, the emergence of detente in the 1960s and 1970s,
the new cold war of the 1980s, and the post–cold war of the 1990s. In each
case the international configuration confronted German leaders with new
policy challenges around the three related issues: military security,
national unity, and the German role between East and West.

Through the end of the cold war, military security issues revolved
around the perceived Soviet threat.[23] From its founding, the Federal
Republic was exposed to powerful Soviet military forces and dependent on
the U.S. conventional and nuclear deterrent. Both the Soviet deployments
in Central and Eastern Europe and the U.S. presence in the FRG placed
Bonn at the center of subsequent security controversies. Only five years
after World War II the intensification of the cold war moved the issue of
rearmament to the top of the German and European agenda. During the
late 1960s and early 1970s the trend toward East-West detente raised new
questions concerning the nature of the Soviet threat and the German role
in arms control. The new cold war of the early 1980s reached its climax
with the INF-crisis surrounding the proposed deployment of new U.S.
missiles on German soil. And during the early 1990s the end of the Soviet
threat coincided with a new security challenge for the FRG: whether and
how to participate in multilateral military operations outside NATO's
defensive perimeter.

Over the postwar period, major shifts in East-West relations also generated new problems around the issue of national unity.[24] From the outset
the Federal Republic upheld the goal of national unity—a commitment set
down in its 1949 constitution, the Basic Law. The intensification of the
cold war and the emergence of the rearmament issue during the early
1950s went hand in hand with a flurry of international diplomacy around
the issue of reunification. During the 1960s and 1970s the trend toward

23. For overviews of German security policy, see Helga Haftendorn, *Security and
Detente: Conflicting Priorities in German Foreign Policy* (New York: Praeger, 1985); Han-
rieder, *Germany, America, Europe,* chaps. 1–4; Cathleen McArdle Kelleher, *Germany and the
Politics of Nuclear Weapons* (New York: Columbia University Press, 1975).

24. On the evolution of the unity issue, see A. James McAdams, *Germany Divided:
From the Wall to Reunification* (Princeton: Princeton University Press, 1993); Garton Ash, *In
Europe's Name;* Hans Buchheim, *Deutschlandpolitik 1949–1972: Der politisch-diplomatische
Prozeß* (Stuttgart: Deutsche Verlags-Anstalt, 1984).

detente on the basis of the status quo of the German and European division confronted Bonn with a difficult dilemma: whether and how to recognize the reality of a second German state and the integrity of postwar borders without sacrificing the commitment to national unity. The INF struggle complicated FRG-GDR relations during the new cold war of the early 1980s, as each superpower demanded loyalty from its German ally. And the collapse of the Soviet bloc and the incorporation of the GDR into the Federal Republic in 1989–90 forced German leaders to define the role of a united Germany in a new Europe.

Broad changes in superpower relations also compelled FRG leaders to define their role between East and West at critical junctures.[25] The circumstances of the state's creation—a fusion of the United States, French, and British zones of occupation—left German leaders without an alternative to a basic Western orientation. For economic, political, and security reasons, Bonn cultivated good relations with Washington, Paris, and London over the postwar decades. At the same time, however, successive shifts in the international environment raised difficult questions about the nature of Western ties and their implications for Ostpolitik. During the cold war of the early 1950s, controversy centered on the terms and timing of Western integration and its implications for dialogue with the Soviet Union on reunification. The emergence of superpower detente in the late 1960s and early 1970s raised the problem of how to combine close ties with the allies and a more active Ostpolitik. During the INF struggle of the early 1980s, German leaders faced different ways to combine deterrence with the United States and detente with the Soviet Union. And in the 1990s they confronted the problem of how best to maintain solid ties with the West while addressing policy challenges in the East.

Attention to international structure constitutes a necessary but not sufficient step in the explanation of postwar German foreign policy. Structural analysis, applied in isolation, tends to be deterministic and inattentive to the existence of choice amid constraints. Given its position at the crux of superpower rivalry, the Federal Republic was sensitive to overall shifts in the international environment and their implications for military security, national unity, and the German role between East and West. At no point, however, did the East-West climate dictate the direction of FRG foreign policy. There was no self-evident way to respond to the policy challenges posed by shifts from cold war to detente, to the end of the cold war, and the collapse of the whole bipolar order. In order to explain those

---

25. On German relations with the superpowers, see Frank A. Ninkovich, *Germany and the United States: The Transformation of the German Question since 1945* (New York: Twayne Publishers, 1995); Michael J. Sodaro, *Moscow, Germany and the West from Khrushchev to Gorbachev* (Ithaca: Cornell University Press, 1990).

responses, the analysis must move beyond international structure to an assessment of the particular institutional constellations that framed German choices.[26]

The importance of institutions—an enduring theme in international relations theory—is particularly evident in the case of postwar German foreign policy.[27] Institutions were not a completely new context for German foreign policy after 1945. After unification, in 1871, and increasingly after 1918, German policy evolved in the context of bilateral and multilateral accords, from Bismarck's complex diplomatic arrangements, to the Treaty of Versailles and the League of Nations. After World War II, however, international institutions proved a more extensive and effective framework for German foreign policy. Globally, German foreign policy unfolded within the context of the United Nations and U.S.-sponsored monetary and trade regimes. In Europe, the focus of this book, three sets of institutions molded German choices at successive critical junctures—the Three- and Four-Power regimes; NATO and the EC; and the Eastern Treaties and the CSCE.

The Three- and Four-Power regimes had their roots in the wartime diplomacy of the Anti-Hitler Coalition.[28] After unconditional surrender in 1945 the Four Powers—the United States, the Soviet Union, Britain and France—placed German territory east of the Oder-Neisse Rivers under Polish administration and assumed legal responsibility for matters relating to Germany as a whole and the status of Berlin. During the early years of the Federal Republic this Four-Power regime existing alongside a Three-Power regime, which endowed the Western powers with ultimate responsibility for FRG foreign policy. When Bonn regained its sovereignty within NATO in 1955, the Three-Power regime dissolved. The Four-Power regime, however, persisted until reunification in 1990. During the early

---

26. On the inadequacy of realist analysis, particularly after reunification, see Volker Rittberger and Frank Schimmelfennig, "Deutsche Außenpolitik nach der Vereinigung: Realistische Prognosen auf dem Prüfstand," *Tübinger Arbeitspapiere zur internationalen Politik und Friedensforschung,* no. 28 (1997).

27. On international institutions, see Robert O. Keohane and Lisa L. Martin, "The Promise of Institutionalist Theory," *International Security* 20, no. 1 (summer 1995): 39–51; Robert O. Keohane, *International Institutions and State Power: Essays in International Relations Theory* (Boulder: Westview, 1989); John Gerard Ruggie, ed., *Multilateralism Matters: The Theory and Praxis of an Institutional Form* (New York: Columbia University Press, 1993).

28. On the emergence of the Three-Power regime, see Theodor Eschenburg, *Jahre der Besatzung 1945–1949* (Stuttgart: Deutsche Verlags-Anstalt, 1983). On the evolution of the Four-Power regime, see Philip Zelikow and Condoleezza Rice, *Germany Unified and Europe Transformed: A Study in Statecraft* (Cambridge: Harvard University Press, 1995), chap 2.

1950s it framed East-West discussions on the unity issue. After the integration of both German states into opposing alliances, it lay dormant—apart from efforts to manage affairs in Berlin. Over the postwar decades, the Four-Power regime precluded a unilateral FRG policy aimed at reunification or revision of the Oder-Neisse border. The German approach to the national unity and border issues, a source of disaster during the interwar period, unfolded within a restrictive institutional framework.

A second set of institutions, NATO and the EC, became a central part of the context of German foreign policy from the early 1950s onward.[29] In 1951 the Federal Republic was a founding member of the European Coal and Steel Community (ECSC), the core of an emergent European Community. In 1955 it joined NATO. Both Western institutions placed constraints on German foreign policy in subsequent decades. Membership in the EC committed the FRG to the creation of a common market and ruled out a return to the protectionist foreign economic policies of the past. At the same time, membership in the multilateral military alliance—as well as the German renunciation of a national general staff and a national nuclear arsenal—precluded the pursuit of a unilateral security policy. Both the EC and NATO evolved over time as the East-West climate shifted from confrontation to cooperation and back. But both institutions continued to frame German approaches to shifting policy problems—before and after reunification.

A third set of institutions, the Eastern Treaties and the CSCE, became an additional framework for German foreign policy beginning in the 1970s.[30] The Moscow, Warsaw, and Basic Treaties—bilateral accords with the Soviet Union, Poland and the GDR in 1970–72—forged a new institutional foundation for Ostpolitik. The CSCE Final Act of 1975, which outlined areas for East-West economic, political and security cooperation, created a further multilateral framework for German foreign policy. With the Eastern Treaties and through participation in the CSCE, Bonn recognized the reality of the division of Europe and Germany, but held open the prospect of reunification at some point in the future. German commit-

---

29. On NATO and the EC as contexts for German foreign policy, see Stanley Hoffmann, *The European Sisyphus: Essays on Europe, 1964–1994* (Boulder: Westview, 1995); Simon Bulmer and William Paterson, *The Federal Republic of Germany and the European Community* (London: Allen and Unwin, 1987).

30. On the Eastern Treaties and the CSCE as a framework for German foreign policy, see Garton Ash, *In Europe's Name;* William E. Griffith, *The Ostpolitik of the Federal Republic of Germany* (Cambridge: MIT Press, 1978); Angela Stent, *From Embargo to Ostpolitik: The Political Economy of West German–Soviet Relations* (Cambridge: Cambridge University Press, 1981).

ments to recognize existing borders—and regimes—constituted a new starting point for Ostpolitik. The Eastern Treaties and the CSCE, like NATO and the EC, evolved over the decades that followed. After the collapse of the Soviet bloc, they lost some of their salience. In renegotiated form, however, they continued to provide an institutional framework for relations with Russia and Central and Eastern Europe.

Bringing in institutions provides a necessary supplement to structural analysis. While shifts in the overall international environment confronted German leaders with policy challenges, particular arrays of institutions framed their choices. But even attention to institutions cannot explain the content of those choices. At all four postwar junctures, ambiguity within and across institutions left German leaders with some freedom of action. The constraints posed by the different institutions linking the Federal Republic with its neighbors, East and West, often pulled German leaders in different directions. At the same time, particular institutional norms such as multilateralism and supranationalism were open to widely varying interpretations. How should the Federal Republic respond to the alternatives posed by the institutional constellation? Exactly how multilateral and supranational should its foreign policy be? German answers to these questions are best analyzed at the national level of analysis.

At each postwar turning point, contrasting foreign policy ideas structured the political struggle over German foreign policy.[31] Different perceptions of international realities and the lessons of the past informed different foreign policy priorities. Here, the analytical focus is those priorities espoused by top rivals for the chancellorship, the leaders of the CDU/CSU and the SPD. The views of many other people clearly mattered as well: other Christian Democrats and Social Democrats, leaders of the FDP and other small parties, bureaucratic officials, interest group leaders, and policy intellectuals. Moreover, the priorities of leading contenders for national leadership had complex sources. They grew out of complex processes of socialization and interaction with different kinds of elites in German society and abroad. A detailed examination of the origins of foreign policy ideas would have to trace those processes. Here, however, the analytical focus is the substance of the foreign policy debate, not its origins. A focus

---

31. Scholarship on foreign policy ideas includes Judith Goldstein and Robert O. Keohane, eds., *Ideas and Foreign Policy: Beliefs, Institutions, and Political Change* (Ithaca: Cornell University Press, 1993); Albert S. Yee, "The Causal Effects of Ideas on Policies," *International Organization* 50, no. 1 (winter 1996): 69–108; Markus Jachtenfuchs, "Ideen und internationale Beziehungen," *Zeitschrift für internationale Beziehungen* 2, no. 2 (1995): 417–43. Earlier work includes Richard Little and Steve Smith, eds., *Belief Systems and International Relations* (Oxford: Basil Blackwell, 1988).

on major rivals for the chancellorship isolates the priorities that mattered most—those that gave the domestic debate its contours and were most likely to shape the direction of foreign policy in practice.

Different analyses of the international configuration underpinned the contrasting priorities espoused by CDU/CSU and SPD rivals: Adenauer and Kurt Schumacher in the early 1950s; Kurt Georg Kiesinger and Brandt in the late 1960s; Kohl and Helmut Schmidt in the early 1980s; and Kohl and Rudolf Scharping in the early 1990s. In each of these cases, perceptions of the international configuration tended to diverge along two dimensions—the power and intentions of other states, and the relative prominence of different institutions. Christian Democratic leaders, for example, usually professed greater concern about Soviet military strength and expansionist aims, while SPD leaders were more likely than their CDU/CSU counterparts to be critical of U.S. power and intentions. Social Democratic leaders tended to focus on the Eastern Treaties as a salient institutional framework for German foreign policy, while CDU/CSU leaders were more likely than their SPD counterparts to stress the absolute centrality of NATO and the EC. These priorities diverged more at some times than at others. At every postwar turning point, however, they situated the FRG in different ways within an international constellation marked by some degree of ambiguity and openness.[32]

Contrasting historical narratives—interpretations of the past and its significance for the present—also shaped assessments of the German policy alternatives.[33] Historical memory often informs foreign policy controversies to one degree or another. In the case of the Federal Republic, the experience of the catastrophe of national socialism allowed historical narratives a particularly broad impact on the policy debate. Rivals for the chancellorship tended toward agreement on two broad themes—that prewar German foreign policy represented a disaster to be left behind; and that postwar German foreign policy constituted a positive legacy to be sustained into the future. On this common foundation, however, party leaders often articulated contrasting historical narratives with divergent prescriptive implications. Christian Democrats, for example, more often drew links between the legacy of Nazism and the imperative of Western integration, while Social Democrats were most likely to posit connections

32. On the range of German foreign policy ideas after reunification, see Gunther Hellmann, "Goodbye Bismarck? The Foreign Policy of Contemporary Germany," *Mershon International Studies Review* 40 (1996): 1–39.

33. On historical narrative, see Hayden White, *The Content of the Form: Narrative Discourse and Historical Representation* (Baltimore: Johns Hopkins University Press, 1987); Paul Ricoeur, *Time and Narrative,* vol. 1 (Chicago: University of Chicago Press, 1984); Donald Polkinghorne, *Narrative Knowing and the Human Sciences* (Albany: State University of New York Press, 1988).

between Hitler's war and the imperative of a "peace policy" toward the East. And, while CDU/CSU leaders highlighted Adenauer's Western integration as a positive historical legacy, SPD leaders later placed somewhat more emphasis on Brandt's New Ostpolitik. In the German context, historical narratives tended to shape national responses to the international configuration of power and institutions.[34]

Successive political debates about the implications of history for German foreign policy evolved alongside several highly charged historiographical controversies. In the aftermath of World War II most leading historians in the FRG clung to a national conservative perspective. While critical of Hitler and national socialism, they still considered Bismarck's Reich—and the imperative of national unity—a point of orientation for postwar Germany. This orthodoxy, at odds with Adenauer's focus on Western integration and Brandt's drive for reconciliation with the East, came under sharp attack in the 1960s. Fritz Fischer and his allies were much more critical of Bismarck's legacy: they posited lines of continuity between the autocratic structures of the Reich, the outbreak of war in 1914, and Hitler's war of aggression three decades later. While problematic in many respects, the thesis of a negative "special path" [*Sonderweg*] from Bismarck to Hitler had a clear policy implication—that Germans should break with their nationalist, militarist past and embrace reconciliation, peace, and cooperation with their neighbors, East and West. During the 1980s and 1990s more nationally oriented historians, eager to resurrect Bismarck's Reich and the "national interest" as points of reference for the Federal Republic, attacked the "special path" thesis. But their calls for a more self-confident, power-conscious, and independent German foreign policy had little impact on the political debate within and across the parties.[35]

Attention to foreign policy ideas provides an important supplement to analysis centered at the level of the international system. While structural shifts and institutional configurations constrained German foreign policy at successive junctures, they also allowed for a significant range of choice. Given the existence of alternatives, foreign policy priorities—the way that German leaders situated the Federal Republic with respect to policy challenges—had a significant impact. Those priorities were con-

---

34. Thomas Banchoff, "Historical Memory and German Foreign Policy: The Cases of Adenauer and Brandt," *German Politics and Society* 14, no. 2 (summer 1996): 36–53; "German Policy towards the European Union: The Effects of Historical Memory," *German Politics* 6, no. 1 (April 1997): 60–76.

35. For an overview of postwar historiographical controversies, see Stefan Berger, *The Search for Normality: National Identity and Historical Consciousness in Germany since 1800* (Berghahn: Providence, 1997), chaps. 3–4.

tested, to differing degrees, over the entire postwar period. Rivals for national leadership articulated contrasting potential foreign policy paths rooted in divergent perceptions of the international configuration and the lessons of the past. While ideas mattered, however, only those with adequate political support shaped the direction of German foreign policy in practice. A persuasive explanatory strategy must therefore address the political dynamics that favored some policy priorities over others.

In order to explain the course of postwar FRG foreign policy, one has to trace the political struggle for control of authoritative political institutions.[36] In the German context the office of the chancellor is the crucial prize. The Basic Law of 1949 relegates the German presidency to symbolic status; invests the chancellor with the power to select a cabinet and set overall policy guidelines; and includes a "constructive vote of no confidence"—the provision that the lower house of parliament, the Bundestag, can only topple a chancellor if it can also agree on a successor. Despite these sources of strength, the "chancellor democracy" label is somewhat misleading. In order to maintain power and implement policies, chancellors face three ongoing tests at the level of party politics. First, because the office is not directly elected, chancellors must win and hold the support of their own parliamentary parties. Second, because the primarily proportional electoral system makes single party majorities difficult, chancellors must maintain the support of smaller coalition parties in the Bundestag. Third, even when a majority is securely in place, opposition parties can sometimes impede the implementation of foreign policy through recourse to two powerful institutions—the Constitutional Court and the Federal Chamber, the Bundesrat.[37]

---

36. On domestic politics and foreign policy, see Andrew Moravcsik, "Taking Preferences Seriously: A Liberal Theory of International Politics," *International Organization* 51, no. 4 (autumn 1997): 513–53; Peter B. Evans, Harold K. Jacobson, and Robert D. Putnam, eds., *Double-Edged Diplomacy: International Bargaining and Domestic Politics* (Berkeley and Los Angeles: University of California Press, 1993); Robert D. Putnam, "Diplomacy and Domestic Politics: The Logic of Two-Level Games," *International Organization* 42, no. 3 (summer 1988): 427–60. Earlier work in this vein includes James N. Rosenau, ed., *Domestic Sources of Foreign Policy* (New York: Free Press, 1967).

37. On "chancellor democracy," see Stephen Padgett, ed., *Adenauer to Kohl: The Development of the German Chancellorship* (London: Hurst, 1994); Karlheinz Niclauß, *Kanzlerdemokratie: Bonner Regierungspraxis von Konrad Adenauer bis Helmut Kohl* (Stuttgart: W. Kohlhammer, 1988). On the German party system and its policy effects across a range of issue areas, see Peter J. Katzenstein, *Policy and Politics in West Germany: The Growth of a Semisovereign State* (Philadelphia: Temple University Press, 1987). For a political history of the Federal Republic, see Dennis C. Bark and David R. Gress, *A History of West Germany,* 2 vols. (Oxford: Blackwell, 1988).

Given these constraints, the implementation of foreign policy at all four postwar junctures required success at three levels of party competition. First, prospective chancellors had to anchor their priorities within one of the two major parties. The CDU/CSU, founded after World War II, gathered centrist and pro-democratic conservative forces under one banner. And the SPD, which traced its existence back to the Kaiserreich, occupied the Left-Center of the political spectrum. In both parties—hierarchical, mass-based organizations—chairpersons were generally best placed to claim to the chancellor candidacy in the run-up to national elections, usually held every four years. In order to become chancellor and implement particular priorities, CDU/CSU and SPD leaders not only had to anchor their priorities within their party organizations. Before and after winning office, they also had to maintain the support of their parliamentary groups, a task that often proved difficult. In the case of the CDU the semi-autonomous status of the Bavarian Christian-Social Union (CSU) complicated contests for party leadership. During the 1970s, for example, then CSU leader Franz Josef Strauss, a foreign policy hardliner, challenged Kohl for the national Christian Democratic leadership—ultimately without success.[38]

A second, necessary task for the implementation of particular foreign policy priorities was success at the level of coalition politics. The failure of any party to win an outright Bundestag majority—with the exception of the CDU/CSU in 1957—obliged Christian Democrats and Social Democrats to seek coalitions with smaller parties, and the Liberals in particular. The Free Democratic Party secured the 5 percent of the vote necessary for representation in the Bundestag in every postwar election, enabling it to form a ruling coalition with one of the major parties over most of the postwar decades. For CDU/CSU and SPD leaders, who only ruled together during the Grand Coalition of 1966–69, forging and maintaining coalitions with the FDP required agreement on basic foreign policy matters—especially as the Liberals made control of the foreign ministry a precondition for a governing alliance after 1969. While secure leadership atop one of the major parties was a first step toward the implementation of foreign

---

38. On the CDU/CSU and the SPD, see Geoffrey Pridham, *Christian Democracy in Western Germany: The CDU/CSU in Government and Opposition, 1945–1976* (London: Croom Helm, 1977); Hans-Otto Kleinmann, *Geschichte der CDU 1945–1982* (Stuttgart: Deutsche Verlags-Anstalt, 1993); Gerard Braunthal, *The German Social Democrats since 1969: A Party in Power and Opposition* (Boulder: Westview, 1994); Susanne Miller and Heinrich Potthoff, *Kleine Geschichte der SPD: Darstellung und Dokumentation 1848–1983* (Bonn: Verlag Neue Gesellschaft, 1983). The CSU has its own party organization but has formed a single parliamentary group with the CDU since the 1950s. See Alf Mintzel, *Die CSU: Anatomie einer konservativen Partei 1945–1972* (Opladen: Westdeutscher Verlag, 1975).

policy priorities, the creation and maintenance of an alliance with the Liberals was a second. This, too, often proved extremely difficult.[39]

A final political task crucial for the implementation of foreign policy priorities concerned relations between the major parties. At critical postwar turning points, foreign policy issues often figured prominently in the national election campaigns that pitted the chancellor candidates of the CDU/CSU and SPD against each other. But, even after the successful formation of a ruling coalition, chancellors sometimes had to overcome opposition resistance to their foreign policies. From the cold war 1950s through the post–cold war 1990s, the party in opposition periodically challenged the direction of foreign policy in several different ways: by wooing individual deputies from the coalition parties; questioning the conformity of foreign policy with the Basic Law; wielding majorities in the Bundesrat; or mobilizing extraparliamentary opposition. Adenauer's Western integration, Brandt's New Ostpolitik, Kohl's INF policy and his post-reunification foreign policy all met and eventually overcame at least one such form of opposition.

Adenauer, Brandt, and Kohl managed to place their foreign policy priorities on a solid domestic foundation only after prolonged partisan struggles. The course of those struggles, and their attendant compromises, shaped German foreign policy in practice. In order to explain the foreign policy of the Federal Republic, then, one must trace the political conflict over its implementation. Attention to domestic politics in isolation cannot provide an adequate account. Other dimensions of the explanatory strategy employed here capture the forces that framed the political struggle: the problems generated by the international environment; the alternatives posed by the institutional constellation; and the priorities articulated by party leaders. Only in combination with structure, institutions, and foreign policy ideas can domestic politics contribute to a persuasive account of German foreign policy at key postwar turning points.[40]

The structured analysis carried out in each chapter allows for a systematic comparison of the critical junctures—a task undertaken in the conclusion. That comparison establishes the book's core argument about path dependence. It shows how institutional and political configurations, once in place, influenced subsequent foreign policy choices, before and after reunification. There was nothing inevitable about the postwar path of German foreign

---

39. On the FDP, see Peter Lösche and Franz Walter, *Die FDP: Richtungsstreit und Zukunftszweifel* (Darmstadt: Wissenschaftliche Buchgesellschaft, 1996).

40. On the reciprocal effects of international structure on domestic politics, see Peter Gourevitch, "The Second Image Reversed: The International Sources of Domestic Politics," *International Organization* 32, no. 4 (autumn 1978): 881–912.

policy and its continuity across the 1990 divide. At no critical juncture did the international constellation dictate foreign policy choices. Political forces and foreign policy ideas pushed FRG foreign policy in some directions rather than others. Efforts to predict the German future, the book concludes, must acknowledge both the contingency of the past and the salience of historical memory in the Federal Republic. Whether or not the new Germany continues to embrace multilateralism and supranationalism will depend not only on international and domestic political developments, but also on German views of history and its policy implications.

CHAPTER 2

The Cold War and
Western Integration

German foreign policy underwent a startling transformation during the decade after World War II. The Four Powers—the United States, the Soviet Union, Britain, and France—defeated and occupied Germany in 1945. In May 1949 the three Western powers combined their zones of occupation, encompassing most of the country's prewar territory and population, to form the Federal Republic. Only five years later, the FRG regained its sovereignty as a member of NATO and the nascent European Community. Chancellor Konrad Adenauer's policy of Western integration marked a sharp break with the tradition of seesaw diplomacy between East and West. Bonn did not abandon the goal of national unity or rule out dialogue with Moscow. But integration within the Atlantic Alliance and the EC marked a new point of departure for Ostpolitik. In the mid-1950s, only a decade after war's end, German foreign policy rested on a new institutional foundation.[1]

The first postwar German government, formed in September 1949, quickly moved to anchor the Federal Republic in Western institutions. Upon taking office, Adenauer immediately pressed for German membership in the newly formed Council of Europe. A deliberative body without any formal powers, the Council brought together parliamentarians from across Western Europe committed to the ideal of European unity. With

---

1. On German foreign policy during the Adenauer era, see Konrad Adenauer, *Erinnerungen,* 4 vols. (Stuttgart: Deutsche Verlags-Anstalt, 1965–68); Waldemar Besson, *Die Außenpolitik der Bundesrepublik: Erfahrungen und Maßstäbe* (Munich: Piper, 1970). For overviews of relevant primary and secondary sources, see Klaus A. Maier and Bruno Thoss, eds., *Westintegration, Sicherheit und deutsche Frage: Quellen zur Außenpolitik in der Ära Adenauer* (Darmstadt: Wissenschaftliche Buchgesellschaft, 1994); Anselm Doering-Manteuffel, ed., *Adenauerzeit: Stand, Perspektiven und methodische Aufgaben der Zeitgeschichtsforschung (1945–1967)* (Bonn: Bouvier, 1993).

the support of the Western powers, who retained ultimate sovereignty over FRG foreign policy through 1955, Bonn joined the Council in July 1950. French leaders considered the matter of Council membership an extension of their policy toward the Saar, a disputed area on the Franco-German border. They calculated that separate FRG and Saar delegations to the Council would strengthen their efforts to secure the region's political independence from Bonn. U.S. and British leaders supported German membership for different reasons—in order to shore up the FRG's new democratic institutions and contribute to overall Western unity amid the emergent cold war.[2]

During the course of 1950 the German government supplemented the largely symbolic step of FRG membership in the Council of Europe with support for two more far-reaching French initiatives: the ECSC and the European Defense Community (EDC). French Foreign Minister Robert Schuman proposed the European Coal and Steel Community in May 1950. Conceived by the chief architect of postwar French economic policy, Jean Monnet, the project called for the reorganization of two key West European industrial sectors under a single supranational authority. Both Monnet and Schuman were committed to the ideal of European unity. From their perspective, however, the ECSC also promised tangible benefits: a spur to France's economic recovery and some leverage over heavy industry in the Ruhr basin, the backbone of successive German war efforts. The United States, eager to spur economic recovery in Western Europe and to assuage French security concerns, backed the project. In April 1951 the Federal Republic and France, together with Italy and the Benelux countries, became founding members of the ECSC. Britain, supportive of the process of European integration but jealous of its sovereignty, opted not to join.[3]

The German government also backed a more ambitious initiative for supranational integration, the EDC. Outlined by French Defense Minister René Pleven in October 1950, the proposal envisioned German rearmament within the context of an integrated Western European force. From the perspective of Paris, London, and Washington, the EDC made sense for two reasons. It both promised to strengthen the Western alliance

---

2. The Saar finally voted in a 1956 referendum to become part of the FRG. See Jacques Freymond, *The Saar Conflict, 1945–1955* (New York: Praeger, 1960). On links between the Saar and Council of Europe controversies, see Hans-Peter Schwarz, *Die Ära Adenauer: Gründerjahre der Republik 1949–57* (Stuttgart: Deutsche Verlags-Anstalt, 1981), 86–96.

3. On the ECSC, see John Gillingham, *Coal, Steel, and the Rebirth of Europe, 1945–1955: The Germans and French from Ruhr Conflict to Economic Community* (Cambridge: Cambridge University Press, 1991); Klaus Schwabe, ed., *Die Anfänge des Schuman-Plans 1950–51* (Baden-Baden: Nomos, 1988).

against a possible Soviet threat and to provide a framework for FRG rearmament that ruled out a revival of German militarism. In May 1952 all six ECSC governments endorsed the EDC Treaty. That same month the Federal Republic and the three Western powers signed the Bonn Conventions, which granted German sovereignty within the context of an integrated West European military force. Over the next two years, however, a drawn-out ratification struggle in France delayed the implementation of EDC. Despite overt pressure from the United States—Secretary of State John Foster Dulles warned of an "agonizing reappraisal" of the U.S. commitment to Europe should the project collapse—the French ratification debate dragged through 1953 and on into 1954.[4]

As long as the terms of German integration within the Western alliance were unresolved, Adenauer pursued a confrontational policy toward the East. The Federal Republic refused to recognize the creation of the GDR in the Soviet zone of occupation in October 1949 and staked its international claim to represent all Germans [*Alleinvertretungsanspruch*]. Adenauer subsequently dismissed Soviet security concerns in connection with German rearmament. And the German government flatly rejected Soviet leader Josef Stalin's March 1952 offer of reunification in exchange for neutrality as an insincere, transparent effort to torpedo German rearmament and drive a wedge between Bonn and Western capitals. As the EDC ratification controversy wore on, Adenauer's government remained skeptical of international negotiations on the unity issue and insisted instead on the absolute priority of rearmament within the West. Only as part of a united Western front, the chancellor insisted, should Bonn support dialogue with Moscow on the issue of reunification.[5]

The final terms of German integration into the alliance had to wait until the fall of 1954. After a series of divisive debates, the French National Assembly finally rejected the EDC in August 1954. The foundation of Adenauer's proposed policy of Western integration had collapsed. Over the next two months, however, U.S., British, and German leaders managed to set up an alternative framework for German rearmament. British Foreign Minister Anthony Eden proposed that the Federal Republic join both NATO and the Brussels Pact, a Western European alliance founded in 1948. Dulles and Adenauer greeted the proposal and French leaders

---

4. On German security policy during this period, see Roland G. Foerster et al., *Anfänge westdeutscher Sicherheitspolitik: 1945–1956,* 4 vols. (Munich: R. Oldenbourg, 1982–97). On the diplomacy of EDC, see Rolf Steininger, "John Foster Dulles, the European Defense Community, and the German Question," *John Foster Dulles and the Diplomacy of the Cold War,* ed. Richard H. Immerman (Princeton: Princeton University Press, 1990), 79–108.

5. For Adenauer's approach to the Stalin Note and relations with the Moscow, see Adenauer, *Erinnerungen,* 2:63–131.

went along—with somewhat less enthusiasm. At the Paris Conference of October 1954, Adenauer pledged to create a German army and to renounce any future production of atomic, biological and chemical weapons. In return, the Western allies granted the FRG its sovereignty as a member of NATO and the West European Union (WEU), the designation for the enlarged Brussels Pact. With the successful ratification of the Paris Treaties, the FRG became a member of the Western alliance in May 1955.[6]

The mid-1950s also saw a further intensification of the Federal Republic's economic ties with its Western allies. After complex negotiations, the leaders of the ECSC member states met in Rome in March 1957 to found the European Economic Community, later known simply as the European Community, or EC. The Treaty of Rome extended economic integration beyond the coal and steel sectors, committing Community members to the goal of a common market. At the same time, it set up a complex set of supranational and intergovernmental institutions to oversee joint economic policies. The Federal Republic and its partners created the European Commission, responsible for the initiation of EC-wide legislation, and the European Parliament, a legislative body with a mainly advisory role. While member states could still pursue their particular interests through the powerful Council of Ministers, the Community's main legislative body, the EC represented more than an international organization writ large. As a founding member, the Federal Republic linked itself more closely, economically and politically, with its West European allies.[7]

The integration of the Federal Republic into NATO and the emerging European Community did not preclude contacts with the Soviet Union. In September 1955, for example, Adenauer and a large German delegation made a highly publicized trip to Moscow. But his visit, the only one of his chancellorship, did not mark the start of an active Ostpolitik. During the talks Adenauer underscored the absolute priority of German ties with the West, while Nikita Khrushchev and other Soviet leaders railed against German rearmament. Both sides agreed to establish diplomatic relations and Adenauer managed to secure the release of German prisoners of war. On the central issue of German unity, however, hostility prevailed. While

---

6. A useful account remains Karl W. Deutsch and Lewis J. Edinger, *Germany Rejoins the Powers: Mass Opinion, Interest Groups, and Elites in Contemporary German Foreign Policy* (Stanford: Stanford University Press, 1959).

7. On the roots of European institutions within the ECSC construct, see Ernst B. Haas, *The Uniting of Europe: Political, Social, and Economic Forces 1950–1957* (Stanford: Stanford University Press, 1958), chaps 12–13. On the Treaty of Rome, see Hans-Jürgen Küsters, *Die Gründung der europäischen Wirtschaftsgemeinschaft* (Baden-Baden: Nomos, 1982).

the German side demanded free all-German elections as the basis for reunification, the Soviet leadership insisted on the reality of two German states and on recognition of the GDR as a first step toward any settlement. In the years that followed, the FRG not only refused to recognize the status quo of Germany's division. Bonn also withheld diplomatic recognition from states that exchanged ambassadors with East Berlin, the thrust of the so-called Hallstein Doctrine. A decade after war's end the Federal Republic was firmly anchored in the West and locked in confrontation with the East.[8]

Cold War Challenges: Rearmament and Reunification

What explains this postwar transformation of German foreign policy? Changes at the level of international structure—the division of Germany and the onset of the cold war—provide part of the answer. Following unconditional surrender, in May 1945, the Four Powers divided Germany into zones of occupation and placed its territory East of the Oder-Neisse Rivers under Polish administration, effectively recognizing the expulsion of millions of Germans living there.[9] At the Potsdam Conference of July–August 1945 the victors agreed to extract reparations from their respective zones. At the same time, they pledged to maintain the overall economic and political unity of the country—a commitment embodied in their joint occupation of Berlin, the capital of the defeated Reich. The Western powers and the Soviet Union were determined to root out Nazism and prevent any reemergence of a German military threat. From the outset, however, ideological differences among the victors undermined any joint approach to German reconstruction. Economic and political life developed differently in eastern and western Germany.[10]

The division of Germany, which took concrete shape in the years

---

8. On the origins of the Hallstein Doctrine, named after one of Adenauer's top foreign policy advisors, Walter Hallstein, see Rüdiger Marco Booz, *"Hallsteinzeit": Deutsche Außenpolitik 1955–1972* (Bonn: Bouvier, 1995), 15–49. The Soviet Union, as one of the Four Powers responsible for reunification, was exempted from its application. On German-Soviet relations during the early 1950s, see Klaus Erdmenger, *Das folgenschwere Mißverständnis: Bonn und die sowjetische Deutschlandpolitik 1949–1955* (Freiburg: Rombach, 1967). For Adenauer's detailed account of the visit, see Adenauer, *Erinnerungen,* 2:487–556.

9. On the Four-Power approach to the border issue, see Hans Georg Lehmann, *Der Oder-Neiße Konflikt* (Munich: Beck, 1979), chap. 3. France officially joined the group only after the Potsdam Conference.

10. On the immediate postwar years, see Norman M. Naimark, *The Russians in Germany: A History of the Soviet Zone of Occupation, 1945–1949* (Cambridge: Harvard University Press, 1995); Theodor Eschenburg, *Jahre der Besatzung 1945–1949* (Stuttgart: Deutsche Verlags-Anstalt, 1983).

after 1945, was both a catalyst and a consequence of the emergent cold war. The gradual integration of the three Western zones, in economic, administrative, and political terms, worsened U.S.-Soviet relations in 1946–47, as did the step-by-step introduction of a one-party dictatorship under the Socialist Unity Party (SED) in the Soviet zone. At the same time, the U.S. announcement of the Marshall Plan in June 1947 and the Soviet refusal to participate in the proposed economic aid package escalated East-West tensions, undercutting the sporadic efforts of newly formed German parties and regional governments to maintain national unity across all four zones of occupation. The June 1948 currency reform in the Western zones and the Western sectors of Berlin proved a critical turning point. The introduction of the Deutschmark provoked an unsuccessful, yearlong Soviet blockade of West Berlin, and accelerated momentum toward the founding of both German states in 1949.

During the early years of its existence the Federal Republic's foreign policy unfolded within an international constellation characterized by both the height of the cold war and first indications of detente. The outbreak of the Korean War in June 1950 intensified the cold war in Europe. The North Korean invasion redoubled Western concerns about a Soviet attack on Western Europe, while U.S. military intervention on the side of the South heightened Soviet fears of global encirclement. The stabilization of the front in Korea by late 1951 dampened fears of an imminent superpower confrontation. But a thaw in the cold war had to await Stalin's death in March 1953 and the emergence of a reformist leadership under Khrushchev. An armistice ended the Korean War in July 1953, and East-West dialogue intensified over the next several years. The onset of detente was particularly evident in the European context. With the Austrian State Treaty of May 1955 the Four Powers guaranteed the unity and neutrality of the country. And the Geneva Summit of July 1955 marked the first meeting of the "Big Four" since the end of World War II.

Two related policy challenges dominated the German foreign policy agenda during the early 1950s: rearmament and reunification. The outbreak of the Korean War made rearmament a salient issue. With varying degrees of urgency, U.S., British, and French leaders sought to harness German military potential for the Western alliance—and simultaneously to preclude any future German military threat. At different junctures they considered the EDC and NATO appropriate institutional means to both these ends. German rearmament not only came to dominate Bonn's relations with Western capitals. It also moved to the center of East-West relations in Europe. First Stalin and then Khrushchev adamantly opposed the creation of a U.S.-German military alliance. They condemned what they perceived as a concerted effort to change the postwar status quo through force—or the threat of force. Through the mid-1950s Soviet leaders countered the rearmament project with threats and intimidation, on the one hand, and disarmament proposals, on the other. The issue of Germans in uniform, emotionally charged only years after the end of the war, confronted the Federal Republic with a first major foreign policy challenge.[11]

Through 1955 the issue of rearmament was closely bound up with that of reunification. As part of a concerted effort to prevent German integration into Western security institutions, the Soviet leadership launched a series of reunification initiatives from November 1950 onward. Stalin's March 1952 offer of unity in exchange for neutrality was the most significant. The Stalin Note sparked an extended but ultimately futile diplomatic exchange about the domestic and international contours of a German settlement. The foreign ministers of the Four Powers met in Berlin to discuss reunification in January 1954. The Geneva Summit took up the issue the following year. And the foreign ministers met to discuss the topic again in December 1955. Throughout this diplomatic activity Soviet leaders repeatedly warned their Western—and German—counterparts that rearmament would obstruct any future progress toward reunification. For the FRG this constellation created a clear tradeoff between the pursuit of security in alliance with the West and the pursuit of unity, which was impossible without Soviet cooperation.[12]

The resolution of the rearmament and reunification issues was in doubt through 1955. U.S. and British leaders, while supportive of reunification in principle, strongly backed German rearmament in order to counter a perceived Soviet military threat. French leaders, more concerned than their allies about a possible *German* military threat, flirted at times with the alternative of a neutral, reunified Germany through negotiations with Moscow. Soviet leaders, for their part, were strictly opposed to German participation in the Western alliance. On the unity issue, however, they appeared to vacillate between two goals: consolidation of the GDR as a first step toward the Sovietization of all of Germany; and a reunified, neutral Germany through negotiations with the West. Only the integration of the Federal Republic into NATO in May 1955—exactly a decade after

---

11. On the onset of the rearmament controversy, see Rolf Steininger, *Wiederbewaffnung: Die Entscheidung für einen westdeutschen Verteidigungsbeitrag* (Straube: Erlangen, 1989).

12. For contrasting views of this diplomacy and its prospects, see Rolf Steininger, *The German Question: The Stalin Note of 1952 and the Problem of Reunification* (New York: Columbia University Press, 1990); Hans-Peter Schwarz, ed., *Die Legende von der verpaßten Gelegenheit: Die Stalin Note vom 10. März 1952* (Stuttgart: Belser, 1982).

war's end—resolved the ambiguity at the heart of the postwar configuration. Through the mid-1950s the openness of the rearmament and reunification issues confronted German leaders with difficult policy choices.[13]

Institutions and Alternatives: Variations with the West

Two interlocking institutions, the Three- and Four-Power regimes linking the victors of World War II, framed the German response to this international constellation. The Three-Power regime consisted of rules and norms linking the FRG with the United States, Britain, and France. Most clearly embedded in the Occupation Statute, the regime limited German external sovereignty and ruled out a purely nationally oriented German foreign policy. The Four-Power regime, by contrast, consisted of norms linking the Western powers and the Soviet Union. Grounded primarily in the Potsdam Accord of August 1945, it made the sovereignty of Berlin and matters relating to German unity the legal preserve of the Anti-Hitler Coalition. During the early 1950s both sets of institutions framed German policy toward the interrelated policy challenges of rearmament and reunification.

The Three-Power regime emerged during the immediate postwar years. Under the watchful eye of the occupying powers German leaders reconstructed political institutions in the Western zones. The Parliamentary Council, a constituent assembly with representatives from all three zones, drafted the Federal Republic's Basic Law, a constitution deemed provisional pending reunification. The new constitution, subject to approval by the allies, reflected norms shared by both the victors and the vanquished. It not only set up democratic, federal institutions. It also set down norms relevant for the conduct of German foreign policy. The preamble of the Basic Law bound the new state to "achieve, by free self-determination, the unity and freedom of Germany." Other key articles related to foreign policy reflected a strong consensus between German and allied leaders. Article 26 precluded preparations for wars of aggression. And with Article 24, the proscription of German defense policy outside a system of collective security, the Basic Law laid the foundation for a multilateral security policy. A joint allied-German construct, the new constitu-

---

13. For recent historical work on the Four Powers' contrasting approaches to rearmament and reunification, see Wilfried Loth, ed., *Die deutsche Frage in der Nachkriegszeit* (Berlin: Akademie Verlag, 1994). According to Loth, "in light of the new sources, the openness of the German Question seems to have been remarkably substantial into the mid-1950s" (8).

tion effectively outlawed a return to the nationalist, expansionist policies of the past.[14]

The core of the Three-Power regime during the early 1950s was the Occupation Statute of September 1949. In assenting to the creation of the Federal Republic, the United States, France, and Britain not only helped to place its foreign policy on a new constitutional foundation. They also continued to limit its external sovereignty. The statute, promulgated the same month that Adenauer was elected chancellor, replaced the military administration in the three Western zones with a single Allied High Commission. Direct allied interference in internal German affairs, most evident in ongoing dismantling of German heavy industry, receded in the years that followed. But the three high commissioners—not the German government—continued to exercise legal responsibility for the Federal Republic's relations with the outside world. Legal restrictions on German foreign policy eased in the years that followed. In March 1951, for example, statute revisions allowed for the creation of a German foreign ministry. But only after the FRG joined NATO did it gain full control of its own foreign policy. Through 1955 Bonn was legally bound to conduct its foreign affairs with and not against the allies.[15]

The Four-Power regime also constituted the institutional context of German foreign policy during the first postwar decade. Rooted in the wartime anti-Hitler coalition, the regime found its clearest formal expression in the Potsdam Treaty of August 1945. With the treaty the Four Powers not only formalized their joint occupation of Berlin and the division of Germany west of the Oder-Neisse into zones of occupation. They also embraced shared norms to guide German reconstruction: demilitarization, denazification and democratization. In the years after 1945 Western and Soviet interpretations of these norms diverged and two sharply contrasting German states began to take shape. Western leaders condemned the SED's consolidation of power as a violation of Potsdam's democratization provisions, while Soviet leaders attacked the integration of the Western zones as a violation of Four-Power responsibility. Still, the division of Germany during the late 1940s did not destroy the Four-Power regime. The Western powers and the Soviet Union continued to assert their responsibility for questions relating to German unity and the status of Berlin. Four-Power rights removed legal competence for the unity issue from German hands. The Federal Republic could not pursue a national reunification policy.

---

14. *Documents on Germany, 1944–1985* (Washington, D.C.: U.S. Department of State, 1985), 226–27. On the origins of the Basic Law, see Eschenburg, *Jahre der Besatzung,* 459–514.

15. On the Statute, see Schwarz, *Gründerjahre,* 42–48.

The salience of the Four-Power regime as a context for German foreign policy was evident during the early 1950s. The Western powers, for example, blocked Bonn's efforts to make West Berlin a full part of the Federal Republic. And Soviet leaders sought to obstruct political and economic links between Bonn and West Berlin. The Four-Power regime not only limited the FRG presence in the former Reich capital. It also excluded German leaders from direct participation in the East-West dialogue on reunification. In keeping with the principle of Four-Power responsibility, Soviet leaders addressed their reunification initiatives to Western capitals, not Bonn. And the official allied responses bore the signature of the Western powers. The subordinate legal standing of the Federal Republic was most obvious during the 1954 Berlin Conference. While the foreign ministers of the Four Powers discussed the unity issue, representatives of both the FRG and the GDR were relegated to observer status.

These interlocking Three- and Four-Power regimes narrowed but did not eliminate German freedom of action with respect to the rearmament and reunification issues. The Three-Power regime, with its sovereignty restrictions, ruled out a German foreign policy in theory but not in practice. From 1945 onward new democratic elites, first at the local and then at the regional and zonal levels, conducted foreign policies to the extent that they dealt with foreign occupiers. From the outset German leaders could and often did insist on treatment as partners, not simply subordinates. Adenauer vividly demonstrated the German claim to equality during his first meeting with the High Commission in September 1949. To the surprise of those present he slighted protocol by delivering his speech on the carpet reserved for the three allied commissioners. This "carpet diplomacy" set the tone for the months and years that followed. Adenauer exploited bilateral contacts with individual commissioners and interviews with the world press to create an independent German foreign policy profile. From the November 1949 Petersberg Treaty, which phased out the dismantling of German industry, through the ECSC and EDC negotiations, Bonn emerged as an important European player in its own right.[16]

The outbreak of the Korean War and the eruption of the rearmament issue revealed the full extent of German foreign policy within the confines of the Three-Power regime. The allies' concerns about a Soviet threat to Western Europe made it increasingly clear how much they needed the Federal Republic, and not just vice versa. Washington, averse to large

---

16. On Adenauer's "carpet diplomacy" and his interaction with the High Commission in general, see Hans-Peter Schwarz, *Adenauer: Der Aufstieg 1876–1952* (Stuttgart: Deutsche Verlags-Anstalt, 1986), 671–90.

increases in the U.S. military presence in Europe, backed German rearmament, but could not bring it about without close consultation with Bonn. Adenauer immediately exploited German leverage derived from the new situation, that fact that—as he put it in a November 1950 Bundestag speech—the "voice of the FRG must be heard and respected."[17] In the ensuing negotiations concerning the terms of rearmament the German government forcefully pressed the demand for full and equal partnership in the Western alliance. In May 1952 the allies and the FRG endorsed the Bonn Conventions, which called for German sovereignty upon EDC ratification. The crisis and eventual collapse of the EDC postponed formal sovereignty until the ratification of the Paris Treaties in 1955. But the continued existence of the Three-Power regime did not preclude an active German foreign policy throughout the rearmament controversy.

Ambiguity at the heart of the Four-Power regime, too, allowed German leaders some freedom of action. The Potsdam Treaty removed the unity issue from the control of the Germans in legal terms. But the norm of Four-Power responsibility also opened up practical ways for the Federal Republic to shape East-West diplomacy concerning Germany as a whole. On the one hand, the Potsdam Treaty envisioned German ratification of any reunification settlement. In their discussions of the unity issue, the Four Powers had to be attentive to German concerns. On the other hand, Western leaders were bound to consult Bonn in the formulation of their positions. With the Basic Law, the allies had endorsed the Federal Republic's claim to be the sole legitimate representative of the German people. And with the Occupation Statute, they explicitly committed themselves to the pursuit of the unity of the German people. In practice, the Western allies, while jealous of their ultimate responsibility for the unity issue and the status of Berlin, arrived at most positions in close cooperation with the Germans.

The extent of German influence within the context of the Four-Power regime was most evident in the context of the Stalin Note controversy. Formally, the diplomatic exchange it unleashed took place between the Western powers and the Soviet Union. Informally, however, Moscow's initiative was directed as much at Bonn as Washington, London, or Paris. Its key provision—unity in exchange for neutrality—aimed to deflect the Federal Republic from the path of Western integration. Provisions for a *national* German army, in particular, appeared designed to turn Germans against the EDC. Not only was the Soviet diplomatic offensive directed at the FRG; German leaders were able to shape the thrust of the allied

---

17. Address of November 8, 1950, *Verhandlungen des deutschen Bundestages. Stenographischer Bericht,* ser. 1, 3565.

response. Some Western leaders, while skeptical of Soviet intentions, were nevertheless open to testing the seriousness of the proposal. But Adenauer, anxious to press ahead with Western integration, successfully advocated an uncompromising response. After consultations with Bonn, the allies outlined tough counterdemands: all-German elections as a first step toward unity; the freedom of a united Germany to choose its alliances; and nonrecognition of the Oder-Neisse border pending the successful negotiation of a German settlement.[18]

German leverage over Four-Power dialogue was again evident during the thaw that followed Stalin's death. In May 1953 Winston Churchill called for a Four-Power conference on Germany. The administration of Dwight Eisenhower, concerned that such a meeting might impede EDC ratification, remained skeptical. Only in June 1953, when Adenauer temporarily reversed his opposition, did Eisenhower and Dulles agree to the Berlin foreign ministers conference the following January. While Adenauer's reversal made the conference possible, his uncompromising stance in the negotiations helped to assure its failure. In his consultations with the Western allies, he insisted on a new demand—that free elections in the GDR take place in conjunction with the organization of all-German elections. This demand was clearly unacceptable to the Soviet Union and exasperated even allied negotiators—not to mention many of Adenauer's own political supporters. As it happened, fundamental differences between allied and Soviet positions made a breakthrough at the Berlin Conference unlikely. Nevertheless, Adenauer's tough stance, and his eagerness to break off the talks as soon as possible, certainly contributed to its failure.[19]

Ambiguity at the core of the Three- and Four-Power regimes, then, allowed German leaders some leeway in their approach to the rearmament and reunification issues. At no point in the early 1950s did German leaders face a stark choice between East and West. Given their economic and material dependence on the United States, no real alternative to a basic Western orientation for the Federal Republic existed. Nor, given international tensions, did German leaders face a clear choice between Western integration and reunification. The distance between the Western and

---

18. On Adenauer's central role in the formulation of the Western response, see Steininger, *German Question,* chaps. 1–2. Wilfried Loth has even argued that "that the decision about the Soviet offer was first and foremost a German one" (*Die deutsche Frage,* 24). For an alternative account that stresses constraints on German choices, see Hermann-Josef Rupieper, *Der besetzte Verbündete: Die amerikanische Deutschlandpolitik, 1949–1955* (Opladen: Westdeutscher Verlag, 1991), 240–300.

19. On Adenauer's stance and the concerns it raised, see "The Secretary of State to the Embassy in the United Kingdom," October 13, 1953, and "Memorandum of Conversation," February 6, 1954, in *Foreign Relations of the United States, 1952–1954* (Washington, D.C.: U.S. Government Printing Office, 1986), 7:654–56, 976–77.

Soviet negotiating positions concerning the domestic political institutions and foreign policy orientation of a united Germany made reunification unlikely, no matter what the details of the German position. What remained open was the precise nature of ties with the West and the possibility of rapprochement between Soviet and Western positions on the unity issue. Within this context German choices revolved around how much relative emphasis to place on rearmament and how much on reunification; how much to press for Western integration and how much to prod the allies toward Four-Power dialogue.

It seems paradoxical that a weak Federal Republic, still without its external sovereignty, should have faced significant foreign policy alternatives in the early 1950s. The United States, with its crushing economic and military superiority, supported rearmament within Western institutions. And through both the Three- and Four-Power regimes Washington exercised considerable institutional leverage over Bonn. Nevertheless, both the openness of rearmament and reunification issues in the early 1950s and ambiguities within the institutional configuration left German leaders with significant foreign policy alternatives. While eager to enlist Bonn's security cooperation, U.S. leaders were also careful not to impose their will on would-be allies. In his biography of High Commissioner John J. McCloy, Thomas Schwartz concludes that U.S. leaders insisted "that German leaders make a choice between pressing for negotiations for reunification and following the path of European integration and tight association with the United States."[20] That choice emerged out of a domestic political struggle.

Contested Priorities amid the Cold War

During the early 1950s both the project of rearmament and the prospects for reunification were the object of fierce political controversy within the Federal Republic. Economic and social reconstruction at home remained the overriding concern; the "economic miracle" associated with Economics Minister Ludwig Erhard did not fully take hold until the mid-1950s. During the postwar decade, the absence of several million war dead robbed the country of human resources, and the integration of about ten million Germans expelled from territories east of the Oder-Neisse complicated the recovery. So too did wartime damage to industry and the postwar reparations burden. During the early years of the Federal Republic, however, the problems of economic recovery and social integration did not drive foreign policy issues off the political agenda. The persistence of the Three-Power

---

20. Thomas Alan Schwartz, *America's Germany: John J. McCloy and the Federal Republic of Germany* (Cambridge: Harvard University Press, 1991), 268.

regime and the strictures on German sovereignty constituted a continuing source of controversy. And the rearmament and reunification issues that erupted during the early 1950s found political resonance in a society still recovering from war and wrestling with the effects of national division.[21]

The major parties that emerged during the postwar years—the Christian Democrats, the Social Democrats, and the Liberals—converged around a basic pro-Western foreign policy orientation. With the exception of a pro-Soviet communist party and certain nationalist splinter groups, the new German democratic political elite backed cooperation with the allies, and the United States in particular.[22] With the onset of the cold war, however, the rearmament and reunification issues gave rise to sharp divisions in German society and politics. A vocal peace movement protested the prospect of Germans in uniform under the slogan "count me out!" (*ohne mich*).[23] And a radical Right dominated by unrepentant Nazis, while politically insignificant, kept nationalist and revanchist themes in the public eye. Within this shifting international and domestic context, the leaders of the established parties articulated contrasting foreign policy priorities— different ways to combine security and association with the West and the pursuit of national unity in the East. During the late 1940s and early 1950s Adenauer and Kurt Schumacher, the leading rivals for the chancellorship, structured the domestic political debate. Adenauer backed rapid integration within the Western alliance, while Schumacher supported looser Western ties and more active efforts to pursue reunification.

To some degree these divergent foreign policy priorities reflected different political biographies.[24] Adenauer, mayor of Cologne and an influ-

---

21. On the interpenetration of foreign policy and domestic politics during the early years of the Federal Republic, see Wolfram F. Hanrieder, *West German Foreign Policy, 1949–1963: International Pressure and Domestic Response* (Stanford: Stanford University Press, 1967); Anselm Doering-Manteuffel, *Die Bundesrepublik Deutschland in der Ära Adenauer: Außenpolitik und innere Entwicklung* (Darmstadt: Wissenschaftliche Buchgesellschaft, 1983).

22. For an overview of postwar positions, see Hans-Peter Schwarz, *Vom Reich zur Bundesrepublik: Deutschland im Widerstreit der außenpolitischen Konzeptionen in den Jahren der Besatzungsherrschaft, 1945–1949* (Neuwied: Luchterhand, 1980). On the importance of the United States for postwar German leaders, see Hans-Jürgen Grabbe, *Unionsparteien, Sozialdemokratie und Vereinigte Staaten von Amerika, 1945–1966* (Düsseldorf: Droste, 1983), chaps. 1–5.

23. Alice Holmes Cooper, *Paradoxes of Peace: German Peace Movements since 1945* (Ann Arbor: University of Michigan Press, 1996), chap. 2.

24. On Adenauer, see Schwarz, *Adenauer: Der Aufstieg;* Henning Köhler, *Adenauer: Eine Politische Biographie* (Frankfurt am Main: Ullstein, 1994). On Schumacher, see Peter Merseburger, *Der schwierige Deutsche: Kurt Schumacher* (Stuttgart: Deutsche Verlags-Anstalt, 1995); Lewis J. Edinger, *Kurt Schumacher: A Study in Personality and Political Behavior* (Stanford: Stanford University Press, 1965).

ential member of the Catholic Center party during the Weimar Republic, spent the Nazi years in retirement in his native Rhineland. During the immediate postwar years, he struggled for—and achieved—leadership of the newly formed Christian Democratic movement, which had strongholds in western and southern Germany. Schumacher, who hailed from Prussia, served in the Reichstag toward the end of the Weimar Republic and spent most of the Nazi period in concentration camps. He quickly assumed leadership of the postwar SPD, which was stronger in the Protestant North and Soviet-occupied East. From these very different starting points Adenauer and Schumacher emerged as the dominant figures in postwar German politics. They helped to craft the Basic Law as members of the Parliamentary Council, contested the FRG's first national campaign, and defined its most prominent policy controversies through Schumacher's death in August 1952.

The foreign policy differences between Adenauer and Schumacher rested on three broad points of agreement. First, both insisted that the Federal Republic belonged squarely within the community of Western democracies. This entailed more than a pragmatic recognition of the presence of the allies and the strictures on German sovereignty. Both Adenauer and Schumacher were ardent anti-fascists and anticommunists. Mistrustful of their compatriots' political instincts, they insisted that Germans break with their authoritarian habits and embrace parliamentary democracy once and for all. As Adenauer put it in 1946, the "German people has been afflicted with a false view of the state, power, and the role of the individual."[25] Links with the Western allies, he and Schumacher contended, would safeguard German institutions and prevent a revival of the nationalist and militarist politics that followed World War I. After 1945 both men saw the greatest threat to German democracy embodied in Soviet communism. They condemned the progressive Sovietization of the Eastern zone—particularly the subjugation of the CDU-East and the forced merger of Social Democrats into the communist-dominated SED. Association with the West, Adenauer and Schumacher both maintained, was necessary to counter the *political* threat posed by communism.[26]

Second, Adenauer and Schumacher shared the commitment to national unity set down in the Basic Law. Both considered the GDR a nonentity, a mere Soviet puppet, and demanded free all-German elections

---

25. Address as CDU leader in the British Zone of Occupation, March 24, 1946, in Konrad Adenauer, *Reden, 1917–1967: Eine Auswahl* (Stuttgart: Deutsche Verlags-Anstalt, 1975), 85.

26. See, for example, Schumacher's speech at the first postwar SPD party conference, May 9, 1946, in Kurt Schumacher, *Reden—Schriften—Korrespondenzen, 1945–1952* (Berlin: Dietz, 1985), 387–418.

as a first step toward reunification. In response to the creation of the GDR, in October 1949, Adenauer and Schumacher led the major parties in reiterating the Federal Republic's claim to be the sole legitimate representative of the German people. And they both refused to recognize the permanence of the Oder-Neisse line. This commitment to unity within Germany's prewar borders, the object of broad consensus across the German political spectrum, reflected a historical identification with Bismarck's Reich. As a Rhinelander and a Catholic, Adenauer had ambivalent feelings toward the Prussian-dominated Reich. But he did not view a separate West German state as preferable to a united Germany—the charges of his critics notwithstanding. Like Schumacher, whose Prussian background made him less ambivalent on this score, Adenauer considered the Reich a national frame of reference.[27]

A third broad similarity concerned support for a strong defense against a Soviet military threat. Neither Adenauer nor Schumacher was enthusiastic about the prospect of German rearmament: both feared that a revival of German militarism might undermine new democratic institutions. As the cold war intensified, however, neither voiced principled objections to a German military contribution. Both Adenauer and Schumacher calculated that the Western powers could not effectively counter the Soviet threat without German military support. And while fiercely opposed to militarism, both nevertheless rejected the German pacifist tradition with strong roots on the German left. The only way to meet the threat posed by an aggressive and expansionist Soviet Union, they reasoned, was through an adequate military counterweight. The example of Hitler's aggression, Adenauer and Schumacher both maintained, underscored the importance of strength and determination in the face of a dictatorship.[28]

During the late 1940s and early 1950s these broadly similar stances on Western orientation, national unity, and military security served as a common foundation for contrasting foreign policy priorities. For Adenauer Western orientation entailed more than close ties with the Western powers. As early as 1945, he made the integration of western Germany into a set of tight-knit Western economic, political, and security institutions his over-

---

27. For a discussion of the problematic thesis that Adenauer was not committed to national unity, see Josef Foschepoth, ed., *Adenauer und die deutsche Frage* (Göttingen: Vandenhoeck and Ruprecht, 1988). For an opposing view, see Rudolf Morsey, *Die Deutschlandpolitik Adenauers: Alte Thesen und neue Fakten* (Opladen: Westdeutscher Verlag, 1991).

28. See, for example, Schumacher before an SPD audience, September 17, 1950, in Schumacher, *Reden,* 850–52. Adenauer invoked the negative analogy of Western appeasement in a party conference speech of October 20, 1950, in Adenauer, *Reden,* 184–85.

riding foreign policy priority.[29] Adenauer's support for European integration, rooted in the perception of cultural and historical affinities between Germany and its Western neighbors, went back to the post–World War I years. After World War II he backed integration for a number of strategic reasons as well. In Adenauer's view Western integration constituted the most effective way to win back German sovereignty from the Western powers. In addition, membership in a military alliance promised security against the Soviet threat, while participation in the EC promised an accelerated economic recovery. In pursuit of these strategic ends, Adenauer was willing to countenance some discriminatory measures against the FRG— for example, the limits on national German armed forces envisioned within the EDC framework.[30]

Schumacher, by contrast, conceived of a Western orientation in terms of cooperation, not integration. He did not reject an alliance with the United States, Britain, and France or progress toward European unity. Schumacher pointed to the importance of strategic links with the Western powers and invoked his party's traditional support for a "United States of Europe."[31] At the same time, however, he rejected any institutional arrangement that discriminated against the Federal Republic or—in the context of economic integration—weakened the position of organized labor. The allies, he insisted, should abandon their economic controls, grant the FRG its political sovereignty, and treat it as an equal in any security arrangement. During one of the first Bundestag debates, in September 1949, he stressed that "Europe means equal rights" and—with an eye toward France—warned that using Europe as a cover for hegemonic power would only devalue the European idea.[32] In the years that followed, Schumacher condemned the ECSC as anti-labor and the EDC as an effort to keep the Federal Republic weak and subordinate. While Adenauer backed greater sovereignty through integration, Schumacher insisted on full sovereignty as a starting point for cooperative Western ties.

These different approaches to relations with the West went hand in

---

29. See, for example, Adenauer to Sollmann, March 16, 1946, in Hans-Peter Mensing, ed., *Adenauer: Briefe 1945–47* (Berlin: Siedler, 1983), 189–91. On Adenauer's approach to European integration in particular, see Werner Weidenfeld, *Konrad Adenauer und Europa. Die geistigen Grundlagen der westeuropäischen Integrationspolitik des ersten Bonner Bundeskanzlers* (Bonn: Europa Union Verlag, 1976).

30. On continuity between Adenauer's pre- and postwar approaches to Western integration, see Arnulf Baring, *Im Anfang war Adenauer: Die Entstehung der Kanzlerdemokratie* (Munich: Deutscher Taschenbuch Verlag, 1971), 86–109.

31. Party conference address of May 9, 1946, in Schumacher, *Reden,* 407.

32. Schumacher addresses of September 21, 1949, *Verhandlungen des deutschen Bundestags,* ser. 1, 42.

hand with contrasting views of the unity issue. After the war both Adenauer and Schumacher expressed confidence that a democratic and prosperous western Germany would exert a magnetic pull on the East, laying the groundwork for reunification.[33] And both insisted that the Western powers commit themselves to German unity—a goal only realizable through talks with Moscow. During the early 1950s, however, their attitudes toward Four-Power dialogue diverged. Adenauer opposed such dialogue until Western integration was secure. Before then, he argued, talks would only complicate integration and might even generate a Four-Power accord at German expense—Adenauer's "Potsdam Nightmare."[34] Once the FRG regained its sovereignty, he reasoned, it could fully protect its interests in any future unity negotiations. And once Soviet leaders realized that the FRG was not vulnerable and the GDR was not viable, they would be open to reunification on Western terms. Adenauer adhered to this policy of strength throughout the controversies of the early 1950s.

Schumacher, by contrast, insisted that Western integration would make a German settlement with Moscow less, not more likely. While suspicious of Soviet intentions, he urged that the FRG combine association with the West and dialogue with the East. Germans, he insisted, should avoid thinking about East and West in "either-or" terms.[35] The government should do everything in its power to promote a settlement with the East before fixing the terms of its association with the West. In response to the Stalin Note, for example, Schumacher pressed for a more active diplomacy. "Any German government," he wrote the chancellor at the time, "should feel obliged to press for the acceleration of Four-Power talks."[36] It is by no means clear that Schumacher was ready to entertain the Soviet offer of unity in exchange for neutrality. But he certainly rejected the premise of Adenauer's approach—that Western integration would make

---

33. Schumacher referred to the "irresistible magnetism" of the Western zones as early as 1947. See his party conference address of June 29, 1947, in Schumacher, *Reden,* 493. Adenauer set out this argument before the CDU leadership during the 1950s. See Günther Buchstab, ed., *Adenauer: "Wir haben wirklich etwas geschaffen": Die Protokolle des CDU-Bundesvorstands, 1953–1957* (Düsseldorf: Droste, 1990), 431–32.

34. On Adenauer's anxieties concerning Four-Power diplomacy, see, for example, his conversation with McCloy on December 16, 1950, in *Foreign Relations of the United States 1950,* 4:675. The "Potsdam Nightmare" reference is cited in Schwarz, *Adenauer: Der Aufstieg,* 833.

35. Address at an SPD party conference, June 29, 1947, in Schumacher, *Reden,* 488. See also his address of May 22, 1950, ibid., 750–57.

36. Radio address of July 15, 1952, ibid., 967. More than a year earlier, Schumacher had also called for a more active reunification policy in a major Bundestag debate, March 9, 1951, *Verhandlungen des deutschen Bundestags,* ser. 1, 4761–67.

both the allies and the Soviet Union more likely to engage in serious negotiations on reunification.[37]

Contrasting perspectives on security accompanied these different approaches to ties with the West and national unity. Adenauer, determined to integrate any new German armed forces tightly into a Western institutional framework, was willing to accept some discriminatory controls and the possibility that rearmament might set back the prospects for reunification. Schumacher did not object to Adenauer's alarmist rhetoric concerning a Soviet threat, his depiction of the FRG as a "dam against the East" and part of the Western "defensive front"[38] But he rejected any discriminatory controls and insisted that alliance strategy reflect German interests—that war, should it come, be fought in the East and not on German soil.[39] More important, in the context of German domestic politics, he insisted that the Federal Republic exhaust the possibilities of Four-Power diplomacy before committing itself to rearmament within the Western alliance. During the early 1950s the issues of reunification and rearmament were linked not only at the level of international politics but also in the German foreign policy debate.[40]

The contrasting foreign policy priorities of Adenauer and Schumacher reflected different appraisals of the international situation. Adenauer's overriding concern was the Soviet threat. As early as 1945, he saw Stalin committed to exploiting differences among the Western powers and drawing all of Germany into the Soviet orbit. Before a CDU audience in 1946 he charged Moscow with seeking to "cast all of Europe into the greatest disorder" in order to "extend its power" to Germany, France and the rest of Western Europe.[41] In the years that followed, he dismissed conciliatory Soviet gestures—whether reunification offers or arms control initiatives—as transparent efforts to undermine Western unity and subjugate the Federal Republic. Adenauer's basic anti-Soviet orientation underpinned his strong pro-Western stance and his policy of strength with

---

37. For Schumacher's distinction between political and military neutrality and his openness to the latter, see his address before the Parliamentary Council, April 20, 1949, in Schumacher, *Reden,* 642.

38. These phrases are taken from a party conference address of October 20, 1950, in Adenauer, *Reden,* 187; and a Bundestag speech of November 8, 1950, *Verhandlungen des deutschen Bundestags,* ser. 1, 3567.

39. Debate of November 8, 1950, *Verhandlungen des deutschen Bundestags,* ser. 1, 3569.

40. On Schumacher's views of the links between the rearmament and reunification issues, see Ulrich Buczylowski, *Kurt Schumacher und die deutsche Frage* (Stuttgart: Seewald, 1973).

41. Quoted in Schwarz, *Vom Reich zur Bundesrepublik,* 464.

respect to the unity issue. It remained remarkably constant during the early 1950s and through the end of his chancellorship in 1963.[42]

Schumacher's view of Soviet intentions was no more positive. He also saw Moscow determined to bring all of Germany under its control. His view of the Western powers, however, was more negative than Adenauer's. He discerned a determination to keep the FRG subordinate and a lack of enthusiasm for German unity. Schumacher was critical of France in particular, and its "hegemonic tendencies," evident in efforts to discriminate against the FRG in the ECSC and EDC contexts. And he missed more active Western efforts to address the unity issue. Soviet leaders, Schumacher acknowledged, had subjugated eastern Germany and deepened the German division. But if Moscow bore most of the responsibility for the German division, "the lack of interest on the part of the western allies" had also helped to bring it about.[43] While Adenauer's perception of the international constellation informed support for rapid integration in Western institutions, Schumacher's suggested a looser association with the West and more attention to dialogue with the East.

These contrasting foreign policy priorities also rested on different views of the past and its lessons. The legacy of Hitler's rule not only overshadowed the reconstruction of German society and politics in the decade after World War II.[44] It also shaped the public foreign policy debate. Adenauer's self-confident but respectful approach to the allies reflected his view of the Nazi period and its implications.[45] He sought to reestablish West German sovereignty as quickly as possible, but insisted that the legacy of German aggression necessitated an incremental approach. Given the crimes committed in Germany's name, he considered the creation of trust an absolute necessity. As he put it upon assuming the chancellorship, "We Germans must not forget what happened between 1933 and 1945. We also should not forget the disaster [*Unglück*] that the National Socialist Regime brought upon the entire world." From Adenauer's perspective, not just German weakness but also historical experience dictated patience in relations with the allies. Given the salience of psychological considera-

---

42. Adenauer's memoirs, written in the mid-1960s, attest to this continuity. Their main foreign policy themes—the imperative of Western integration and an anti-Soviet stance—inform his account of the two postwar decades. See Adenauer, *Erinnerungen.*

43. Address before SPD party conference, August 1948, in Schumacher, *Reden,* 604.

44. Norbert Frei, *Vergangenheitspolitik: Die Anfänge der Bundesrepublik und die NS-Vergangenheit* (Munich: Beck, 1996); Ulrich Brochhagen, *Nach Nürnberg: Vergangenheitsbewältigung und Westintegration in der Ära Adenauer* (Hamburg: Junius Verlag, 1994).

45. For a discussion of Adenauer's understanding of history, see Anneliese Poppinga, *Konrad Adenauer. Geschichtsverständnis, Weltanschauung und politische Praxis* (Stuttgart: Deutsche Verlags-Anstalt, 1975), 119–57.

tions, "Germans should not expect or demand a high level of trust from the outset."[46]

Adenauer's view of the past and its implications also reinforced the substance of his foreign policy priorities, especially his support for close ties with France and European integration. In his first government declaration as chancellor in September 1949, Adenauer insisted that the "rivalry that dominated European politics for hundreds of years and has caused so many wars and so much destruction and bloodshed must be abolished once and for all."[47] Adenauer also drew a link between German responsibility for World War II and the imperative of deeper European integration. "The catastrophe brought the German people to the realization that an excessive nationalism had more than once destroyed peace," he argued in December 1951. "From this," he continued, "there emerged the recognition that our existence, along with that of all other European peoples, can only be maintained within a community that transcends national borders."[48] While Adenauer's backing for the alliance with the United States derived mainly from strategic considerations, his support for Franco-German reconciliation and European integration reflected a particular view of the past and its lessons.

Schumacher drew different policy conclusions from the same historical experience. While Adenauer invoked the past in support of his patient, incremental approach to the allies, Schumacher enlisted it in support of his more assertive stance. Pointing to the interwar precedent, Schumacher warned that Western efforts to discriminate against the Germans on economic and security matters would prove counterproductive. He openly admonished the Western powers not to repeat post–World War I mistakes, when antipathy toward Germany—and fear of German power—culminated in the harsh provisions of the Versailles Treaty of 1919. The West's "security sickness," he suggested, had sparked draconian policies, which led in turn to a nationalist German reaction with catastrophic consequences—dictatorship and war.[49] The allies, in his view,

46. Adenauer Bundestag address of November 24, 1949, *Verhandlungen des deutschen Bundestags,* ser. 1, 472. Moral and historical considerations also shaped Adenauer's support for reparations payments to Israel. On this, see Lily Gardner Feldman, *The Special Relationship between West Germany and Israel* (Boston: Allen and Unwin, 1984), 49–86.

47. Adenauer address of September 20, 1949, *Verhandlungen des deutschen Bundestags,* ser. 1, 30 . He had also sounded this theme in his CDU address of March 1, 1946, Adenauer, *Reden,* 105.

48. Adenauer address in London, December 6, 1951, in Adenauer, *Reden,* 235. Adenauer drew similar links between past conflicts and integration efforts in his declaration of October 20, 1953, ibid., ser. 2, 11–22.

49. Schumacher address before an SPD party conference, May 9, 1946, in Schumacher, *Reden,* 397.

were risking a repeat of their interwar mistake of depriving Germans of control over their own affairs. Given the interwar precedent, Schumacher considered German leaders justified in pressing assertively for sovereignty and equality.

Schumacher's support for a more assertive stance did not represent a renewed German nationalism. He condemned the ideology of nationalism that had "isolated Germany in the world not once but twice."[50] And he viewed close ties with the West, and Paris in particular, as crucial for the success of peace and freedom in Europe. Moreover, like Adenauer, Schumacher censured the "Rapallo-Policies" of the interwar years, when Germany pursued its national interests by playing off East against West. Nevertheless, Schumacher drew different lessons from the past for the present.[51] If recent German history had discredited nationalism, it had also, in Schumacher's view, underscored the importance of a self-confident national stance. The failure of Weimar democrats to articulate national concerns effectively, Schumacher contended, had left those concerns to the militant nationalists, with terrible consequences for democracy and peace. Only a self-confident democratic Germany could make a positive contribution to postwar Europe. For Schumacher *national* and *nationalism* represented "irreconcilable contradictions."[52]

Interestingly, Schumacher's view of the past and its lessons dovetailed with that of the dominant conservative current of German historiography during the first postwar decade. The traditional "primacy of foreign policy" school, with its focus on the national interest and the balance of power, survived the Nazi era and maintained its strongholds within German universities. Leading representatives, including Gerhard Ritter, Friedrich Meinecke, and Hans Rothfels, were sharply critical of Hitler's dictatorship and its disastrous consequences. Like Schumacher, however, they refused to conflate destructive nationalism with the responsible pursuit of national interest. In their postwar scholarship they upheld Bismarck's Reich and the pre–World War I balance of power as relevant models for foreign policy in the new Europe. Irresponsible leadership, they argued, and not the international system of sovereign states, had precipitated both world wars. In an influential work published in 1954, Ritter put it most succinctly: Hitler was the "demon" responsible for ruining Ger-

---

50. Ibid., 409.

51. On the importance of the Franco-German relationship, see his address of June 29, 1947, ibid., 489. For his reference to Rapallo, the German-Soviet conference of April 1922 that stunned Western capitals, see the party conference address of May 22, 1950, ibid., 750.

52. On the importance of national identity as a counter to nationalism, see Schumacher's address of May 22, 1950, ibid., 778.

many's "good name."[53] This perspective, which contrasted sharply with Adenauer's view of history and its consequences, resonated with opponents of Western integration even more vehement than Schumacher. Paul Sethe, for example, the influential editor of the conservative *Frankfurter Allgemeine Zeitung,* argued that the FRG should come to terms with its central position within the European balance of power and embrace a more independent policy between East and West.[54]

The perspectives articulated by Adenauer and Schumacher, and the views of history that underpinned them, defined opposing poles in the postwar German foreign policy debate. Their broadly similar approaches to links with the West, national unity, and security were reflective of a broad foreign policy consensus across the most of the political spectrum. The experience of fascism, the Soviet threat, and the imperatives of reconstruction generated broad support for economic, political, and security cooperation with the Western powers. At the same time, the important differences separating Adenauer and Schumacher reflected deep divisions in German society concerning the relative priority of national unity and links with the West. While Adenauer made integration within Western institutions his top priority, Schumacher insisted on a tougher approach to negotiations with the allies and more active efforts to bring about a German settlement. Both men articulated contrasting priorities in the face of the alternatives posed by the international constellation. The struggle to implement those priorities was ultimately decided at the level of party politics.

The Political Clash over Western Integration

Adenauer's priorities prevailed not because they better fit international realities, but because they triumphed in domestic politics. There is no doubt that the Western allies preferred Adenauer to Schumacher. In September 1949, for example, U.S. Secretary of State Dean Acheson had a confrontational encounter with the SPD leader that left a lasting negative impression.[55] In

---

53. Gerhard Ritter, *Staatskunst und Kriegshandwerk: Das Problem des "Militarismus" in Deutschland* (Munich: R. Oldenbourg, 1954), 1:9. Another influential book in the same tradition was Friedrich Meinecke, *The German Catastrophe: Reflections and Recollections* (Cambridge: Harvard University Press, 1950). On historians' efforts to condemn Hitler while upholding a national orientation, see Georg G. Iggers, *The German Conception of History: The National Tradition of Historical Thought from Herder to the Present* (Middletown, Conn.: Wesleyan University Press, 1983), chap. 8.

54. Paul Sethe, *Zwischen Bonn und Moskau* (Frankfurt am Main: Scheffler, 1956), 40–46.

55. See Dean Acheson, *Present at the Creation: My Years in the State Department* (New York: Norton, 1969), 341–42.

setting up the Federal Republic, however, the allies agreed to respect its new democratic institutions. Had Schumacher become chancellor in 1949, as many observers expected, German foreign policy would have taken a different path than it did. It is certainly true that, confronted with the Western powers and ongoing restrictions on German sovereignty, Schumacher would have had to adjust his priorities once in office. Amid the cold war of the early 1950s some kind of Western integration was probably inevitable. Had Schumacher become chancellor, however, that integration would certainly have taken place less smoothly, and probably only after the exhaustion of Four-Power diplomacy. Because the international constellation allowed for alternatives to rapid integration in the West, Adenauer's capacity to place his foreign policy priorities on a stable political foundation ultimately proved decisive.

That foundation was far from secure through the mid-1950s. Among Christian Democrats, for example, Adenauer's priorities were sharply contested during the postwar years. During the late 1940s his bid for CDU/CSU leadership was bound up with a clash over the party's foreign policy stance.[56] Jakob Kaiser, a favorite to emerge as the national Christian Democratic leader in 1945–46, countered Adenauer's priority of Western integration with his idea of Germany as a "bridge between East and West." The concept had related domestic and foreign policy dimensions. As postwar Christian Democratic leader in Berlin and the Soviet zone, Kaiser favored his own brand of Christian socialism, a quixotic mixture of capitalism and socialist values. In terms of foreign policy, Kaiser's "bridge" concept was not a call for a return to the seesaw diplomacy of the past. Like Adenauer and Schumacher, Kaiser supported strong ties with the Western democracies to counter Soviet military power. At the same time, however, he favored an alignment with the West even looser than Schumacher's, one designed to maximize the prospects for reunification through dialogue with Moscow. During the immediate postwar years, Kaiser argued that German leaders in all four zones should seize the unity issue and move it to the top of the European agenda.[57]

The leadership struggle between Adenauer and Kaiser revolved mainly around different understandings of Christian Democracy and its implications for economic and social policy. While Kaiser's views overlapped with those of the SPD, for example on the question of the nation-

---

56. On Adenauer's rise during the late 1940s, see Arnold J. Heidenheimer, *Adenauer and the CDU: The Rise of the Leader and the Integration of the Party* (The Hague: Nijhof, 1960).

57. On Kaiser's views, see the speeches and interviews collected in Jakob Kaiser, *Wir haben Brücke zu sein: Reden, Äußerungen, und Aufsätze zur Deutschlandpolitik* (Cologne: Verlag Wissenschaft und Politik, 1988).

alization of major industry, Adenauer aligned himself with the FDP's more free-market orientation. Nevertheless, the outcome of the struggle had far-reaching implications for the CDU/CSU's foreign policy stance. The critical turning point was the first national conference of regional Christian Democratic leaders, held in April 1947 in Königstein. In the run-up to the conference Kaiser laid claim to the chair of a proposed CDU foreign policy committee, the party's first national office. Kaiser's narrow defeat on the key vote—orchestrated by Adenauer with the help of the Bavarian CSU—weakened his position in the leadership struggle. So, too, did the progressive Sovietization of the Eastern zone. Soviet leaders removed Kaiser as chairman of the CDU-East in December 1947, though he remained head of the Christian Democrats in West Berlin. In the meantime Adenauer exploited his position as head of the CDU in the British zone to secure the CDU/CSU chancellor candidacy for the 1949 elections.[58]

Adenauer's defeat of Kaiser in the postwar leadership struggle, in and of itself, did not secure party approval of his foreign policy priorities. Kaiser's notion of Germany as bridge between East and West lost relevance with the Berlin Blockade and the creation of two German states. But one of his core foreign policy differences with Adenauer, an insistence on the priority of reunification over Western integration, persisted into the 1950s. As minister for All-German Questions in early 1950, for example, Kaiser joined Minister of the Interior Gustav Heinemann in opposing German membership in the Council of Europe. Parallel membership in the Council for the FRG and the Saar, they argued, was incompatible with the imperative of German national unity. Adenauer countered that proposed Saar membership neither signaled that territory's separation from Germany nor implied any acceptance of the German division. He was able to rally the cabinet behind his stance. Several months later Adenauer's drive for a German defense contribution generated further divisions within the CDU leadership. Heinemann, concerned about rearmament and its implications for national unity, quit both the government and the party. Kaiser stayed on.[59]

Differences between Kaiser and Adenauer erupted again in the con-

---

58. On this struggle, see Werner Conze, *Jakob Kaiser: Politiker zwischen Ost und West 1945–1949* (Stuttgart: W. Kohlhammer, 1969), chap. 3. For a colorful account of the Königstein conference from a CSU perspective, see Franz Josef Strauss, *Die Erinnerungen* (Berlin: Siedler, 1989), 117–18.

59. On the controversy, see Schwarz, *Adenauer: Der Aufstieg,* 713–14. On ongoing differences among these three men, see Anselm Doering-Manteuffel, "Konrad Adenauer—Jakob Kaiser—Gustav Heinemann: Deutschlandpolitische Positionen in der CDU," in *Die Republik der fünfziger Jahre: Adenauers Deutschlandpolitik auf dem Prüfstand,* ed. Jürgen Weber (Munich: Olzog, 1989), 18–46. Heinemann founded his own, unsuccessful political party and later joined the SPD.

text of the Stalin Note. Adenauer, who opposed anything short of reunification within the Western alliance, rejected the offer of unity in exchange for neutrality out of hand. In the domestic political context he played down his categorical opposition to negotiations, focusing instead on specific aspects of the Soviet proposals, particularly the procedures for free elections and the recognition of the Oder-Neisse border. Kaiser infuriated Adenauer by speaking out in favor of an allied response to test Soviet intentions. Where Adenauer perceived a Soviet ruse designed to torpedo Western integration and bring all of Germany into its orbit, Kaiser welcomed the possibility of a compromise German settlement. In putting Western integration ahead of talks with the East, Kaiser claimed in a heated cabinet meeting, Adenauer was acting "more American than the Americans." As in the case of the Council of Europe, however, Adenauer proved able to win internal party support for his stance.[60]

The balance of forces within the CDU/CSU was different in the context of the "binding clause" controversy of May 1952. During the negotiation of the EDC and the Bonn Conventions, Adenauer sought to bind a future united Germany to membership in the Western alliance. Kaiser and other prominent CDU/CSU politicians, such as Heinrich von Brentano, a future foreign minister, and Kurt Georg Kiesinger, a future chancellor, voiced a concern that the clause would burden any future negotiations with the Soviet Union. Faced with a party revolt, Adenauer retreated. In last-minute negotiations with the allies, the offending clause was attenuated. While Adenauer's defeat on the "binding clause" controversy did not threaten his overall policy of Western integration, it revealed ongoing differences within his party concerning the absolute priority of integration over Four-Power talks with the Soviet Union. These differences emerged later, in less dramatic fashion, over Adenauer's hard line in the run-up to the 1954 Berlin Conference. His objection to any recognition of GDR authorities as part of an eventual reunification process struck some leading Christian Democrats as too extreme.[61]

Adenauer was aware of the fragility of party support for his policy of rapid integration within the West. In his keynote speeches before annual party conferences in the early 1950s he tirelessly set out and defended his conviction that Western strength and unity were the best means to the end

---

60. For Kaiser's response to the Stalin Note—and his criticism of Adenauer—see Kaiser, *Wir haben Brücke zu sein,* 551–55.

61. On the binding clause controversy, see Schwarz, *Ära Adenauer,* 160–64. On dissatisfaction with Adenauer's uncompromising stance inside the CDU/CSU leadership in the context of the Berlin Conference, see "Conant to the Office of the United States High Commissioner for Germany," January 21, 1954, in *Foreign Relations of the United States 1952–54,* 7:775–77.

of reunification. In meetings of the CDU executive committee he sounded the same themes, ignoring several appeals from Kaiser and his allies that he prod the Western allies to seek a German settlement with the Soviet Union.[62] His concerns about Christian Democratic resistance to his policy of Western integration were most acute in the aftermath of the French rejection of EDC in August 1954. If the edifice of Western integration should collapse, he argued, German national conservatism might revive. There might be "an inevitable drift toward a more independent policy and Germany's traditional interest in the East."[63] Only with the October 1954 Paris Treaties and FRG membership in NATO did Adenauer's anxieties subside. The existence of contrasting views within the CDU/CSU through the mid-1950s underscores the importance of Adenauer's authority as party leader for the direction of German foreign policy.

The implementation of Western integration also required success at the level of coalition politics. The CDU/CSU emerged from the August 1949 general election as the largest single party, but fell far short of an absolute majority. In the ensuing negotiations to form a government, Adenauer rejected Kaiser's call for a Grand Coalition with the SPD, opting instead to work with smaller parties. He managed to put together a fragile Center-Right coalition that included the liberal FDP and the smaller, nationally oriented German Party (DP). In September 1949 the Bundestag elected Adenauer chancellor by a margin of one vote—his own. The survival of the coalition for the duration of its four-year term was, however, far from assured. The implementation of Adenauer's foreign policy depended on his capacity to maintain a fractious coalition with parties ambivalent about its direction.

The Liberals were the CDU/CSU's most important partner in government. Founded in 1948, the FDP was an uneasy amalgam of the national and social strands of German liberalism. It included former supporters of two Weimar parties: Gustav Stresemann's nationally oriented German Peoples' Party and the more progressive German Democratic Party. While Liberal leaders rallied behind most of Adenauer's domestic program, particularly Erhard's free-market economic policies, they were

---

62. See, for example, Adenauer's keynote address at the CDU's 1952 party conference, October 19, 1952, *Dritter Parteitag der Christlich-Demokratischen Union Deutschlands* (Bonn: CDU, 1952), 24–34; and Adenauer before the CDU Executive Committee, January 26, 1953, in Günther Buchstab, ed., *Adenauer: "Es mußte alles gemacht werden": Die Protokolle des CDU-Bundesvorstandes* (Stuttgart: Klett-Cotta, 1986), 318–29.

63. Adenauer made the remarks to an acquaintance, Fabian von Schlabrendorff, who brought them to the attention of the State Department. See "Memorandum of Conversation," July 8, 1954, in *Foreign Relations of the United States, 1952–1954*, 7:582. On Adenauer's concerns in the summer of 1954, see also Schwarz, *Ära Adenauer*, 246–47.

sharply divided on the issue of Western integration. Through the mid-1950s the party's national wing, represented by Baden-Württemberg governor Reinhold Maier and federal justice minister Thomas Dehler, pressed for a more assertive approach toward the Western allies and for greater efforts to prod the Four-Powers toward a German settlement. They opposed Adenauer's efforts to accommodate France on the Saar issue, for example, and backed Four-Power talks on German unity. At a party conference in June 1953 Maier publicly cast doubt on "the seriousness of Bonn's efforts to bring about the reunification of Germany."[64]

Whatever their reservations about the course of Western integration, FDP leaders proved unable to alter its thrust. Adenauer made full use of his constitutional prerogative to set foreign policy guidelines. He often used cabinet meetings to announce foreign policy decisions, rather than to discuss them—and when the allies agreed to create a German foreign ministry in March 1951, Adenauer claimed it for himself. While both the substance and the style of Adenauer's foreign policy irritated the Liberals, they possessed little political leverage in the political constellation of the early 1950s. The FDP had no other prospective coalition partner: its free-market policies clashed with the economic program of the SPD, which still incorporated Marxist elements. Moreover, Adenauer skillfully exploited rifts among the Liberals, cultivating ties with FDP leaders more sympathetic to his policy of Western integration. When Dehler, elected party leader in 1954, pulled out of the coalition in 1956, the FDP split. Most Liberal ministers and some Bundestag deputies continued to back Adenauer, helping to preserve his ruling majority. Adenauer's mastery of coalition politics, like his control over the CDU/CSU, made the implementation of his foreign policy priorities possible.[65]

In order for Adenauer to implement his foreign policy priorities it was not enough to secure the support of the CDU/CSU and the FDP. He also had to overcome an ongoing political and parliamentary challenge from the Social Democrats. In the immediate postwar years the SPD appeared well positioned to become the leading German party. Even when the CDU/CSU won a narrow victory in the August 1949 elections, SPD lead-

64. Cited in Christof Brauers, *Liberale Deutschlandpolitik 1949–1969: Positionen der F.D.P. zwischen nationaler und europäischer Orientierung* (Hamburg: Lit, 1992), 55. Within the FDP Karl Georg Pfleiderer, an advisor to Maier, was the most articulate advocate of a more active reunification policy during the early 1950s. See Karl Georg Pfleiderer, *Politik für Deutschland: Reden und Aufsätze, 1948–1956* (Stuttgart: Deutsche Verlags-Anstalt, 1961).

65. On coalition politics and FDP development through the mid-1950s, see Jörg Michael Gutscher, *Die Entwicklung der FDP von ihren Anfängen bis 1961* (Königstein: Hain, 1984), chaps. 3–4.

ers held out some hope for a Grand Coalition. Adenauer, however, was intent on excluding the Social Democrats from power, not least in order to secure a freer hand in the conduct of his foreign policy. Only by relegating the SPD to the opposition in 1949, repulsing its political and legal challenges to his foreign policy in the years that followed, and decisively defeating the Social Democrats at the polls in 1953 was he able to secure the implementation of Western integration.[66]

Schumacher's opposition to Western integration was not an object of consensus among SPD leaders. Ernst Reuter, the mayor of West Berlin, and Carlo Schmid, a leading Social Democratic parliamentarian, were more open to the thrust of Adenauer's foreign policy. But Schumacher, whose claim to SPD leadership was uncontested after 1945, defined the party's confrontational stance. A dramatic clash with Adenauer in the first foreign policy debate in the Bundestag in November 1949 set the tone. On the occasion of the Petersberg Treaty, Schumacher stepped up his attacks on continued allied dismantling of German industry—and Adenauer's failure to stop it. His cry of "Federal Chancellor of the allies!" unleashed a tumult and earned him a parliamentary censure. When Adenauer and Schumacher conferred on foreign policy matters in private, their tone was not acrimonious. The public foreign policy debate between them and their parties, by contrast, was sharply polarized.[67]

During the early 1950s rearmament, reunification, and the links between the two were central to the struggle between government and opposition. Social Democratic objections to the EDC project—that the proposed European force would discriminate against the Federal Republic and prejudice Four-Power talks on reunification—initially resonated with German public opinion. A series of SPD victories in state elections in 1950–51 made the ratification of the EDC and the Bonn Conventions an uncertain prospect. The government parties' majority in the Bundesrat, or Federal Chamber, necessary for ratification, evaporated. Schumacher called for new national elections, claiming that Adenauer's government, formed before the eruption of the rearmament controversy, had no mandate to address the issue. Adenauer contemptuously dismissed this argument. But he still faced the difficult task of securing parliamentary approval for his foreign policy.

The final months of Schumacher's life saw an escalation of the conflict between government and opposition. In January 1952 the SPD

---

66. On SPD opposition to Adenauer's approach to rearmament and national unity, see Gordon D. Drummond, *The German Social Democrats in Opposition, 1949–1960: The Case against Rearmament* (Norman: University of Oklahoma Press, 1982).

67. For Schumacher's remark, see the debate of November 25, 1949, *Verhandlungen des deutschen Bundestags,* ser. 1, 525.

tried unsuccessfully to block the ratification of the ECSC in the Bundestag. In March the Stalin Note led to a bitter exchange between Adenauer and Schumacher. And two months later Schumacher stated that anyone who supported the EDC and the Bonn Conventions "would cease to be a German."[68] Both before and after his death in August this strident opposition to Adenauer's Western integration continued to define Social Democratic foreign policy. The SPD first challenged the EDC Treaty in the courts, charging that its provisions for rearmament required constitutional changes. While the complex legal controversy dragged on, Adenauer secured ratification in the Bundestag in March 1953, after a final, acrimonious debate pitting government against opposition.[69] In the months that followed, the SPD shifted its efforts to the Bundesrat, where the CDU-led states were in a minority. Speculation centered around the votes of Baden-Württemberg, a state where Maier and the Liberals governed in coalition with the Social Democrats. Maier had misgivings about the treaties' implications for national unity. Unwilling to risk the collapse of the Christian-Liberal coalition in Bonn, however, he did not oppose them in the decisive May 1953 vote.

The ratification of EDC did not secure Adenauer's policy of Western integration. The prospects for EDC approval in the French National Assembly continued to dwindle. In the context of this uncertainty the issues of rearmament and reunification moved to the center of the 1953 national election campaign. Adenauer attacked the SPD's opposition to rearmament as capitulation before Soviet power: a prominent CDU campaign poster charged, "All Marxist Roads Lead to Moscow." Erich Ollenhauer, Schumacher's successor atop the SPD, condemned rearmament in the West as an obstacle to reunification. Sensitive to this criticism, Adenauer temporarily reversed his opposition to a Four-Power conference in June 1953.[70] Two months earlier, during his first visit to the United States as chancellor, he had secured Eisenhower's pledge in support of reunification—a gesture that boosted his election prospects. In September the coalition, buoyed by the onset of the German "economic miracle," handily won reelection. The CDU/CSU fell just short of an absolute majority. With the support of the FDP and other smaller parties, however,

---

68. Schumacher's open letter to Adenauer of May 15, 1952, in Schumacher, *Reden,* 902. On Schumacher's efforts to block Western integration, see also Merseburger, *Der schwierige Deutsche,* 505–30; Drummond, *German Social Democrats in Opposition,* 12–33.

69. Bundestag ratification debate of March 19, 1953, *Verhandlungen des deutschen Bundestages,* ser. 1, 12296–361.

70. On the link between his shift in position and the campaign, see Adenauer before the CDU leadership, July 15, 1953, in Buchstab, *Adenauer: "Es mußte alles neu gemacht werden,"* 584, 647.

Adenauer managed to forge a two-thirds Bundestag majority—enough votes for any constitutional changes necessary to secure rearmament.[71]

With his position more secure after the elections, Adenauer still faced adamant SPD opposition to his foreign policy. After the collapse of the EDC the move toward a NATO solution also met with attacks from Social Democratic ranks. While Schumacher's main objection to rearmament had been its negative implications for reunification, the new SPD leadership also stressed its adverse impact on European security. The party's leading security expert, Fritz Erler, articulated the Social Democrats' concept of a European Collective Security System as an alternative to two opposing military blocs.[72] Both themes—concerns about reunification and opposition to the militarization of the East-West conflict—resonated in the final Bundestag debate on the Western Treaties, in February 1955. Erler and other SPD leaders warned that rearmament within the West would both deepen the German division and heighten East-West tensions. But the government had the votes to secure ratification. A drawn-out but ultimately successful struggle with the opposition enabled the realization of Adenauer's policy of Western integration.[73]

Enduring Effects of Western Integration

An adequate explanation of the postwar transformation of German foreign policy requires attention to the international constellation as well as domestic political controversies. Shifts at the level of international structure—the deepening division of Germany and the onset of the cold war—marked a first critical juncture in the foreign policy of the Federal Republic. Two institutions, the Three- and Four-Power regimes, framed German responses to two pressing issues: rearmament and reunification. The intensity of the cold war and strictures on German sovereignty left no reasonable alternative to a Western orientation, but allowed different approaches to its realization. Adenauer made integration within Western institutions an absolute priority over East-West dialogue on reunification. Schu-

---

71. For Adenauer's request to Eisenhower that he make a public commitment to the goal of reunification, see his letter of June 21, 1953, *Foreign Relations of the United States 1952–1954,* 7:1591. On the transition from Schumacher to Ollenhauer, see Michael Longerich, *Die SPD als "Friedenspartei"—mehr als nur Wahltaktik?* (Lang: Frankfurt am Main, 1990), 73–79.

72. Hartmut Soell, *Fritz Erler: Eine Politische Biographie* (Berlin: Dietz, 1976), 1:164–88.

73. On changes in SPD security policy in the mid-1950s, see Udo F. Löwke, *Die SPD und die Wehrfrage: 1949 bis 1955* (Bonn: Verlag Neue Gesellschaft, 1976), chap. 4. The climactic Bundestag debate took place on February 24–25, 1955, *Verhandlungen des deutschen Bundestages,* ser. 2, 3511–858.

macher, while generally pro-Western and anti-Soviet in outlook, pressed for a more independent approach to the allies and a more active policy on the national issue. While these contrasting priorities constituted the main contours of foreign policy debate, the struggle within and across the parties decided its outcome. Only by anchoring his priorities within the CDU/CSU, in coalition with the FDP, and in competition with the SPD was Adenauer able to forge a new German foreign policy.

The postwar transformation of German foreign policy had enduring institutional and political effects. With his embrace of NATO and the EC, Adenauer contributed to a new institutional context for subsequent German foreign policy. Membership in NATO effectively precluded a reversion to a national orientation. As a member of the alliance, the FRG both embraced multilateralism and accepted continued important restrictions on its armed forces—the absence of a national general staff and a renunciation of nuclear weapons. At the same time, membership in the EC—and the broader global trade regime within which it was embedded—ruled out a return to protectionist, nationalist foreign economic policies. The transition from the Three-Power regime to NATO and EC membership marked the end of postwar strictures on German sovereignty. At the same time, however, it represented the start of a durable multilateral, supranational framework for subsequent German foreign policy. During the late 1950s and early 1960s the importance of that framework was evident amid three prominent controversies.

The first controversy concerned the deployment of nuclear missiles on German soil. By the mid-1950s Soviet progress toward nuclear parity sparked a gradual shift in U.S. military strategy. Once deprived of its nuclear monopoly, the United States could no longer credibly threaten massive retaliation in the event of a Soviet conventional attack on Western Europe. In order to strengthen extended deterrence Washington moved to deploy medium-range nuclear missiles in West Europe and to grant shared access to the allies—including the Federal Republic. Adenauer and his defense minister, Franz Josef Strauss, pressed for such access, unleashing a barrage of Soviet criticism and some concerns in Paris and London—as well as a peace movement at home. The outcome of the controversy highlighted the salience of institutional constraints. Bonn did gain some indirect access to some missiles, but a more ambitious plan to create a sea-based Multilateral Force with German participation failed during the early 1960s. While France and Britain developed their own nuclear arsenals, the FRG had to make do with a seat in NATO's Nuclear Planning Group. The Federal Republic's nonnuclear status, a condition for its alliance membership in 1955, continued to circumscribe its military security options. The FRG remained directly dependent on NATO—and the U.S. nuclear deterrent—for its defense.[74]

The continued salience of Western institutions as a context for German foreign policy was also evident during the Berlin Crisis. In an effort to stop the flow of refugees from East to West Berlin and consolidate the SED regime, Khrushchev announced an ultimatum in November 1958: the Western allies should either agree to a peace treaty with both German states and an independent status for West Berlin, or the Soviet Union would sign a separate peace treaty with the GDR and hand over control of access to the divided city to East Berlin authorities.[75] The Soviet ultimatum, which the Western powers rejected out of hand, challenged the Federal Republic's commitment to national unity; it endangered the survival of West Berlin and threatened to secure international recognition for the GDR. At the same time, the crisis illustrated Bonn's dependence on its allies within the context of both NATO and the Four-Power regime. Adenauer rejected negotiations on anything but technical issues bearing on the situation in Berlin. He was powerless, however, to prevent some revival of East-West dialogue about Germany as a whole in 1959–60, which he feared might culminate in a Four-Power settlement at Bonn's expense. As it happened, that dialogue went nowhere. But the ultimate resolution of the Berlin Crisis also illustrated the salience of institutional constraints on German foreign policy. Khrushchev and GDR leader Walter Ulbricht stopped the refugee flow in August 1961 with the construction of the Berlin Wall, to which the Western powers acquiesced. The Federal Republic was powerless to prevent this deepening of the German division.

A third foreign policy controversy, the growing rift between France and the United States, also underscored the resilience of international institutions as a framework for German foreign policy. Charles de Gaulle came to power as the first president of the Fifth Republic in 1958, determined to assert Paris's independence with respect to Washington. He built an independent French nuclear arsenal, withdrew France from NATO's military integration, and embarked on an active Ostpolitik. At the same time, de Gaulle vetoed Great Britain's entry into the EC, a step that angered both London and Washington. Adenauer expressed growing sym-

---

74. On the controversy, see Mark Cioc, *Pax Atomica: The Nuclear Defense Debate in West Germany during the Adenauer Era* (New York: Columbia University Press, 1988); Cathleen McArdle Kelleher, *Germany and the Politics of Nuclear Weapons* (New York: Columbia University Press, 1975), chaps. 3–5.

75. The text of Khrushchev's ultimatum of November 27, 1958, in *Documents on Germany*, 552–59.

pathy with de Gaulle's political vision of a Europe more independent from the United States, with France and the Federal Republic at its core.[76] In January 1963 he and de Gaulle signed the Franco-German Treaty, the capstone of postwar reconciliation and a foundation for future political and security cooperation. To de Gaulle's chagrin, however, Bonn did not loosen its institutional links with Washington. Dependent on the U.S. troop presence and nuclear deterrent for its security, the FRG continued to make NATO a crucial multilateral framework for its foreign policy. Rivalry between Washington and Paris did not leave Bonn with a choice between an Atlantic and a West European orientation. As a member of both NATO and the EC, the Federal Republic had to find ways to combine both.

The years after 1955 also revealed enduring effects of Western integration at the level of domestic politics. Sharply contested during the early 1950s, Adenauer's foreign policy priorities gradually became an object of broad consensus. Opposition to Adenauer's basic foreign policy orientation subsided in the CDU/CSU. Kaiser and other more nationally minded members of the Christian Democratic leadership did occasionally raise the national issue. But Adenauer continued to insist—successfully—on the absolute priority of Western strength and unity, particularly in the context of the Berlin Crisis. During the early 1960s Erhard, eager to succeed Adenauer as chancellor, criticized certain aspects of his Western policy. He supported EC membership for Britain and unequivocally considered Washington, not Paris, the Federal Republic's most important international partner. While it continued through the middle of the decade, the clash between "Atlanticists" and "Gaullists" within the CDU/CSU did not affect the overriding importance of Western integration as a foundation for Christian Democratic foreign policy. While differences concerning the relative importance of the United States and France persisted, Adenauer's pro-Western, anti-Soviet stance remained an object of internal party consensus.[77]

The FDP, which had followed Western integration with ambivalence during the early 1950s, gradually embraced it fully. After the Liberals left the government, in 1956, they initially stepped up their attacks on Ade-

---

76. On German-American differences emerging out of this constellation during the Kennedy administration, see the memoirs of the German ambassador in Washington at the time, Wilhelm G. Grewe, *Rückblenden 1976–1951* (Frankfurt am Main: Propylaen, 1979), 545–74. On the struggle over the EC's future, see Hans von der Groeben, *Aufbaujahre der Europäischen Gemeinschaft: Das Ringen um den Gemeinsamen Markt und die Politische Union (1958–1966)* (Baden-Baden: Nomos, 1982).

77. On development of the CDU during the mid-1960s, see Klaus Dedring, *Adenauer—Erhard—Kiesinger: Die CDU als Regierungspartei 1961–69* (Pfaffenweiler: Centaurus, 1989), chap. 4.

nauer's handling of the unity issue. In a blistering January 1958 speech, for example, Dehler accused Adenauer of having missed a historic opportunity with his negative response to the Stalin Note.[78] And party leaders, whose rhetoric still contained references to Germany's "middle position" in Europe [*Mittellage*], initially pressed for reunification initiatives in the context of the Berlin Crisis. Gradually, however, both the fait accompli of Western integration and a poor showing in the 1957 elections sparked a foreign policy shift. The FDP, which had voted against the Treaty of Rome in the Bundestag, gave up its objections to European integration. And, confronted with Soviet belligerence during the Berlin Crisis, Liberal leaders embraced Western integration as the necessary foundation for any active Ostpolitik.[79]

The Social Democratic embrace of Western integration also took place slowly and unevenly. During the late 1950s the SPD fought the creation of the Bundeswehr, opposed German access to nuclear weapons, and showed interest in Soviet "disengagement" plans—proposals that envisioned the dissolution of the blocs in combination with possible movement toward German unity.[80] Faced with the reality of NATO and the EC, however, and with two devastating electoral defeats, in 1953 and 1957, Social Democratic leaders began to reconsider their opposition to Western integration. They welcomed the 1957 Treaty of Rome and affirmed the principle of national defense [*Landesverteidigung*] in their March 1959 Godesberg Program. The clearest change in the SPD stance took place, unexpectedly, in a June 1960 Bundestag debate. Herbert Wehner, one of the party's parliamentary leaders, stunned his listeners with the statement that membership in the Western alliance represented a new foundation for German foreign policy.[81] The gulf that separated government and opposition foreign policies during the early 1950s had begun to disappear.

By the early 1960s the foreign policy of the Federal Republic was not only securely anchored within a new institutional framework. It also rested on a new domestic political foundation. Adenauer's transformation of Ger-

---

78. Dehler's address of January 23, 1958, *Verhandlungen des deutschen Bundestags,* ser. 3, 384–99.

79. On shifts in the tone of FDP foreign policy in the context of the Berlin Crisis, see Brauers, *Liberale Deutschlandpolitik,* 119–23

80. On SPD opposition to nuclear armament under the motto "struggle against atomic death," see Drummond, *German Social Democrats in Opposition,* 212–41.

81. Wehner's address of June 30, 1960, *Verhandlungen des deutschen Bundestags,* ser. 3, 7052–61. On the shift in SPD security policy, see Lothar Wilker, *Die Sicherheitspolitik der SPD, 1956–1966: Zwischen Wiedervereinigungs- und Bündnisorientierung* (Bonn: Neue Gesellschaft, 1977). On SPD European policy during this period, see William E. Paterson, *The SPD and European Integration* (Lexington, Mass.: Lexington Books, 1974).

man foreign policy, implemented against considerable opposition, became the object of a broad partisan consensus. Just as that consensus was taking shape, however, an underlying change in East-West relations—the shift from cold war to detente—began to confront German leaders with new fundamental policy challenges. Both the trend toward strategic parity and the deepening German division, most obvious after the construction of the Berlin Wall, led the Western allies to engage the Soviet Union in dialogue on the basis of the division of Europe. In this emerging constellation Adenauer's confrontational policy toward the Soviet Union and refusal to recognize the existence of the GDR threatened to isolate the FRG in Europe. Pro-Western and anti-Soviet policies no longer reinforced each other as they had a decade earlier.

During the final years of his chancellorship Adenauer sought in vain to slow momentum toward detente on the basis of the postwar status quo. But his strong anti-Soviet stance on Berlin and security issues was increasingly at odds with the new East-West climate. The failure of his policy of strength, premised on the view that Western might and unity would compel the Soviet Union to accept a favorable German settlement, became increasingly evident after the resolution of the Berlin Crisis and the subsequent consolidation of the SED regime.[82] Adenauer acknowledged this himself. Confronted with the prospect of German isolation amid detente, he entertained the possibility of a new departure. He communicated several secret plans to Soviet leaders, offers to place a moratorium on consideration of reunification in exchange for democratic reforms in the GDR. But Khrushchev, committed to the further consolidation of the SED regime, refused to respond. While some observers have portrayed this and other related initiatives as a precursor to the New Ostpolitik, they had more in common with the hard-line policies of the 1950s. Adenauer still refused any recognition of East Berlin or the Oder-Neisse border. And his public rhetoric remained overwhelmingly confrontational.[83]

This pattern did not change fundamentally once Erhard succeeded Adenauer as chancellor in late 1963. Erhard and his foreign minister, Gerhard Schröder, sought to breathe life into a stagnant Ostpolitik. The new government's "policy of movement" led to the establishment of German

82. On the GDR's growing stability during the 1960s, see A. James McAdams, *East Germany and Detente: Building Authority after the Wall* (Cambridge: Cambridge University Press, 1985).

83. Two versions of Adenauer's proposals, dating from 1959 and 1960, are reprinted in Rudolf Morsey and Konrad Repgen, eds., *Adenauer-Studien III* (Mainz: Matthias-Grünewald-Verlag, 1974), 202–9. For the problematic argument that Adenauer's approach foreshadowed the detente of the 1970s, see Peter Siebenmorgen, *Gezeitenwechsel: Aufbruch zur Entspannungspolitik* (Bonn: Bouvier, 1990).

trade missions in several Central and East European states and an improvement of bilateral relations below the level of full diplomatic recognition.[84] It remained encumbered, however, by demonstrative nonrecognition of the GDR and the Oder-Neisse border—positions that also burdened relations with the Soviet Union. Erhard's "Peace Note" of March 1966 was illustrative. It offered bilateral renunciation of force agreements to the states of the Warsaw Pact—but excluded the GDR. Moreover, it insisted that Germany's prewar borders, "the borders of 1937," form the basis for a future German settlement. Not surprisingly, the Soviet reaction was hostile.[85] Through the mid-1960s German foreign policy remained largely isolated from the overall trend toward detente in Europe. This changed dramatically in the years that followed.

---

84. On the "policy of movement," see William Griffith, *The Ostpolitik of the Federal Republic of Germany* (Cambridge: MIT Press, 1978), 107–30. On Erhard's foreign policy, see Horst Osterheld, *Außenpolitik unter Bundeskanzler Ludwig Erhard 1963–1966: Ein dokumentarischer Bericht aus dem Kanzleramt* (Düsseldorf: Droste, 1992).

85. On Soviet-German relations in the mid-1960s, see Michael J. Sodaro, *Moscow, Germany and the West from Khrushchev to Gorbachev* (Ithaca: Cornell University Press, 1990), chaps. 2–3. Text of the Peace Note of March 25, 1966, in *Documents on Germany*, 914–18.

CHAPTER 3

Detente and the New Ostpolitik

The New Ostpolitik of the 1970s marked a second major turning point in the foreign policy of the Federal Republic. During the early 1950s, membership in NATO and the EC—and an eventual political consensus around them—provided a new Western foundation for German foreign policy. At the same time, however, Konrad Adenauer and his successor, Ludwig Erhard, remained locked in political and ideological confrontation with Moscow and East Berlin. During the Grand Coalition of 1966–69 Chancellor Kurt Georg Kiesinger (CDU/CSU) and Foreign Minister Willy Brandt (SPD) sought to improve ties with the East. Only when Brandt succeeded Kiesinger as chancellor, however, did a significant new departure take place. Brandt broke with two decades of FRG foreign policy, embracing a dialogue with the Soviet Union and its allies based upon the reality—if not the permanence—of the division of Germany and Europe. The New Ostpolitik did not dismantle close ties with the West. The FRG continued to support European integration and the Atlantic Alliance. Nevertheless, a series of bilateral Eastern Treaties and the multilateral Conference on Security and Cooperation in Europe constituted an additional institutional basis for its subsequent foreign policy. Firmly anchored in the West, the Federal Republic opened to the East.[1]

The New Ostpolitik took shape immediately after Brandt assumed the chancellorship. In his first government declaration, in October 1969, Brandt signaled a readiness to engage Soviet leaders in a wide-ranging bilateral dialogue on the basis of the territorial status quo. The central passage of his declaration, a reference to "two states in Germany," repre-

---

1. On the New Ostpolitik in general, see Timothy Garton Ash, *In Europe's Name: Germany and the Divided Continent* (New York: Random House, 1993); William Griffith, *The Ostpolitik of the Federal Republic of Germany* (Cambridge: MIT Press, 1978); Peter Bender, *Neue Ostpolitik: Vom Mauerbau bis zum Moskauer Vertrag* (Munich: Deutscher Taschenbuch Verlag, 1986); Egbert Jahn and Volker Rittberger, eds. *Die Ostpolitik der BRD: Triebkräfte, Widerstände, Konsequenzen* (Opladen: Westdeutscher Verlag, 1984).

sented a sharp break with two decades of total nonrecognition of the SED regime in East Berlin. Brandt quickly added that both German states could not consider each other foreign countries—that their relationship was of a special nature. The Federal Republic, he underlined, remained committed to the constitutional goal of unity and freedom through self-determination. In recognizing the reality of the GDR as a state, however, Brandt jettisoned the Federal Republic's traditional claim to be the only legitimate international representative of the German people. That claim had persisted even into Brandt's tenure as foreign minister during the Grand Coalition of the late 1960s.[2]

Brandt's willingness to acknowledge—if not accept—the division of Germany eliminated the single most important obstacle to an improvement of ties with the Soviet Union. Almost immediately, the bilateral negotiations began that culminated with the Moscow Treaty of August 1970. Endorsed by Brandt and Soviet leader Leonid Brezhnev during a summit in the Soviet capital, the treaty marked a sharp break with two decades of hostility in bilateral relations. Its most important provisions were the mutual renunciation of force and the recognition of the inviolability of existing borders in Europe. More generally, the Moscow Treaty committed the Federal Republic and the Soviet Union to economic and cultural cooperation, as well as joint efforts to further peace and detente in Europe. During the final negotiations Brandt and his foreign minister, Walther Scheel, reminded the Soviet leadership of Bonn's unbroken commitment to reunification in a "Letter on German Unity." Yet in practice the Moscow Treaty confirmed the elimination of reunification from the Ostpolitik agenda. German-Soviet relations improved dramatically. The Federal Republic emerged as the Soviet Union's most important political and economic partner in Western Europe.[3]

The breakthrough with Moscow enabled better ties with the rest of the Soviet bloc. Upon taking office, Brandt also engaged the Polish leadership in negotiations on a normalization of bilateral ties. The Warsaw Treaty of December 1970, like the Moscow Treaty, included a renunciation of force and a recognition of existing borders. The border issue proved particularly sensitive, given the legacy of Hitler's war and the sub-

---

2. Brandt's declaration of October 28, 1969, *Verhandlungen des deutschen Bundestags. Stenographischer Bericht,* ser. 6, 21–32. On the onset of the New Ostpolitik, see Günther Schmid, *Entscheidung in Bonn: Die Entstehung der Ost-und Deutschlandpolitik, 1969–1970* (Cologne: Verlag Wissenschaft und Politik, 1979).

3. On the origins of the Moscow Treaty, see the memoirs of one of its main architects, Egon Bahr, *Zu meiner Zeit* (Munich: Karl Blessing Verlag, 1996), chap. 6; Griffith, *Ostpolitik,* 181–96. Text of the Moscow Treaty and "Letter on German Unity," in *Documents on Germany, 1944–1985* (Washington: U.S. Government Printing Office, 1985), 1103–5.

sequent transfer of German territory to Poland. In the treaty the Federal Republic explicitly recognized the Oder-Neisse line as Poland's western border. From a legal perspective the German government insisted—in keeping with Four-Power responsibility—that the final determination of the border would have to await a German settlement. Politically, though, the Warsaw Treaty signified a German renunciation of territorial claims for the present and the future. Other issues continued to burden bilateral ties—the rights of the German minority in Poland and compensation for Polish laborers in wartime Germany. But the treaty, together with Brandt's dramatic kneeling gesture at the monument to the Warsaw Ghetto uprising during his December 1970 visit, marked a new start for German-Polish reconciliation.[4]

The initial breakthrough in ties with the GDR proved more difficult. Early in his term Brandt underlined his willingness to increase economic and cultural cooperation with East Berlin. But his offer of dialogue ran up against GDR insistence on full diplomatic recognition and an exchange of ambassadors. Two meetings between Brandt and GDR prime minister, Willi Stoph, in 1970 produced no concrete accords. Only after Erich Honecker—then a moderate—assumed the leadership of the ruling SED in May 1971 did the bilateral dialogue intensify. In December 1972 the FRG and the GDR endorsed a Basic Treaty setting out institutional foundations for the bilateral relationship. The treaty outlined areas for practical economic, cultural and political cooperation, bracketing fundamental differences on the issue of German unity. And it called for the exchange of permanent representatives, not ambassadors. Both German states pledged to apply for admission to the United Nations—a step they took in June 1973. The Basic Treaty inaugurated an inter-German modus vivendi.[5]

During the early 1970s the Federal Republic flanked its Ostpolitik with an active policy toward the West. The new government brought its arms control policies into line with those of its allies, dropping the long-standing German demand that any accords be linked with progress toward German unity—or at least not recognize the GDR as a signatory. Brandt also supported plans to modernize NATO's conventional forces. Just as

---

4. On the subsequent development of bilateral ties, see Werner Plum, ed. *Ungewöhnliche Normalisierung: Beziehungen der Bundesrepublik Deutschland zu Polen* (Bonn: Verlag Neue Gesellschaft, 1984). For the text of the Warsaw Treaty, see *Documents on Germany,* 1125–27.

5. On inter-German relations in the early 1970s, see A. James McAdams, *Germany Divided: From the Wall to Reunification* (Princeton: Princeton University Press, 1993), 79–95; Ernest D. Plock, *The Basic Treaty and the Evolution of East-West German Relations* (Boulder: Westview, 1986).

significant from a political perspective, the chancellor coordinated his engagement in the East with the allies, and the United States in particular. Bonn informed Western capitals of the progress of its dialogue with Moscow, while the allies consulted Bonn on the negotiations that culminated in the Berlin Treaty of September 1971. The treaty delineated the rights and obligations of the Four Powers and both German states in the former Reich capital. It permitted links between the Federal Republic and West Berlin but dictated that the latter was not to be considered a constituent part of the former. By clarifying the legal status of the city, the Berlin Treaty normalized a complex situation that had twice—in the late 1940s and late 1950s—sparked crises in East-West relations.[6]

The Federal Republic also demonstrated its continued commitment to Western unity through support of ambitious efforts to strengthen the EC. During the 1960s the integration process had stagnated. Some progress was made toward the completion of a single market, particularly with the creation of a Common Agricultural Policy. But de Gaulle's veto of British membership and refusal to endorse stronger European political institutions brought integration momentum to a standstill through the French president's retirement in April 1969. At an EC summit in The Hague that December, two months after Brandt took office, European leaders sought to relaunch the integration process. They pledged to complete the single market and move toward a single currency; to extend Community membership to Britain, Ireland, and Denmark; and to intensify and institutionalize their foreign policy cooperation. The new German government was one of the most enthusiastic supporters of this ambitious agenda.[7]

While Brandt did not neglect relations with the Western allies, he focused his energies on ties with the East. The Moscow, Warsaw, and Basic Treaties served as the foundation of an active Ostpolitik through his resignation from office in May 1974. Brandt and Brezhnev signed far-reaching accords on economic cooperation at a summit in Bonn in May 1973. And that December the FRG and Czechoslovakia completed a treaty normalizing their ties. There were some persistent Ostpolitik tensions. Soviet leaders continued to object to any FRG political presence in West Berlin and refused to sign bilateral cultural and technical accords

---

6. On the Berlin Accord, see Honore M. Catudal Jr., *The Diplomacy of the Quadripartite Agreement on Berlin: A New Era in East-West Politics* (Berlin: Berlin Verlag, 1977); David M. Keithly, *Breakthrough in the Ostpolitik: The 1971 Quadripartite Agreement* (Boulder: Westview, 1986).

7. On Germany and the EC during the 1960s and 1970s, see Werner J. Feld, *West Germany and the European Community: Changing Interests and Competing Policy Objectives* (New York: Praeger, 1981).

with their German counterparts that incorporated the divided city. At the same time, the Honecker regime sought to curb the interaction between East and West Germans envisioned in the Basic Treaty—a policy of limited contacts [*Abgrenzung*] designed to buttress its domestic authority. Still, there was no return to the confrontation of the past, with its bitter controversies over the national issue. With the New Ostpolitik, Bonn came to terms with the status quo of Europe's division. The CSCE Final Act, signed in Helsinki in August 1975, marked the culmination of this development. The NATO and Warsaw Pact states—the FRG and GDR included—endorsed existing borders and pledged to deepen their economic, political and security cooperation.[8]

Policy Challenges: Relations with the Soviet Union and the GDR

The second key juncture in postwar German foreign policy—the combination of Western integration and engagement in the East—was a response to a gradual and uneven international shift from cold war to detente. That trend, which began with Stalin's death in March 1953, reached a first high point at the July 1955 Geneva Four-Power Summit. With the "Spirit of Geneva" the Western powers and the Soviet Union began to shift their attention from the issues of German reunification and rearmament to questions of East-West dialogue and arms control.[9] They gradually moved to embrace detente on the basis of the status quo of the German and European division. This trend, which accelerated during the 1960s, confronted German leaders with difficult policy problems. To adhere to Adenauer's anti-Soviet stance and principled refusal to recognize East Berlin risked the FRG's growing political isolation between East and West. At the same time, to embrace an active dialogue with Moscow and its allies risked undermining ties with the West and cementing the division of Germany.

The contours of the new international configuration only gradually became apparent. First signs of detente in the mid-1950s gave way to renewed confrontation after the 1956 Soviet invasion of Hungary, the Berlin Crisis of 1958–61, and the Cuban Missile Crisis of October 1962. The outcome of each crisis, in turn, accelerated momentum toward detente

---

8. On the limits on Ostpolitik and the German contribution to the CSCE in the early 1970s, see Karl Dietrich Bracher, Wolfgang Jäger, and Werner Link, *Republik im Wandel 1969–1974: Die Ära Brandt* (Stuttgart: Deutsche Verlags-Anstalt, 1986), 231–33.

9. On the start of this shift in East-West ties, see John Van Oudenaren, *Detente in Europe: The Soviet Union and the West since 1953* (Durham: Duke University Press, 1991), 25–45.

on the basis of the European status quo. While the Western powers objected vehemently to the Soviet suppression of the Hungarian revolution, their unwillingness to intervene underscored Europe's de facto division into two opposing ideological, military, and political blocs. Two years later Khrushchev's efforts to drive the Western allies from Berlin sparked a drawn-out confrontation. The resolution of the crisis, however, created momentum for detente. The August 1961 construction of the Berlin Wall stopped the flow of refugees to the West, stabilized the GDR, and ultimately reduced East-West tensions in the divided city. In assenting to the division of the Reich capital, the Western powers effectively signaled their recognition of the reality of the German division. The resolution of the Cuban Missile Crisis also furthered detente in Europe. The superpowers stepped back from the brink of a nuclear confrontation and embraced arms control. They signed a Test Ban Treaty in 1963 and began negotiations on a Non-Proliferation Treaty (NPT) concluded in 1968.[10]

Despite this overall relaxation of tensions, a breakthrough in U.S.-Soviet detente did not take place until the early 1970s. The escalation of the Vietnam War in the late 1960s and the Soviet crushing of the Prague Spring in August 1968 set back superpower relations. A wide-ranging dialogue only took hold after Richard Nixon became president in January 1969. At several summits, he and Brezhnev endorsed a series of economic, political, and security accords including the May 1972 Strategic Arms Limitation Treaty (SALT I). The Four Powers completed the Berlin Treaty in September 1971. And NATO and Warsaw Pact states jointly established the CSCE and began Mutual and Balanced Force Reductions talks (MBFR). The early 1970s were not free of East-West tensions. The last phase of the Vietnam War and the beginning of U.S.-Chinese rapprochement placed strains on U.S.-Soviet relations, as did the October 1973 war in the Middle East. Nevertheless, the trend toward detente in the late 1960s and early 1970s constituted a sharply different environment for German foreign policy than had the cold war of the 1950s.[11]

In the decade after Adenauer left office in October 1963, the trend toward detente on the basis of the status quo placed two related problems on the German foreign policy agenda: ties with Moscow and approaches

---

10. On the transition from cold war to detente during the early 1960s, see Richard Löwenthal, *Vom Kalten Krieg zur Ostpolitik* (Stuttgart: Seewald, 1974).

11. On these developments, see Adam B. Ulam, *Dangerous Relations: The Soviet Union in World Politics, 1970–1982* (New York: Oxford University Press, 1983). On the central role of strategic arms negotiations in U.S.-Soviet detente, see John Newhouse, *Cold Dawn: The Story of SALT* (New York: Holt, Rinehart and Winston, 1973).

to East Berlin.[12] Each involved complex tradeoffs. Better relations with the Soviet Union promised to avert German diplomatic isolation amid detente. At the same time, however, strong German-Soviet ties threatened to strain links with the Western allies. The United States, France, and Britain backed a more flexible German policy toward Moscow but were anxious about the possible negative effects of an active Ostpolitik on the unity of the alliance. U.S. ambassador to Bonn George McGhee, for example, noted that some leading policy experts, including Henry Kissinger, were unsure what role the Germans should play in detente.[13] Later, as national security advisor to Nixon, Kissinger supported a more flexible German stance, but recalled that from "Bismarck to Rapallo it was the essence of Germany's nationalist foreign policy to maneuver freely between East and West." French Presidents Charles de Gaulle and Georges Pompidou harbored similar concerns about a possible German turn eastward and drift into neutrality. In these international circumstances German leaders faced the challenge of improving ties with Moscow without undermining relations with their Western allies.[14]

Coming to terms with the reality of the GDR involved a linked set of tradeoffs. The Soviet Union demanded recognition of the GDR—and the division of Germany and Europe—as a precondition for better bilateral ties. From Bonn's perspective, however, such recognition risked further consolidating the SED regime and undermining the constitutional commitment to national unity. Through the late 1960s the Federal Republic managed to uphold its international claim to be the sole representative of the German people. Its threat to break off diplomatic relations with any state that exchanged ambassadors with East Berlin—the "Hallstein Doctrine"—deterred non–Warsaw Pact states, with the exception of Yugoslavia and several developing countries, from establishing diplomatic rela-

---

12. For a discussion, see Karl Kaiser, *German Foreign Policy in Transition: Bonn between East and West* (London: Oxford University Press, 1968).

13. See George McGhee, *At the Creation of a New Germany: From Adenauer to Brandt* (New Haven: Yale University Press, 1989), 241–43. The memoirs of George Ball, assistant secretary of state under the Johnson administration, also relate such concerns. See George W. Ball, *Diplomacy for a Crowded World: An American Foreign Policy* (Boston: Little, Brown, 1976), 110–11. Once the New Ostpolitik got under way Dean Acheson and John J. McCloy, influential former architects of U.S. policy toward Germany, warned that it threatened to unravel the Western alliance.

14. Henry Kissinger, *The White House Years* (Boston: Little, Brown, 1979), 409. On French concerns about Ostpolitik, see Haig Simonian, *The Privileged Partnership: Franco-German Relations in the European Community, 1969–84* (Oxford: Clarendon Press, 1984), 94–99; Renata Fritsch-Bournazel, "The French View," in *Germany between East and West,* ed. Edwina Moreton (Cambridge: Cambridge University Press, 1987), 64–82.

tions with the GDR. Within this constellation any inter-German relationship, even one intended to improve living conditions for Germans in the East, necessarily implied some recognition of GDR authorities. And any such recognition would strengthen the SED regime's authority at home and abroad, undercutting Bonn's longstanding self-conception as the only legitimate representative of the German nation. Amid detente FRG leaders faced the problem of how to acknowledge the reality of the GDR without deepening the German division.

The resolution of both problems—ties with Moscow and approaches to East Berlin—remained open through the early 1970s. Some scholars have cast the New Ostpolitik, in retrospect, as a necessary response to the challenge of detente. The Federal Republic, in this interpretation, had no alternative to an active dialogue with Moscow and the recognition of the GDR as a second German state. The straightforward argument from international structure presents two main problems. First, it obscures the instability of detente: its uneven development in the 1950s and 1960s and its subsequent setbacks during the late 1970s and early 1980s. The checkered emergence and subsequent decline of detente revealed it to be a fragile construct. Second, the structural argument neglects the difficult tradeoffs that confronted German leaders. A new approach to Moscow and East Berlin, necessary to avoid diplomatic isolation, had potential negative implications for ties with the West and the prospects for German unity. Given these tradeoffs, the New Ostpolitik was not "the result of a readiness to acquiesce in a political and moral necessity."[15] It was a choice in the face of difficult problems, one framed by an array of European institutions.

Institutions and Alternatives: What Kind of Ostpolitik?

The Federal Republic of the late 1960s and early 1970s was much more powerful than that of the 1950s. Sustained economic growth and rearmament transformed it, after 1955, into a leading—if not *the* leading—power in Western Europe. The "economic miracle" that persisted into the early 1960s generated levels of production and trade greater than those in Britain and France. And the Bundeswehr created during the second half of the 1950s emerged as a formidable military force. Amid the trend toward detente, however, this greater power did not translate into greater independence. The Federal Republic continued to participate within a dense

---

15. Wolfram F. Hanrieder, *Germany, America, Europe: Forty Years of German Foreign Policy* (New Haven: Yale University Press, 1989), 20.

set of international institutions. Anchored in NATO and the EC, the FRG still depended on cooperation with the allies, and the United States in particular, for its military security and economic prosperity. The Four-Power regime, too, persisted as a constraint on German foreign policy—especially in the context of Berlin. During the late 1960s and early 1970s these institutions framed potential German responses to an emergent East-West detente.

From the mid-1950s onward the EC constituted an increasingly important institutional context for German foreign policy. The 1957 Treaty of Rome called for foreign policy consultation and cooperation among the six, but such activity remained sporadic over subsequent years. The Franco-German Treaty of January 1963 formalized political and security consultations between Paris and Bonn; Adenauer and de Gaulle sought to create a bilateral foundation for the articulation of European interests. Yet at the European Community level the French president's emphasis on national sovereignty—and on France's claim to speak for Europe—impeded the emergence of the EC as an international actor. The 1969 Hague Summit proved an important turning point. European leaders created the institution of European Political Cooperation (EPC), a framework for regular contacts among foreign ministers and top foreign policy officials. In the years that followed, EPC served as a forum for consultation on East-West issues. It was one of the multilateral contexts in which Bonn informed its allies about the course of its Ostpolitik.[16]

During the late 1960s and early 1970s NATO represented a much more salient institutional constraint on German foreign policy. From the outset NATO was both a military and a political alliance. It not only placed restrictions on the exercise of German military power, but also constituted a multilateral framework for Bonn's overall foreign policy. In the context of detente, NATO's Harmel Report of December 1967 was an important marker. Noting that the political tasks of the alliance had taken on a new "dimension," the report set out a two-pronged strategy of defense and dialogue. It called both for the maintenance of an adequate nuclear and conventional deterrent and for efforts to engage the Soviet Union and the Warsaw Pact in arms control talks.[17] The Harmel Report

---

16. On the development of EPC, see Elfriede Regelsberger, Phillippe de Schoutheete de Tervarent, and Wolfgang Wessels, eds., *Foreign Policy of the European Union: From EPC to CFSP and Beyond* (Boulder: Lynne Rienner, 1997).

17. Report excerpted in *Außenpolitik der Bundesrepublik Deutschland: Dokumente von 1949 bis 1994* (Cologne: Verlag Wissenschaft und Politik, 1995), 311–13. On its origins, see Helga Haftendorn, "Entstehung und Bedeutung des Harmel-Berichtes der NATO von 1967," *Vierteljahreshefte für Zeitgeschichte* 40, no. 2 (April 1992): 169–221.

laid the groundwork for security dialogue between the blocs: for the conventional arms control that began through MBFR and for the wider political and security dialogue inaugurated with CSCE. It reinvigorated NATO as a political as well as a military framework for German foreign policy.

NATO did not completely displace the Four-Power regime as a context for FRG foreign policy in the 1960s and 1970s. Even after the integration of both German states into opposing alliances, the Four Powers continued to insist on their responsibility for the status of Berlin and Germany as a whole. The Federal Republic could not unilaterally place reunification on the East-West agenda. During the mid-1960s, for example, Erhard's proposal for an international body to address the unity issue found no echo in Moscow and Western capitals. The Four-Power regime also constrained the Federal Republic in the context of Berlin. Although not a signatory of the 1971 Berlin Treaty, Bonn was bound by its outcome—a compromise that allowed for links between the FRG and West Berlin but stressed the latter's political independence. German leaders welcomed the city's greater stability, but had to abandon any efforts to integrate it into the Federal Republic. This absence of sovereignty in the former capital also constrained the overall course of German policy during the late 1960s and early 1970s. Through its leverage in West Berlin, Kissinger realized that the United States could curtail the development of any German-Soviet bilateralism detrimental to allied interests.[18]

Amid the trend toward detente Western institutions and the Four-Power regime framed, but did not determine German foreign policy choices. Ambiguity within and across both sets of institutions left German leaders with significant alternatives in their approach to relations with the Soviet Union. EC efforts to forge a common foreign policy did not move beyond consultations of various kinds. And within NATO, efforts to establish multilateralism in practice ran up against assertions of national sovereignty. During the mid-1960s the collapse of the Multilateral Force and the creation of independent British and French nuclear deterrents undermined the unity of the alliance. So, too, did de Gaulle's decision to withdraw France from NATO's military integration in 1966. Even the Harmel Report, which rallied the alliance around the principle of detente with the Soviet Union the following year, allowed for contrasting national priorities. The report set out a basic foreign policy strategy, but remained vague on the proper mix of defense and dialogue at the heart of it, leaving NATO's "sovereign states" considerable leeway in the formulation of their policy toward Moscow. Within the context of the Atlantic Alliance, then,

---

18. Kissinger, *White House Years,* 823–33.

German leaders were bound to rethink their confrontational Ostpolitik but could decide themselves how to do so.[19]

Freedom of action also existed with respect to East Berlin and the question of national unity. NATO and EC membership and the emergence of a bipolar political order in Europe did rule out a return to the early 1950s, when the Federal Republic was in a position to prod the allies toward negotiations on reunification. During the early 1960s, for example, Adenauer and Erhard were unable to make progress during the Test Ban and NPT negotiations dependent on movement toward a German settlement. At the same time, however, membership in Western institutions did not compel Bonn to recognize the status quo of Germany's division. The Treaty of Rome endorsed the goal of German unity and even handled FRG-GDR trade as internal to the EC. And the Paris Treaties, which sealed German membership in NATO, legally bound the allies to "cooperate to achieve, by peaceful means, their common aim of a reunified Germany enjoying a liberal-democratic constitution, like that of the Federal Republic, and integrated within the European community."[20] As late as 1967, the Harmel Report referred to the German division as a root cause of tensions in Europe and reiterated the NATO commitment to overcoming it.[21] Western support for established German positions on unity were less than solid. In 1959, for example, de Gaulle broke with the United States and Britain and recognized the Oder-Neisse line. But through the 1960s all three Western allies refused to exchange ambassadors with East Berlin and continued to recognize the FRG's claim to represent all Germans in the international arena.

The Four-Power regime, too, did not necessitate FRG recognition of East Berlin and the postwar status quo. While the Western powers and the Soviet Union dropped reunification from the East-West agenda, they continued to exercise their responsibility for questions relating to German unity. The persistence of Four-Power rights kept the unity issue alive—if only in theoretical terms. Interestingly, the openness of the unity issue was acknowledged not only by the Western powers but also by the Soviet Union. During the course of the 1960s Moscow supported a number of confederation plans emanating from East Berlin. The plans, which envisioned close inter-German cooperation on the basis of parity, were a trans-

---

19. Relevant passages from the Harmel Report in *Außenpolitik der Bundesrepublik,* 312. On divisions within the alliance and their implications for German foreign policy, see Roger Morgan, *The United States and West Germany, 1945–1973: A Study in Alliance Politics* (London: Oxford University Press, 1974), chaps. 8–9.

20. *Documents on Germany,* 428.

21. Ibid., 312.

parent effort to secure greater international recognition for the GDR. At the same time, however, they acknowledged the special nature of inter-German ties and the existence of a single German nation. Even the GDR's new 1968 constitution, approved by Moscow, alluded to the existence of a "German nation." On balance, then, the combination of the Four-Power regime and detente made changes in Bonn's established approach to reunification necessary. But they did not dictate recognition of the status quo of the German division.

One could argue that, even though the institutional configuration was permissive, allied pressure—particularly from Washington—created momentum for such recognition. U.S. diplomats did, in fact, show some impatience with the Federal Republic's hard-line stance on relations with East Berlin.[22] At the same time, however, successive U.S. administrations refrained from pressuring Bonn directly on the issue. In view of the growing German contribution to Western defense and ongoing transatlantic irritations over the cost of U.S. forces stationed in the FRG, Washington apparently opted not to pressure Bonn on a matter as sensitive as national unity. If German leaders could not expect reunification initiatives from the allies, Lyndon Johnson told Erhard, they were "encouraged to continue on their own."[23] Even on the Oder-Neisse issue there was no overt U.S. pressure for recognition. In 1968 Ambassador McGhee told then Foreign Minister Brandt that "Americans still held that the final delineation of the German border must await the peace treaty with Germany." The United States, he argued, "did not wish to get ahead of Germany" on the issue. McGhee added only that his government would "support any flexibility the Germans chose to exhibit in their attitude toward their borders."[24]

The institutional constellation of the late 1960s and early 1970s confronted German leaders with significant foreign policy alternatives. It made a continuation of the confrontational policies of the 1950s untenable but was compatible with different approaches to Moscow and East Berlin. The FRG's anti-Soviet stance and uncompromising positions on GDR and Oder-Neisse recognition threatened to isolate it within the multilateral framework of the alliance. At the same time, however, Western institutions

---

22. For an example of such impatience, see the June 1966 testimony of McGeorge Bundy before the Senate Foreign Relations Committee, discussed in Morgan, *United States and West Germany,* 154–55.

23. Memorandum of Conversation, June 10, 1964, cited in McGhee, *At the Creation,* 148.

24. Ibid., 214. On controversy surrounding the financing of U.S. forces in Germany, see Gregory F. Treverton, *The Dollar Drain and American Forces in Germany: Managing the Political Economics of Alliance* (Athens: Ohio University Press, 1978).

allowed German leaders different ways to tone down those demands and engage a more active Ostpolitik—without raising allied concerns about German loyalty to the West. During the late 1960s and early 1970s the Four-Power regime precluded German leaders from placing reunification on the East-West agenda. But it obliged them only to adjust, and not necessarily to abandon, their established policy toward East Berlin. The overall institutional configuration—and the trend toward detente within which it was embedded—confronted the Federal Republic with contrasting options. Bonn could seek to improve relations with Moscow and East Berlin gradually while maintaining but playing down existing positions on nonrecognition. Or it could make the de facto recognition of the political and territorial status quo the starting point for an active Ostpolitik.

Contested Priorities amid Detente

The German response to the alternatives posed by the international constellation emerged out of a prolonged political struggle. The domestic context of German foreign policy shifted in the mid-1960s. With the end of the postwar boom, attention turned from economic growth to problems of consolidation. At the same time, the emergence of the postwar generation moved new issues to the top of the agenda—the still largely unconfronted Nazi past, and authoritarian vestiges in German political culture. Together with the ongoing war in Vietnam and dismal conditions at universities, these trends contributed to student protests and a reform discussion that reached their peak during the Grand Coalition.[25] The 1960s also saw the onset of a societal debate about new directions for German foreign policy. The Berlin Wall sparked a search for new approaches to national unity; some intellectuals began to argue that there was no way around the reality of the GDR. At the same time, new reflection on the enormity of Nazi crimes raised questions concerning the Oder-Neisse border and reconciliation with the victims of Hitler's war in the East. In October 1965, for example, Lutheran Bishops appealed to their compatriots to reconsider their stance on the border and open a new dialogue with their Eastern neighbors.[26]

25. For an influential appeal for further democratic reforms, see Ralf Dahrendorf, *Society and Democracy in Germany* (Garden City, N.J.: Doubleday, 1967), 435–50. On the Grand Coalition, see Reinhard Schmoeckel and Bruno Kaiser, *Die vergessene Regierung: Die Große Koalition 1966–1969 und ihre langfristigen Wirkungen* (Bonn: Bouvier, 1991).

26. Calls for a new approach to the GDR included Eberhard Schulz, *An Ulbricht führt kein Weg mehr vorbei: Provozierende Thesen zur deutschen Frage* (Hamburg: Hoffmann and Campe, 1967); Peter Bender, *Zehn Gründe für eine Anerkennung der DDR* (Frankfurt am Main: Fischer, 1968). An earlier pro-recognition argument was Karl Jaspers, *Freiheit und Wiedervereinigung: Über Aufgaben deutscher Politik* (Munich: Piper, 1960).

Within this shifting societal context, the major parties—Christian Democrats, Social Democrats and Liberals—began to rethink their foreign policy priorities. They remained united around the centrality of Western integration. By 1960 first the CDU/CSU and then the SPD and the FDP embraced NATO and EC membership as a starting point for German foreign policy. The established parties also broadly concurred on the national issue. The goal of unity, set down in the Basic Law and reiterated in the major party programs, remained the object of consensus. On this common foundation, however, the CDU/CSU, SPD, and FDP gradually embraced very different approaches to the challenges posed by detente, and relations with East Berlin and Moscow in particular. During the late 1960s and early 1970s Kiesinger and Brandt, the major rivals for the chancellorship, situated the Federal Republic differently with respect to the international constellation. Kiesinger supported a cautious opening to the East, while Brandt backed a bold new departure. Their views did not exhaust the spectrum of party positions. The Far Right National Democratic Party (NPD), which almost gained a foothold in the Bundestag, endorsed an openly nationalist, pro-reunification and anti-Soviet platform. The leaders of both major parties, however, framed the main foreign policy debate during the Grand Coalition and through Kiesinger's resignation as CDU chairman in July 1971.[27]

As in the case of Adenauer and Kurt Schumacher, different political biographies underpinned contrasting policy stances. Kiesinger, a native of southwest Germany, joined the Nazi party as a youth and served in the foreign ministry during the war. After 1945 he rose quickly in the CDU/CSU, first as a foreign policy expert in the Bundestag under Adenauer and then as governor of Baden-Württemberg, his home state. When Erhard's coalition with the Liberals collapsed, in 1966, the CDU/CSU entrusted Kiesinger, a centrist, with the formation of a Grand Coalition. Brandt, a native of northern Germany, joined the socialist youth movement during the Weimar Republic, spent the Nazi period in exile in Scandinavia, and was active in the resistance. Like Kiesinger, he rose quickly within his party after the war. The most charismatic of the SPD's younger leaders, Brandt was elected mayor of West Berlin in 1957, where he governed through the Berlin Crisis. He also ran as an unsuccessful chancellor

---

27. On the NPD, see John David Nagle, *The National Democratic Party: Right Radicalism in the Federal Republic of Germany* (Berkeley and Los Angeles: University of California Press, 1970); Schmoekel and Kaiser, *Die vergessene Regierung,* chap. 12. National thinking also remained strong among a CDU/CSU minority impatient with the lack of progress toward reunification. See, for example, Hans-Graf Huyn, *Die Sackgasse: Deutschlands Weg in die Isolierung* (Stuttgart: Seewald, 1966).

candidate in 1961 and 1965, before becoming foreign minister in the Grand Coalition.[28]

During the late 1960s and early 1970s the foreign policy priorities of Kiesinger and Brandt overlapped in three important respects.[29] First, both agreed that the Federal Republic must uphold its constitutional commitment to national unity. As a leading CDU foreign policy spokesman during the 1950s and later head of the Bundestag Foreign Affairs Committee, Kiesinger espoused the goal of reunification more forcefully than Adenauer. In May 1952, for example, he was among those who blocked Adenauer's efforts to bind a hypothetical future unified Germany to the Western alliance—partly out of concern that such a "binding clause" might impede a settlement with Moscow.[30] Brandt, too, was firmly committed to the goal of national unity. From his vantage point, as the mayor of West Berlin, he directly confronted the human costs of the deepening German division—families and friends divided, and East Germans deprived of political freedom. Both before and after the 1961 construction of the Berlin Wall, Brandt insisted that national unity remain an overriding priority for German foreign policy. For both Kiesinger and Brandt unity was not just a constitutional injunction; it was also a moral and political imperative.[31]

Second, Kiesinger and Brandt both welcomed the overall trend toward detente. Like Adenauer and Erhard, Kiesinger was strongly anticommunist and suspicious of Soviet intentions. In his first government declaration as chancellor, however, he outlined stronger German support for arms control and for intensified dialogue between the blocs. Kiesinger energetically backed renunciation-of-force accords with Moscow and its allies. And, to the surprise of some of his listeners, he called for the creation of a European "Peace Order" and labeled Germany a "bridge

---

28. The relevant memoirs are Kurt Georg Kiesinger, *Dunkle und helle Jahre: Erinnerungen, 1904–1958* (Stuttgart: Deutsche Verlags-Anstalt, 1989); Willy Brandt, *People and Politics: The Years, 1960–1975* (Boston: Little, Brown, 1978); Willy Brandt, *My Life in Politics* (London: Hamish Hamilton, 1992). See also Dieter Oberndörfer, ed., *Begegnungen mit Kurt Georg Kiesinger: Festgabe zum 80. Geburtstag* (Stuttgart: Deutsche Verlags-Anstalt, 1984); Barbara Marshall, *Willy Brandt: Eine politische Biographie* (Bonn: Bouvier, 1993).

29. For Kiesinger's most important statements as chancellor, see Kurt Georg Kiesinger, *Die Große Koalition, 1966–1969: Reden und Erklärungen des Bundeskanzlers* (Stuttgart: Deutsche Verlags-Anstalt, 1979). For an overview of Brandt's views during the Grand Coalition, see Willy Brandt, *A Peace Policy for Europe* (New York: Holt, Rinehart and Winston, 1969).

30. On this controversy, see Kiesinger, *Dunkle und helle Jahre,* 428–32.

31. The importance of national unity for both was evident during the decisive Bundestag debates on Western integration. See their addresses of February 24, 1955, *Verhandlungen des deutschen Bundestags,* ser. 2, 3531–38 and 3563–68.

between Western and Eastern Europe"—rhetoric reminiscent of Jakob Kaiser's.[32] Brandt was an even more articulate supporter of a German "peace policy." As foreign minister and later as chancellor, he argued that the Federal Republic should support the arms control process and actively seek to improve relations with its Eastern neighbors. Brandt, too, viewed Soviet motives with suspicion. But he argued that the FRG, situated at the center of the bipolar struggle, was in a position to contribute to a relaxation of East-West tensions. Both Kiesinger and Brandt supported detente in principle.[33]

Third, both men conceived of good relations with the East as a precondition for German unity. Adenauer and Erhard had insisted that the German division was a major cause of East-West tension and that lasting detente in Europe was only possible *after* a German settlement. Kiesinger and Brandt both reworked the causal logic: they construed European detente as a means toward national unity, not vice versa. In a June 1967 Bundestag speech, for example, Kiesinger reminded his listeners that a united Germany would have a "critical size" potentially unsettling for both East and West. Therefore, he argued, "the growing together of both parts of Germany can only be conceived as part of the process of overcoming the East-West conflict."[34] Brandt articulated a similar view. From the early 1960s onward he placed the problem of the German division within the larger context of the European division. Only in an all-European framework, Brandt argued, could Germans in East and West preserve the substance of the German nation through the pursuit of closer economic, cultural, and political ties. Both Kiesinger and Brandt reinterpreted the unity injunction of the Basic Law amid the trend toward detente.[35]

On this broad foundation—support for German unity, for detente in

---

32. See the government declaration of December 13, 1966, in Kiesinger, *Die Große Koalition,* 20, 22. For a discussion of the lineage of the term *European Peace Order,* see Garton Ash, *In Europe's Name,* 16–19.

33. For Brandt's approach to detente, see his address before the 1966 SPD party conference in Dortmund, in *Protokoll der Verhandlungen und Anträge vom Parteitag der Sozialdemokratischen Partei Deutschlands vom 1.–5. Juni in Dortmund* (Bonn: Vorstand der SPD, 1966), 82–85.

34. Kiesinger address of June 17, 1967, in Kiesinger, *Die Große Koalition,* 81. Franz Josef Strauss, the leader of the conservative CSU, also downplayed the immediate goal of reunification, while remaining strongly committed to established German legal positions on nonrecognition of the GDR and the Oder-Neisse border. See Strauss, *The Grand Design: A European Solution to German Reunification* (London: Weidenfeld and Nicolson, 1965).

35. See, for example, Brandt's address before an SPD audience, November 30, 1967, Willy Brandt, *Peace. Writings and Speeches of the Nobel Prize Peace Winner* (Bonn: Verlag Neue Gesellschaft, 1971), 49–63.

Europe, and for the realization of the former in the context of the latter—
Kiesinger and Brandt differed on three specific issues: GDR recognition,
the Oder-Neisse line, and dialogue with Moscow. Kiesinger held that the
FRG should de-emphasize but not rescind its nonrecognition of the SED
regime. Like Adenauer and Erhard, he considered the FRG the sole legitimate representative of the German people in world affairs. Kiesinger did
apply the principle more flexibly. In 1967, for example, he agreed to
exchange ambassadors with Romania despite the latter's full diplomatic
ties with the East Berlin—a relaxation of the Hallstein Doctrine. And he
also expressed a readiness to engage the GDR in dialogue on humanitarian issues. At the same time, however, Kiesinger insisted from the beginning of his chancellorship that such contacts, like the relaxation of the
Hallstein Doctrine, "would not signify recognition of a second German
state." When he sent a letter to Willi Stoph in June 1967, for example, he
addressed it simply to "Prime Minister," omitting any mention of the
GDR.[36]

Brandt, by contrast, gradually embraced the view that the established
policy of nonrecognition should be not just downplayed but dropped as a
core component of Ostpolitik.[37] During the 1960s he articulated the idea
that the best way to overcome the German division was to strengthen ties
between Germans in the FRG and the GDR. Brandt rejected full diplomatic recognition for East Berlin. But de facto recognition, he came to
believe, might foster a web of economic, social, and cultural ties between
Germans in East and West, preserving the substance of the German nation
and holding open prospects for reunification in the long term. This
approach, made famous under the label "change through rapprochement," informed Brandt's policy as mayor of West Berlin in coalition with
the FDP during the early 1960s.[38] With the support of the Liberals, who
were also groping toward a new approach to the national issue, Brandt
negotiated several accords with East Berlin facilitating contacts among
Germans in the divided city. As foreign minister under Kiesinger, Brandt
adhered to the latter's nonrecognition policy, although he pushed for its

---

36. Government declaration of December 13, 1966, in Kiesinger, *Die Große Koalition,*
25. Kiesinger's letter to Stoph of June 13, 1967, ibid., 66–67.

37. First contours of this stance were evident in Brandt's address before the SPD's 1964
party conference in Karlsruhe, in *Protokoll der Verhandlungen und Anträge vom Parteitag der
Sozialdemokratischen Partei Deutschlands vom 23.–27. November 1964 in Karlsruhe* (Bonn:
Vorstand der SPD, 1964), 148–51. For Brandt's account, see Brandt, *People and Politics,*
166–97.

38. The term was coined by Brandt's advisor, Egon Bahr, in a much cited February
1963 speech. See Bahr, *Zu meiner Zeit,* chap. 3.

relaxation. But as chancellor, after 1969, he made recognition of the reality of two German states the starting point for a dialogue with the GDR.[39]

Kiesinger and Brandt also differed on the question of Oder-Neisse recognition. More than Adenauer and Erhard, Kiesinger emphasized that the Federal Republic had no territorial claims on Poland. At the same time, however, he continued to refuse Soviet and Polish demands that renunciation-of-force accords include recognition of existing borders. Final borders, he insisted, could only be fixed in a reunification settlement. And such a settlement, in turn, represented a "precondition for a durable, peaceful and good-neighborly relationship" between Germans and Poles.[40] By contrast, Brandt gradually—and carefully—came to support de facto recognition of the Oder-Neisse line as Poland's western border. At a March 1968 SPD party conference in Nuremberg, for example, he suggested that the FRG consider "respecting or even recognizing" the border. Cooperative relations with Warsaw, he maintained, were possible even in the absence of a unity settlement. Brandt's stance on the Oder-Neisse sparked an angry outburst from Kiesinger, who attacked his foreign minister's readiness to recognize the postwar territorial status quo as an unacceptable break with legal and policy precedent.[41]

These different stances on relations with the GDR and the Oder-Neisse went hand in hand with contrasting approaches to detente and relations with the Soviet Union.[42] While he supported detente in principle, Kiesinger had misgivings about its emergence in the 1960s. He perceived two risks—that the superpowers might reach agreement on key issues at German expense, a concern akin to Adenauer's "Potsdam Complex"; and that German-Soviet dialogue might make the Federal Republic less, not more secure. For Kiesinger the Non-Proliferation Treaty best illustrated the risk of a superpower condominium at German expense. He did not go

39. Brandt negotiated a first Transit Accord with East Berlin authorities in 1963. It allowed West Berliners to visit their relatives in the East over the Christmas holidays. See Brandt, *People and Politics,* 94–113. On the FDP's stance on Brandt's approach to inter-German relations during the late 1960s, see Christof Brauers, *Liberale Deutschlandpolitik, 1949–1969: Positionen der F.D.P. zwischen nationaler und europäischer Orientierung* (Hamburg: Lit, 1992), 148–66.

40. Declaration of December 13, 1966, in Kiesinger, *Die Große Koalition,* 21.

41. Brandt's statement before the SPD's 1968 party conference in Nuremberg, March 18, 1968, in *Protokoll der Verhandlungen und Anträge vom Parteitag der Sozialdemokratischen Partei Deutschlands vom März 1968 in Nürnberg* (Bonn: Vorstand der SPD, 1968), 111. For Kiesinger's response clarifying government policy, see his address of March 27, 1968, in Kiesinger, *Die Große Koalition,* 182–85.

42. See, for example, the addresses of Brandt and Kiesinger after the Soviet crushing of the Prague Spring, September 25 and September 26, 1968, *Verhandlungen des deutschen Bundestags,* ser. 5, 10049–56 and 10109–16.

as far as Adenauer, who called the NPT "a tragedy for us Germans." Concerned, however, that the treaty might increase the international legitimacy of the GDR as a cosignatory and preclude FRG participation in a future European nuclear force, Kiesinger withheld his signature during the Grand Coalition.[43] Negotiations with the Soviet Union on a possible renunciation-of-force accord, which began but made little progress during the Grand Coalition, illustrated the second risk: less, not more security through an active Ostpolitik. In Kiesinger's eyes Moscow's insistence that such an accord be linked with recognition of existing borders was a transparent attempt to consolidate its hold in the East and increase its threat to the West.[44]

Brandt's support for detente in general and for better German-Soviet relations in particular was unambiguous. He was far less concerned about U.S.-Soviet bilateralism at German expense. As foreign minister, and later as chancellor, he continually urged the superpowers to expand their conventional and nuclear arms control dialogue. In the context of the NPT, for example, Brandt was untroubled by possible implications for GDR legitimacy or a future European nuclear option. His government endorsed the treaty immediately after taking office. Brandt also did not share Kiesinger's concern that active German-Soviet dialogue might weaken the Western alliance or advance Soviet expansionism. Such dialogue, he argued, was bound to increase mutual trust and advance mutually beneficial cooperation. In Brandt's view revitalizing relations with Moscow by linking a renunciation of force with a recognition of borders—the core of the Moscow Treaty—promised to make the Federal Republic more, not less, secure. Germans, he argued, should overcome their paralyzing fear of Soviet power: "We can afford a self-confident Ostpolitik!"[45]

The differences between the foreign policy priorities of Kiesinger and Brandt—on the national issue and approaches to detente—reflected contrasting views of the international environment and the lessons of history. For Kiesinger, like Adenauer before him, the Soviet threat to a vulnerable Federal Republic remained a prominent feature of the international situation. In an era of detente, the threat was more political than military:

---

43. On Adenauer's position and CDU/CSU opposition to NPT, see Matthias Küntzel, *Bonn und die Bombe: Deutsche Atomwaffenpolitik von Adenauer bis Brandt* (Frankfurt am Main: Campus, 1992), chap. 2.

44. See, for example, Kiesinger's address of January 15, 1970, *Verhandlungen des deutschen Bundestags*, ser. 6, 851–60.

45. The theme of a "self-confident Ostpolitik" can be traced at least as far back as 1960. For Kiesinger's concerns about Soviet expansionism, see his address of May 27, 1970, ibid., 2725–29. See also Brandt's address of April 26, 1972, ibid., ser. 6, 10639–41.

Soviet leaders, in Kiesinger's view, were determined to divide NATO and draw all of Germany into their orbit. Moreover, according to Kiesinger and other CDU/CSU leaders, an active Ostpolitik threatened to provoke concerns about German reliability in the West and undermine the unity of the alliance.[46] Kiesinger did perceive the overall trend toward detente and the consolidation of the GDR as grounds for a more flexible stance toward Moscow. But he also considered the injustice of the German division a salient part of European reality that should not be endorsed through recognition of a second German state.[47]

Brandt, for his part, did not question the existence of a potential Soviet threat to German security. Like Kiesinger, he considered multilateral Western institutions the indispensable foundation for German policy toward the East. As chancellor, for example, he backed the modernization of NATO's conventional forces to counter Soviet forces in central Europe. But unlike Kiesinger, Brandt considered an active Ostpolitik on the basis of the status quo a way to sustain, rather than undermine Western unity— a means to bring German foreign policy into line with that of its most important allies. Moreover, from Brandt's perspective, de facto recognition of the GDR did not represent an endorsement of an unjust status quo. It constituted instead acknowledgment of the postwar reality of division. As he put it in 1967: "In the other part of Germany, a political system exists and governs which we choose to reject rather than accept." However, he continued, "it does exist and it does govern."[48] Only by accepting the reality of two German states, he reasoned, could the Federal Republic ease the human costs of the division.

These different foreign policy priorities also rested on particular interpretations of the past and its lessons. For Kiesinger the experience of Hitler and national socialism made strong ties with the West an absolute priority. Kiesinger did not invoke this argument as frequently as had Adenauer—averse, perhaps, to drawing attention to his own past association with the Nazi party. But he clearly viewed Western integration as a historic repudiation of German nationalism. He insisted, for example, that inroads made by the NPD did not mark "the birth hour of a new nationalism in

---

46. On later CDU/CSU efforts to win allied support for their objections to the New Ostpolitik, see Kurt Birrenbach, *Meine Sondermissionen: Rückblick auf zwei Jahrzehnte bundesdeutscher Außenpolitik* (Düsseldorf: Econ-Verlag, 1984), 324–43.

47. For these perspectives, see Kiesinger's Bundestag address of June 17, 1970, *Verhandlungen des deutschen Bundestags,* ser. 6, 3241–42.

48. Address of November 30, 1967, in Brandt, *Peace,* 60. For Brandt's insistence that his policy brought the FRG into line with the overall Western approach to the East, see his address of April 26, 1972, *Verhandlungen des deutschen Bundestags,* ser. 6, 10641.

Germany."[49] And he rejected Brandt's New Ostpolitik in part because it raised the old specter of a more independent Germany adrift between East and West. At times Kiesinger did articulate the view that the German past required reconciliation with the East. In his first government declaration, for example, he referred to Germany's bridge-building function between East and West as a historic task and alluded to the history of German-Polish suffering in particular. But in that and subsequent major addresses Kiesinger eschewed explicit links between past German aggression and a new approach to Ostpolitik.[50]

In grounding his foreign policy priorities with reference to historical experience, Kiesinger placed less emphasis on prewar disasters than he did on postwar achievements. The policy of Western integration, he reiterated, had secured freedom and security for Germans in the West and held open the prospect of unity with Germans in the East. Adenauer's achievement did not rule out a more active Ostpolitik. In fact, Kiesinger noted with reference to Adenauer's secret proposals to Soviet leaders, the first chancellor had entertained some creative ideas of his own in the years before his retirement.[51] By contrast, Kiesinger argued, Brandt's policies after 1969 threatened to unravel the edifice of Western integration. The New Ostpolitik risked dividing the West, advancing Soviet expansionist designs, and closing off the prospect of reunification. For Kiesinger a more gradual approach, in which NATO and the EC remained the focal points of German policy and the goal of unity persisted as a central component of Ostpolitik, promised to build on, and not undermine, Adenauer's achievement.[52]

Different views of history and its lessons informed Brandt's foreign policy priorities. Like Kiesinger and Adenauer, Brandt viewed Germany's nationalist and militarist pre-1945 foreign policies as a negative legacy—a conviction reinforced by his own wartime activities as an exile and member of the resistance. The New Ostpolitik, Brandt insisted, had nothing to do with the nationalism and seesaw policies of old. Unlike his CDU counterparts, however, Brandt drew clear links between the legacy of German

---

49. Declaration of December 13, 1966, in Kiesinger, *Die Große Koalition,* 26–27. The NPD fared well in several state elections in the late 1960s and fell just short of the 5 percent hurdle in the 1969 Bundestag elections.

50. Address of December 13, 1966, in Kiesinger, *Die Große Koalition,* 20.

51. Address of January 15, 1970, *Verhandlungen des deutschen Bundestags,* ser. 6, 852. On Adenauer's success in committing the Western powers to the goal of German unity, see Kiesinger's address of February 23, 1972, ibid., 9789.

52. For Kiesinger's positive assessment of Adenauer's legacy, see his memorial address of April 24, 1967, in Kurt Georg Kiesinger, *Stationen, 1949–1969* (Tübingen: Wunderlich, 1969), 220–22.

aggression and the imperative of an active Ostpolitik. As early as 1953, Brandt argued that Germans should seek to address "the sad legacy of national socialism" through "real reconciliation and peaceful settlement [*Ausgleich*]" with the East.[53] This perspective, a leitmotif of major policy addresses in the 1960s and 1970s, shaped Brandt's evolving approach to the border question in particular. The victims of Hitler's aggression, he insisted as foreign minister and later as chancellor, had a right to secure frontiers. Acceptance of the territorial status quo in Europe, and the Oder-Neisse border in particular, merely represented recognition of the results of Hitler's lost war. As he put it on the occasion of the Moscow Treaty, "nothing is lost with this Treaty that was not gambled away long ago."[54]

Like Kiesinger, Brandt also grounded his foreign policy priorities in a particular interpretation of the postwar period and its legacies. He recognized Western integration as a historic repudiation of past nationalism— and was one of the first SPD leaders to do so. At the same time, however, he repeatedly criticized Adenauer's failure to move beyond integration in the West toward engagement in the East. During his 1961 election campaign against Adenauer, for example, he labeled the Berlin Wall a poignant symbol of the failure of the government's reunification policy. And in the years that followed, he reiterated the view that Adenauer had failed to exploit possibilities to press the unity issue during his chancellorship. After Adenauer's retirement and death in 1967, Brandt struck a more conciliatory tone. He construed Adenauer's Western policy as a necessary foundation for an active Ostpolitik. And during the early 1970s he even portrayed his own foreign policy departure as an extension of Adenauer's, although he continued to underline the limitations of the latter.[55]

Brandt's view of the past and its lessons dovetailed with new trends in German historiography in the 1960s. Gerhard Ritter and other leading postwar historians had interpreted Hitler and national socialism as an aberration in German history and upheld Bismarck's Reich as a model for the foreign policy of the Federal Republic. They advocated foreign policies

---

53. SPD party conference address of March 6, 1953, in Willy Brandt, *Der Wille zum Frieden: Perspektiven der Politik* (Frankfurt am Main: Hoffmann and Campe, 1971), 60.

54. Brandt, *Peace Policy for Europe,* 99–104, 107. On World War II as a backdrop for the New Ostpolitik, see also Brandt's address in the Eastern Treaties ratification debate of May 10, 1972, *Verhandlungen des deutschen Bundestags,* ser. 6, 10888–98.

55. Willy Brandt, "Konrad Adenauer—Ein schwieriges Erbe für die deutsche Politik," in Dieter Blumenwitz et al., eds., *Konrad Adenauer und Seine Zeit: Politik und Persönlichkeit des ersten Bundeskanzlers* (Stuttgart: Deutsche-Verlags-Anstalt, 1976), 99–107. In a major Bundestag debate, Brandt questioned whether vehement CDU/CSU opposition to the Eastern Treaties was really in the tradition of Adenauer. See his address of April 27, 1972, *Verhandlungen des deutschen Bundestags,* ser. 6, 10711.

grounded in the dispassionate pursuit of the national interest, not reconciliation with the victims of German aggression. During the 1960s the "Fischer Controversy" destroyed this orthodoxy. The Hamburg historian Fritz Fischer argued that German political and military elites had deliberately unleashed World War I in order to shore up an autocratic regime at home. His two major works, informed by a "primacy of domestic politics" [*Primat der Innenpolitik*] perspective, suggested lines of continuity between the autocratic structures of the empire, the institutional weakness of the Weimar Republic, and elite support for Hitler's takeover.[56] The thesis of a negative "special path" [*Sonderweg*] from Bismarck to Hitler, rife with political and policy implications, sparked a furor. For Ritter, Fischer's work was typical of "current political-historical fashion" destructive of "German historical consciousness." The CSU's Franz Josef Strauss even attacked him as a communist fellow traveler. For Fischer's supporters, by contrast, criticism of Germany's nationalist, militarist past, went hand in hand with support for Brandt's new foreign policy departure. Many were vocal supporters of the chancellor's push for reconciliation with the victims of Hitler's war in the East.[57]

The foreign policy priorities espoused by Kiesinger and Brandt in the late 1960s and early 1970s, and the views of history that informed them, both represented viable responses to the alternatives posed by the international configuration. The shift toward detente generated a divisive German debate over policy toward Moscow and East Berlin. With their divergent perceptions of the international situation and the lessons of the past, Kiesinger and Brandt articulated contrasting positions within that debate. Kiesinger's stance was cautious, respectful of established precedent and reticent with respect to bilateral German-Soviet dialogue. Brandt's approach was bold. It called for a fundamental reassessment of the unity issue and a far-reaching dialogue with Moscow, Warsaw, and East Berlin. The struggle between both sets of foreign policy priorities was decided at the level of party politics.

---

56. Fritz Fischer, *Germany's Aims in the First World War* (New York: Norton, 1967); *The War of Illusions: German Policies from 1911 to 1914* (New York: Norton, 1975). Eckart Kehr, an interwar historian, was one of the first proponents of the "primacy of domestic politics" approach. See Eckart Kehr, *Der Primat der Innenpolitik: Gesammelte Aufsätze zur preussisch-deutschen Sozialgeschichte im 19. und 20. Jahrhundert* (Berlin: Walter de Gruyter, 1965).

57. Stefan Berger, *The Search for Normality: National Identity and Historical Consciousness in Germany since 1800* (Providence: Berghahn, 1997), 69–70, 83. On the "Fischer Controversy," see John A. Moses, *The Politics of Illusion: The Fischer Controversy in German Historiography* (New York: George Prior Publishers, 1975); Fritz Fischer, "Twenty-Five Years Later: Looking Back at the 'Fischer Controversy' and Its Consequences," *Central European History* 21, no. 3 (September 1988): 207–23.

The Political Struggle over the New Ostpolitik

Brandt's success in the political contest of the early 1970s ultimately secured the necessary domestic backing for the New Ostpolitik. That success was by no means assured when he became chancellor in October 1969. In order to pursue his priorities in practice, Brandt had to anchor them within the SPD and forge a coalition with a like-minded FDP. He also had to implement them against a powerful opposition. The newly formed social-liberal coalition controlled only a razor-thin Bundestag majority, and the Christian Democrats, out of office for the first time, were determined to undermine it. From the moment Brandt recognized the existence of "two states in Germany" in his first government declaration, the New Ostpolitik injected a high degree of polarization into German politics. Only with the ratification of the Moscow and Warsaw Treaties in May 1972 and Brandt's reelection as chancellor that November did his new foreign policy departure come to rest on a stable political foundation.

Brandt's success in anchoring his foreign policy priorities in the SPD occurred less through an all-out clash than through a gradual generational shift. Erich Ollenhauer, who succeeded Schumacher in 1952, remained party chairman until his death in December 1963. Even before Brandt assumed party leadership in January 1964, however, he and a cohort of emerging SPD leaders, including Fritz Erler and Herbert Wehner, began to move the party toward the political center. In the wake of Ollenhauer's back-to-back losses to Adenauer in the 1953 and 1957 elections, they successfully moderated Social Democratic positions on a variety of domestic and foreign policy issues. The Godesberg Program of March 1959 was a milestone. It broke with the Marxist philosophy of central economic planning and endorsed the principle of national defense. In June 1960 Wehner reversed Social Democratic opposition to the Atlantic Alliance. With Brandt as chancellor candidate in 1961 a rejuvenated SPD began to close the electoral gap that separated it from the CDU/CSU.[58]

The old Social Democratic guard around Ollenhauer did not quarrel with Brandt's strong support for detente and arms control with the Soviet Union. Even more than Schumacher, Ollenhauer had prodded Adenauer to engage the Soviet Union in an active political and security dialogue during the 1950s. During the 1960s, however, Brandt's emerging approach to the national issue and its place within Ostpolitik did spark some controversy within the party. For Schumacher, and later for Ollenhauer, any

---

58. On these developments, see Klaus Hildebrand, *Von Erhard zur Großen Koalition, 1963–69* (Stuttgart: Deutsche Verlags-Anstalt, 1984), 70–83; Abraham Ashkenasi, *Reformpartei und Außenpolitik: Die Außenpolitik der SPD Berlin-Bonn* (Cologne: Westdeutscher Verlag, 1968), chap. 6.

recognition of the GDR was anathema. In some respects the legacy of communist persecution of the SPD in the Soviet zone, and its forced incorporation into the SED in 1946 made Social Democrats even more hostile to the GDR than their Christian Democratic counterparts. Against this backdrop Brandt's efforts as mayor of West Berlin to reach humanitarian accords with East Berlin authorities met some skepticism in the SPD leadership. He was initially careful to insist that a "change through rapprochement" strategy did not entail a shift away from traditional legal positions on the unity issue. At the 1964 party conference in Karlsruhe, for example, Brandt reiterated his party's traditional demand for international progress toward reunification.[59]

Brandt's new approach to the Oder-Neisse issue, too, generated some opposition within the SPD. Schumacher had been particularly vehement in his opposition to the borders of 1945, likening calls for recognition of the Oder-Neisse to demands for German "suicide."[60] And the postwar SPD, like the CDU/CSU, drew on political support from millions of expellees, those driven from the territories East of the Oder-Neisse at the end of World War II. The Godesberg Program, though reformist in its thrust, reiterated established legal positions with respect to the issue, relegating the final delineation of the border between Poland and Germany to a reunification settlement. Established positions on the border issue persisted into the 1960s. In January 1965, for example, Erler suggested that the Federal Republic might have to recognize the Oder-Neisse border as part of future negotiations on national unity. A government spokesman accused him of renouncing long-standing German claims, and the SPD executive committee reiterated the party's official position on the openness of the border issue pending reunification.[61]

Only during the second half of the 1960s, once his position as party chairman was secure, was Brandt able to win broad support in the SPD for his approach to East Berlin and the German-Polish border. The June 1966 Dortmund party conference proved an important turning point. In his keynote speech, Brandt still made reference to the "so-called GDR," a practice he would later drop. At the same time, however, he set out his evolving approach to the unity issue in the clearest terms yet. Germans, he argued, should shift from a focus on reunification within a single state toward the maintenance of the substance of the German nation. And

---

59. Brandt, *People and Politics,* 110–11.

60. Bundestag address of March 9, 1951, in Kurt Schumacher, *Kurt Schumacher: Reden—Schriften—Korrespondenzen, 1945–1952* (Berlin: Dietz, 1985), 934.

61. Hartmut Soell, *Fritz Erler: Eine Politische Biographie* (Berlin: Dietz, 1976), 1:497–500. On controversy around national issues in the SPD during the 1960s, see Peter Arend, *Die innerparteiliche Entwicklung der SPD, 1966–75* (Bonn: Eichholz, 1975), 95–96.

efforts to multiply inter-German contacts—a means to this end—would necessarily involve interaction with GDR authorities. With little dissent the SPD endorsed Brandt's new approach to East Berlin. Two years later, as foreign minister, he also managed to rally Social Democratic support for his new approach to the border issue. His statement that Bonn consider "respecting or even recognizing" the Oder-Neisse border—made at a March 1968 party conference—sparked criticism from Kiesinger and expellee groups. But opposition was muted within the SPD leadership.[62]

As chancellor, Brandt was able to maintain a high degree of support within the SPD for his Ostpolitik. Representatives of the expellees, who had begun to move from the SPD to the CDU/CSU in the 1960s, continued to do so in the 1970s. And the defection of a key expellee leader and SPD deputy to the opposition in early 1972 threatened the government's majority in the run-up to the final ratification debates on the Moscow and Warsaw Treaties. On the whole, however, Brandt's new foreign policy departure served to unite, not divide, the party. In the wake of the 1968 student protests the SPD was racked by dissension between its moderate and radical wings, mainly on economic and social issues. Brandt's New Ostpolitik, which won him the Nobel Peace Prize in December 1971, solidified his authority atop the party, and helped to paper over its internal fissures. After his reelection as chancellor in November 1972, however, those fissures emerged into the open. In the face of internal party squabbles, mounting economic problems, and an espionage scandal—one of his aides worked for the GDR—Brandt resigned in May 1974. While he ceded the chancellorship to Helmut Schmidt, Brandt remained SPD chairman. His New Ostpolitik persisted as a core element of SPD identity from the early 1970s onward.[63]

In order to implement his foreign policy priorities Brandt also had to secure and maintain the support of the FDP for a social-liberal coalition. Given the traditional differences between the two parties, this was no easy task. The FDP, a governing partner of the CDU/CSU from 1949–56 and again from 1961–66, made liberal economic policies its top programmatic priority. The SPD break with its Marxist heritage with the 1959 Godesberg Program reduced the economic and social policy gulf between the parties somewhat, as did the emergence of a reform-oriented "social" wing of the FDP. More than anything else, however, the collapse of the Erhard government and the formation of the Grand Coalition generated momen-

---

62. For Brandt's Dortmund address, see *Parteitag der SPD 1966*, 74–82.

63. On the importance of Ostpolitik for the SPD's internal unity, see Arend, *Die innerparteiliche Entwicklung der SPD*, 75–76, 97–106.

tum for social-liberal rapprochement. Brandt, who had ruled with the FDP for a time in West Berlin, envisioned such a coalition at the national level as the most promising way to capture the chancellorship. And Liberal leaders, thrown into opposition, began to consider an alliance with the SPD as a springboard back into government. During the early 1960s Liberal leader Erich Mende, minister for All-German Questions under Erhard, had supported Brandt's negotiations with East Berlin authorities. As the decade progressed younger leaders around Walter Scheel—including future Foreign Minister Hans-Dietrich Genscher—pushed for further shifts in FDP foreign policy in the direction of Brandt and the SPD. At a pivotal party conference in April 1967 they won majority backing for a number of controversial proposals: de facto recognition of the GDR, normalization of ties with Moscow on the basis of the status quo, and recognition of the Oder-Neisse as Poland's western border. Mende resigned in protest, making way for Scheel to assume the FDP chairmanship the following year. The prospects for a future social-liberal coalition improved.[64]

The cooperation of the SPD and FDP in electing Gustav Heinemann federal president in March 1969 represented a first concrete sign of the rapprochement between the two parties. CDU/CSU and FDP parliamentarians had elected the first two presidents of the Federal Republic, Theodor Heuss and Heinrich Lübke. Although the office was almost exclusively a symbolic one, Liberal support for Heinemann, the SPD candidate, had a double political significance. On the one hand, it signaled FDP readiness to forge a coalition with the SPD after the upcoming September 1969 elections. On the other hand, it pointed to the possibility of a new foreign policy departure. Heinemann, a former minister of the interior under Adenauer, had resigned in protest from the government and the CDU during the rearmament controversy of the early 1950s. During the 1960s he emerged as one of the most articulate spokesmen for detente and reconciliation with the East. Heinemann's election not only marked an embarrassing defeat for Kiesinger and the CDU/CSU. It also signaled a new political and policy constellation.[65]

As it happened, Brandt and the SPD only barely succeeded in forging a coalition with Scheel and the FDP after the September elections. The CDU/CSU remained the largest party in the Bundestag, falling just shy of

---

64. On changes in FDP Ostpolitik in opposition, see Clemens Heitmann, *FDP und neue Ostpolitik. Zur Bedeutung der deutschlandpolitischen Vorstellungen der FDP von 1966 bis 1972* (Sankt Augustin: COMDOK, 1989), 43–77; Hildebrand, *Von Erhard zur Großen Koalition,* 339–52.

65. On the significance of Heinemann's election, see Arnulf Baring, *Machtwechsel. Die Ära Brandt-Scheel* (Stuttgart: Deutsche Verlags-Anstalt, 1982), chap. 1. See also Helmut Lindemann, *Gustav Heinemann: Ein Leben für die Demokratie* (Munich: Kösel, 1978).

an absolute majority. In fact, President Nixon called Kiesinger on election night to congratulate him on his victory. In the days and weeks that followed, however, the SPD and FDP managed to form a government with a parliamentary majority of just six seats. On this slim foundation Brandt and Scheel, now foreign minister, immediately set out to implement their foreign policy. As the New Ostpolitik rapidly unfolded, the coalition grew even weaker. In October 1970 three Liberal deputies, upset about the pace and scope of the rapprochement with the Soviet Union and its allies, switched their allegiance to the CDU/CSU. In February 1972, in the run-up to the key Bundestag vote on the Moscow and Warsaw Treaties, former FDP chairman Mende did the same. The government lost its majority at a critical juncture in the struggle with Christian Democrats.

That struggle, pitting government against opposition, had the greatest impact on the outcome of the New Ostpolitik. It began immediately once Brandt took over as chancellor. CDU/CSU leaders, furious to be excluded from power for the first time since the founding of the Federal Republic, attacked the New Ostpolitik from its inception.[66] Kiesinger in particular did not accept defeat with grace. He insisted that the CDU/CSU, as the largest party in the Bundestag, still had a claim on the chancellorship. And he argued that the social-liberal coalition, given its slim majority, had no mandate to break with two decades of German foreign policy. Kiesinger began an overt campaign to bring down the government and what he called its so-called majority. His strategy was straightforward: to punish the FDP in enough state elections so that its national leadership—or at least enough FDP deputies—would opt to switch allegiance to the CDU/CSU. To this end he branded the SPD the "party of recognition" and condemned Brandt's de facto recognition of the GDR as a "terrible sacrifice of the positions we have held until now."[67] On the eve of Brandt's trip to Moscow, in August 1970, Kiesinger insisted that a normalization of bilateral ties was unacceptable without some "sign of Soviet readiness to work with us to help to bring about a just solution of the German Question."[68]

Not everyone in the CDU/CSU backed Kiesinger's confrontational

---

66. On CDU/CSU opposition to the New Ostpolitik, see Clay Clemens, *Reluctant Realists: The Christian Democrats and West German Ostpolitik* (Durham: Duke University Press, 1989); Christian Hacke, *Die Ost-und Deutschlandpolitik der CDU/CSU: Wege und Irrwege der Opposition seit 1969* (Cologne: Verlag Wissenschaft und Politik, 1975).

67. Kiesinger address of January 15, 1970, *Verhandlungen des deutschen Bundestags,* ser. 6, 859.

68. Kiesinger in the debate of June 17, 1970, ibid., 3242.

course. According to Egon Bahr, Brandt's top foreign policy advisor, future President Richard von Weizsäcker and some other Christian Democrats had been willing to countenance the recognition of two states in Germany during the Grand Coalition.[69] Moreover, once the New Ostpolitik began to unfold, even CDU/CSU parliamentary leader Rainer Barzel warned against its outright rejection. The opposition, Barzel argued, should criticize the Moscow Treaty but reserve final judgment pending the overall development of the New Ostpolitik.[70] By contrast, Kiesinger, together with Franz Josef Strauss and the conservative Bavarian CSU, rejected the Eastern Treaties and the opening to Moscow on principle. Kiesinger charged that the New Ostpolitik would solidify Soviet domination in Central Europe and encourage its "world revolutionary" ambitions. From Strauss's perspective Brandt's policies threatened to abet Soviet expansionism and divide the Western alliance.[71]

This polarization appears to have been a central part of Social Democratic strategy. Given their slim majority, Brandt and Wehner, the SPD parliamentary leader, may have gambled that polarization would reinforce the fragile cohesion of the ruling coalition. Both the calculated surprise of Brandt's "two states in Germany" formula and Wehner's deliberately provocative January 1970 boast that the government did "not need the opposition" support such an interpretation.[72] Whether intended or not, polarization did ultimately work to the benefit of the SPD over the course of 1970. While the government parties did poorly in state elections early in the year and two FDP deputies deserted the coalition, Brandt's trip to the Soviet Union to sign the Moscow Treaty, hailed in the international press as a historic breakthrough, helped to shore up the cohesion of the social-liberal government. By late 1970 the SPD and FDP halted their string of losses in state elections. Kiesinger's efforts to topple Brandt through total rejection of the New Ostpolitik failed.

Still, the ratification of the Moscow and Warsaw Treaties was not

---

69. Egon Bahr, interview by author, Bonn, July 31, 1992.

70. See Barzel to the CDU/CSU Parliamentary Group, August 17, 1970, *Archiv für Christlich-Demokratische Politik,* Werner Marx papers, I-356-A311. For Barzel's account of the struggle over the CDU/CSU position, see Rainer Barzel, *Auf dem Drahtseil* (Munich: Droemer-Knauer, 1978), 104–8.

71. Kiesinger address of January 15, 1970, *Verhandlungen des deutschen Bundestags,* ser. 6, 860. See also his address at the CDU party conference in Düsseldorf, January 27, 1971, in *18. CDU Bundesparteitag* (Bonn: CDU, 1971), 538. For an example of Strauss' rhetoric, see his speech of May 27, 1970, *Verhandlungen des deutschen Bundestags,* ser. 6, 2706–14.

72. Bahr acknowledged that the "two states" formulation, made without warning, polarized the domestic political debate from the start (Bahr, interview). For Wehner's statement, see his interview in *Spiegel,* January 26, 1970.

assured. The government opted to bring them before the Bundestag only after the completion of the Four-Power Berlin Treaty in September 1971. By then, however, the Christian Democrats had made a political recovery. His efforts to bring down the government having failed, Kiesinger stepped down as CDU chairman in July 1971. After an intense leadership struggle Barzel defeated Helmut Kohl, the youthful governor of Rhineland-Palatinate, in a crucial October 1971 party conference vote. As he consolidated his position as party leader, Barzel set out to implement his more moderate line. He first secured the backing of Strauss and the CSU for his chancellor candidacy and then outlined several conditions for CDU/CSU support of the treaties, including Soviet endorsement of the principle of national self-determination and an end to Moscow's opposition to Western European integration. Barzel calculated that Christian Democratic support for the Eastern Treaties would enable a renewed coalition with the Liberals after the national elections scheduled for 1973. A polarized ratification debate, he reasoned at the time, would only consolidate the social-liberal alliance.[73]

Two further defections from the government coalition in early 1972—including one from the SPD—altered the domestic political configuration again. With the government's majority gone Strauss and CDU/CSU hard-liners now pressed Barzel to reject the Moscow and Warsaw Treaties—despite some Soviet efforts to meet the conditions he had set out.[74] Emboldened by a CDU victory in an important state election in April 1972, Barzel embraced a high-risk strategy: to topple Brandt with a constructive vote of no confidence and then travel to Moscow to renegotiate the treaty. In the climactic ballot, however, two Christian Democrats unexpectedly (and secretly) voted for Brandt, keeping him in office. Still without a majority for ratification, Brandt worked with Barzel to include a Joint Declaration in the treaty package that would make a CDU/CSU yes-vote possible. The declaration, which reiterated traditional commitments to the Atlantic Alliance, European integration, and national unity, won the support of the Christian Democratic parliamentary group. But Strauss and CDU/CSU hard-liners still refused to support the treaties themselves.

---

73. Barzel considered the treaties the "linchpin" of the coalition. See Barzel, *Auf dem Drahtseil,* 66–67. On Barzel's December 1971 trip to Moscow to plead for Soviet concessions on some of these issues, see ibid., 140–54.

74. In early 1972 Brezhnev softened Soviet opposition to the European Community, and Foreign Minister Andrei Gromyko agreed to include the "Letter on German Unity" in the Soviet ratification process. For Strauss, however, the Eastern Treaties continued to represent a "massive impediment" to the unification of West Europe (notes for a campaign speech in Baden-Württemberg, April 12, 1972, *Archiv für Christlich-Soziale Politik,* Franz Josef Strauss papers, RA 72 [16]).

In order to preserve some semblance of outward party unity most Christian Democrats abstained on the key May 1972 vote, allowing the Moscow and Warsaw treaties to pass.[75]

The ratification of the third crucial Eastern Treaty, the Basic Treaty with the GDR, proved much less difficult. After the passage of the Moscow and Warsaw Treaties the domestic political constellation rebounded to the advantage of the SPD. Still without a parliamentary majority, Brandt pressed for the dissolution of the Bundestag and early elections that November. In a campaign dominated by the New Ostpolitik the SPD won more seats than the CDU/CSU—for the first time in the history of the Federal Republic.[76] In January 1973 the Christian Democrats fought the ratification of the Basic Treaty in the Bundestag in vain, with Strauss terming it an "important component of a new phase of Soviet expansionism." The Bavarian leader then opted, against Barzel's wishes, to challenge its constitutionality. In July 1973 the Constitutional Court in Karlsruhe ruled that the treaty, understood as a modus vivendi pending reunification, was compatible with the unity injunction of the Basic Law.[77] After a drawn-out battle Brandt had managed to secure the necessary domestic political foundation for the New Ostpolitik.

Enduring Effects of the New Ostpolitik

The New Ostpolitik of the early 1970s emerged out of the interaction of international and domestic forces. The overall trend toward detente on the basis of postwar status quo created pressure for a more flexible German policy toward the East. On two critical issues—relations with the Soviet Union and policy toward the GDR—international institutions framed significant policy alternatives. German leaders could opt to adjust established positions on GDR recognition, the Oder-Neisse line, and dialogue with Moscow. Or they could rework their long-standing positions more extensively. Within this context Kiesinger and Brandt, partners during the

75. For an account of the struggle within the CDU/CSU in early 1972, see Clemens, *Reluctant Realists,* 97–106. Text of the Joint Declaration, *Documents on Germany,* 1188–90.

76. For Bahr's suggestion of an Ostpolitik-centered campaign, see his letter to Brandt of August 2, 1972, *Archiv der sozialen Demokratie,* Brandt papers, BK, folder 2. Just two weeks before the election the government focused the campaign on Ostpolitik by publishing a draft of the Basic Treaty.

77. For Strauss's account of the ratification of the Eastern Treaties and the constitutional challenge, see Franz Josef Strauss, *Die Erinnerungen* (Berlin: Siedler, 1989), 443–58. For his intervention in the ratification debate, see his address of May 9, 1973, *Verhandlungen des deutschen Bundestags,* ser. 7, 1452. For a contrasting account of the May 1972 ratification struggle, see Brandt, *My Life in Politics,* 271–77.

Grand Coalition and rivals after 1969, set out the contrasting foreign policy perspectives that structured the domestic political debate. Kiesinger opted for cautious efforts to reinvigorate Ostpolitik, while Brandt was willing to take a step that no previous chancellor had contemplated: de facto recognition of the GDR and the Oder-Neisse border as a new basis for dialogue with the Soviet Union. In order to reorient FRG foreign policy amid detente Brandt had first to anchor his priorities within the SPD and in coalition with the FDP and then to overcome the fierce resistance of the CDU/CSU in opposition.

This second critical juncture in postwar German foreign policy had far-reaching institutional and political effects. The New Ostpolitik anchored the Federal Republic within a second set of European institutions. While NATO and the EC constrained Bonn to pursue a multilateral, supranational foreign policy, the Eastern Treaties and the CSCE—less salient but nevertheless significant—bound German leaders to cooperate with the Soviet Union and its allies on the basis of the postwar political and territorial status quo. The Moscow, Warsaw, and Basic Treaties did not rule out reunification by peaceful means at some future date. But they effectively removed the unity issue from the Ostpolitik agenda. At the same time, the treaties constituted a framework for bilateral economic and political cooperation—later supplemented by the multilateral CSCE—which precluded a return to the confrontational policies of the 1950s. Within this new, more complex institutional framework Bonn remained an ally of the West while becoming a partner to the East.

The continued salience of both sets of institutions, East and West, was evident in the years after Schmidt succeeded Brandt as chancellor. During the 1970s, intractable international economic problems tested but did not destroy the effectiveness of Western institutions as a context for German foreign policy. With the collapse of the postwar monetary regime and the onset of recession global economic management grew more important. From 1975 onward the Federal Republic and six other leading industrial countries, the "Group of Seven," met annually to coordinate—or at least consult on—pressing economic and political matters. In the face of economic turmoil EC member states put off the goal of a single currency, but proved able to coordinate their monetary policies through the European Monetary System inaugurated in 1978. Over the course of the 1970s the Eastern Treaties, too, emerged as an important context for German economic diplomacy. At summits in October 1974 and May 1978 Schmidt and Brezhnev signed several accords expanding bilateral trade, including an agreement to build a natural gas pipeline between Siberia and Western Europe. Inter-German trade increased significantly over the same period. These economic links with the East paled in comparison with those with the West. Still, the Eastern Treaties emerged alongside the EC as an important political framework for FRG foreign economic policy.[78]

The effects of this more complex institutional configuration were also evident on political and security matters. During the mid-1970s the human rights issue moved to the top of the East-West agenda. Upon taking office in January 1977, President Jimmy Carter made the issue a central component of his policy toward Moscow—and provoked a harsh Soviet reaction. Schmidt, too, admonished the Soviet Union to live up to the human rights provisions it had embraced as part of the CSCE Final Act. At the same time, however, eager to consolidate and build on the political foundation laid by the Moscow Treaty, the German government downplayed the human rights issue as a component of its Ostpolitik. Schmidt was critical of Carter's White House reception for Alexander Solzhenitsyn and did not let the fate of Soviet or East European dissidents complicate his relations with Moscow. The human rights issue illustrated the tensions inherent in the new institutional constellation—between alignment with the West and cooperation with the East.[79]

The international controversy surrounding the neutron bomb in 1977–78 revealed similar tensions. Without consulting the allies, Carter announced his intention to deploy the bomb, a weapon designed to kill people but spare materiel, in an October 1977 speech. The U.S. government made it clear that it expected German support within the NATO framework; most of the eventual deployments were envisioned for the Federal Republic. Over the months that followed, however, Brezhnev publicly warned Bonn that German support for deployment was incompatible with the spirit of the Moscow Treaty and would jeopardize bilateral relations. Schmidt found himself caught between the Atlantic Alliance and a new web of institutional links with the East. In February 1978 he reluctantly agreed to back eventual deployment, sparking Soviet criticism. In the end, however, Carter's unilateral decision to drop the project—only weeks after Schmidt had finally committed to it—defused the controversy.[80]

The New Ostpolitik not only altered the institutional context of German foreign policy. It also shifted its domestic political foundations. Hotly

---

78. See Stent, *From Embargo to Ostpolitik,* chap. 9; Michael Kreile, *Osthandel und Ostpolitik* (Baden-Baden: Nomos, 1978).

79. On German-Soviet relations, see Avril Pittman, *From Ostpolitik to Reunification: West German-Soviet Political Relations since 1974* (Cambridge: Cambridge University Press, 1992). On the German focus on the preservation of detente over the pursuit of human rights, see Garton Ash, *In Europe's Name,* 279–98.

80. On the neutron bomb, see Sherri L. Wassermann, *The Neutron Bomb Controversy: A Study in Alliance Politics* (New York: Praeger, 1983).

contested at the start of the 1970s, Brandt's new departure became the object of growing consensus at decade's end. In the years after Brandt left office, the New Ostpolitik persisted as a core element of SPD identity. The recessions of the 1970s sparked internal party divisions over economic and social policy—divisions later compounded by emotional intraparty conflict around how to deal with terrorism and whether to support nuclear energy. Schmidt and Brandt, still SPD chairman, relied largely on foreign policy and the New Ostpolitik to integrate the party. The Social Democratic Party presented itself as the party of peace, arms control, and dialogue with the East—a profile that contributed to Schmidt's reelection in 1976. Toward the end of the decade foreign policy did gradually reemerge as a divisive issue. The neutron bomb controversy, for example, fed the nascent peace movement and generated dissatisfaction on the SPD left with Schmidt's pro-NATO stance. And some voices within the party called for full diplomatic recognition of the GDR. Despite these differences, however, the SPD remained united around the imperative of detente with the East.[81]

The FDP, too, continued to rally around the New Ostpolitik in the years after Brandt left office. After Scheel replaced Heinemann as federal president in 1974, Genscher took over as FDP chairman and foreign minister. In subsequent years the Liberals highlighted their role in the formulation and implementation of the New Ostpolitik. The stress on foreign policy helped to unify the party, increasingly divided between its "social" and "free-market" wings. At the same time, a focus on points of foreign policy consensus with the SPD served to cement a ruling coalition increasingly threatened by economic and social policy divisions. Toward the end of the 1970s, when irritations in U.S.-German relations surfaced on multiple fronts, Genscher tended to stake out a more pro-Atlantic position than Schmidt. Nevertheless, his party's strong commitment to the New Ostpolitik continued to unite the coalition, and to distinguish it from the CDU/CSU in opposition.

The Christian Democratic embrace of the New Ostpolitik during the 1970s was gradual and incomplete. As early as December 1972, Strauss circumscribed his approach to the Eastern Treaties with the Latin phrase "pacta sunt servanda"—treaties are to be upheld. At the same time, he and other hard-liners insisted that the May 1972 Joint Bundestag Declaration and the July 1973 Constitutional Court Basic Treaty Ruling—and not the treaties themselves—serve as foundations for Ostpolitik. Kohl, who succeeded Barzel as CDU chairman in June 1973, immediately sought to

---

81. Günther Gaus, a former FRG permanent representative in East Berlin, was the most prominent advocate of recognition for GDR citizenship. See Günther Gaus, *Wo Deutschland liegt: Eine Ortsbestimmung* (Hamburg: Hoffmann and Campe, 1983).

move the CDU/CSU toward a pragmatic acceptance of the Eastern Treaties that, as he put it, had "changed the political landscape."[82] The magnitude of the 1972 election loss, his own narrow defeat as chancellor candidate in 1976, and a desire to reforge a ruling coalition with the FDP all pushed Kohl toward a full acknowledgment of the Eastern Treaties and the CSCE as a new institutional foundation for German foreign policy. Embroiled in drawn-out struggle with Strauss for CDU/CSU leadership, however, he was unable to win solid Christian Democratic support for his stance. The political consensus around the New Ostpolitik remained incomplete.

By the late 1970s Brandt's new foreign policy departure had transformed the institutional and political context of German foreign policy. The Federal Republic remained anchored in the West and became engaged in the East. Its new foreign policy orientation rested on a broad, if still incomplete, domestic political consensus. Schmidt, popular at home and respected abroad, managed to combine Western integration and the New Ostpolitik in practice. At precisely this juncture, however, a shift in the international environment posed new problems for the Federal Republic. The gradual downturn in U.S.-Soviet detente, evident in the controversies surrounding human rights and the neutron bomb, accelerated rapidly in the early 1980s. Three developments proved most critical: the Soviet invasion of Afghanistan in December 1979, the rise of Solidarity in Poland in 1980, and the eruption of controversy concerning the deployment of new intermediate-range nuclear forces (INF) on German soil in the early 1980s. In each of these contexts Schmidt sought to slow the erosion of superpower detente and the role it afforded the Federal Republic as an ally of the West and partner of the East.

These efforts were most dramatic in the case of the Afghanistan and Polish crises. Like Carter, Schmidt condemned the Soviet invasion and demanded an immediate withdrawal. He also supported Solidarity and warned against any crackdown by Polish or Soviet authorities. At the same time, however, he sought to maintain dialogue with the Soviet Union and its allies. He only reluctantly joined the U.S. sanctions campaign centered around a boycott of the 1980 Moscow Summer Olympics. And in June 1980, eager to preserve his positive relationship with Brezhnev, he became the first Western leader to visit the Soviet capital since the invasion of Afghanistan. As the Polish crisis escalated, Schmidt was circumspect in his support for Solidarity and only reluctantly withdrew an invitation to

---

82. Kohl interview in *Bild,* June 13, 1973. According to Kurt Biedenkopf, then CDU general secretary, Kohl considered the outcome of the 1972 elections a reason to embrace the New Ostpolitik. Kurt Biedenkopf, interview by author, Bonn, May 11, 1992.

Polish leader Edward Gierek for a visit to the Federal Republic. Schmidt's determination to preserve the New Ostpolitik amid difficult circumstances was most evident in the context of inter-German relations. The chancellor did postpone a visit to the GDR planned for the fall of 1980. Despite the vehement anti-Solidarity campaign launched by the SED leadership, however, he held fast to his travel plans and did make his visit in December of the following year.[83]

Schmidt's efforts to combine Western integration and eastern engagement were most pronounced in the INF context. Alarmed about the Soviet buildup of intermediate-range SS-20s aimed at Western Europe, Schmidt called for a Western response in a much-noted October 1977 speech.[84] In the two years that followed he helped to craft a two-pronged NATO strategy: preparations for counterdeployments combined with arms control negotiations designed to make them unnecessary. Both elements of this strategy informed NATO's Two-Track Decision of December 1979, the plan to deploy new missiles starting in late 1983—mainly in the Federal Republic—and to propose INF negotiations in the interim. Soviet leaders initially refused to negotiate unless NATO rescinded its deployment plans, but Schmidt secured Brezhnev's commitment to begin INF talks during his June 1980 Moscow visit. Preparations for negotiations ceased, however, with Carter's defeat at the hands of Ronald Reagan that November. The new administration's adamant anti-Soviet stance marked a critical juncture in the transition from detente to the new cold war in Europe—a transition that compelled German leaders to redefine their role between East and West amid difficult circumstances.

---

83. On Schmidt's post-Afghanistan diplomatic efforts, see Pittman, *From Ostpolitik to Reunification,* 118–33.

84. On Schmidt's role in the development of the INF issue, see Helmut Schmidt, *Men and Powers: A Political Retrospective* (New York: Random House, 1989), 188–92.

CHAPTER 4

The New Cold War and the INF Struggle

The new cold war of the early 1980s marked a final turning point in the foreign policy of the old Federal Republic. The invasion of Afghanistan, the suppression of Solidarity in Poland, and the collapse of INF negotiations raised East-West tensions to their highest level in two decades. From the German perspective the INF struggle had particularly far-reaching implications. As the country earmarked for the most important U.S. missiles, the Federal Republic was both central to NATO's deployments plans and Soviet efforts to foil them. The governments of Helmut Schmidt and—after October 1982—Helmut Kohl found themselves caught between the hard line of the Reagan administration and the intransigence of the Soviet leadership. They had to strike a difficult balance between solidarity with the United States and the NATO allies, on the one hand, and the continued pursuit of detente with the Soviet Union and East Berlin, on the other. In 1982–83, at the height of the INF struggle, Kohl made solidarity with the United States his top foreign policy priority. His government's strong support for first deployments in November 1983 contributed to alliance cohesion at a critical juncture. The Federal Republic remained engaged in the East. But its focus on Atlantic solidarity strengthened NATO considerably, only years before the Warsaw Pact collapsed.[1]

This unequivocal emphasis on unity with the Western powers emerged only after the social-liberal coalition collapsed and Kohl formed a government with Foreign Minister Genscher and the FDP. In November 1982, on his first official visit to Washington, Kohl underscored his sup-

---

1. On German foreign policy in the early 1980s, see Wolfram F. Hanrieder, *Germany, America, Europe: Forty Years of German Foreign Policy* (New Haven: Yale University Press, 1989), chaps. 4, 7, 11; Christian Hacke, *Weltmacht wider Willen: Die Außenpolitik der Bundesrepublik Deutschland* (Frankfurt am Main: Ullstein, 1993), chap. 7; Jeffrey Boutwell, *The German Nuclear Dilemma* (Ithaca: Cornell University Press, 1990).

port for Reagan's tough "zero-option" stance in the INF negotiations—
the offer to cancel the proposed deployments of U.S. Cruise and Pershing
II missiles only in exchange for the abolition of the Soviet SS-20 arsenal. In
his public statements before, during, and after the visit, Kohl portrayed
the Soviet INF buildup as an effort to intimidate and subdue Western
Europe. He also echoed Reagan's criticism of Soviet expansionism worldwide, condemning the war in Afghanistan in strident terms and censuring
the December 1981 imposition of martial law in Poland. Kohl's tone was
more moderate than Reagan's: he did not embrace the latter's March 1983
depiction of the Soviet Union as an "evil empire." In a government declaration two months later, however, Kohl did call on Moscow to forswear its
"world revolutionary" ambitions.[2]

Less visible, but also important, were the efforts of Kohl and Genscher to strengthen Franco-German ties and reinvigorate the European
integration process. Schmidt and his French counterpart, Valéry Giscard
d'Estaing, had taken an important step forward with the European Monetary System in the late 1970s. But Schmidt's poor relationship with
François Mitterrand, who succeeded Giscard in May 1981, hampered
bilateral relations and undermined EC efforts to articulate a common foreign policy stance amid worsening superpower ties. Mitterrand's strong
support for INF deployments, together with the 1983 abandonment of his
socialist economic program, created a basis for better relations with Kohl.
On the twentieth anniversary of the Franco-German Treaty both leaders
pledged to intensify their security cooperation and deepen the European
integration process. In the years that followed they created a joint Franco-
German brigade and helped to relaunch the drive to complete the single
European market. As they had at earlier critical junctures, German leaders intent on improving ties with the West focused their efforts on Paris as
well as Washington.[3]

Whenever possible, the new German government combined this solidarity with the Western allies with bids to maintain dialogue with Moscow
and East Berlin. In 1982–83 Kohl and Genscher made some efforts,
behind the scenes, to moderate U.S. positions—to encourage a superpower summit, dampen U.S. sanctions imposed after the imposition of

---

2. Government declaration of May 4, 1983, *Verhandlungen des Deutschen Bundestags.
Stenographischer Bericht,* ser. 10, 69. For Kohl's account of his Washington visit, see his Bundestag declaration of November 25, 1982, ibid., ser. 9, 8008–8010.

3. On Franco-German ties in the 1970s and 1980s, see Haig Simonian, *The Privileged
Partnership: Franco-German Relations in the European Community, 1969–84* (Oxford: Claren-
don Press, 1984); Julius W. Friend, *The Linchpin: French-German Relations, 1950–1990* (New
York: Praeger, 1991), chap. 3.

martial law, and further the stalled INF talks.[4] These efforts, a contrast with Kohl's demonstrative support of U.S. positions in his public rhetoric, achieved little. Kohl convinced Reagan to abandon sanctions intended to scuttle a Soviet-German natural gas pipeline. But no superpower summit took place, and the United States continued to adhere to its inflexible zero-option stance in the Geneva negotiations. The Federal Republic's efforts to maintain an active dialogue with the East were most obvious—and successful—in the context of inter-German relations. In July 1983 and again in July 1984 Bonn extended DM 1 billion credits to East Berlin for the support of inter-German trade. Kohl even renewed Schmidt's invitation to GDR leader Erich Honecker to visit the FRG.[5]

The Federal Republic's efforts to combine solidarity with the West and dialogue with the East ran up against Soviet opposition. Kohl's July 1983 trip to Moscow revealed tensions between his strong pro-U.S. orientation and his efforts to maintain good ties with the Soviet Union. During their talks Yuri Andropov, who succeeded Leonid Brezhnev in November 1982, issued a terse warning that FRG support for INF deployments would spark a crisis in bilateral relations and impede the development of inter-German ties. Relations between Bonn and East Berlin, he warned, could not flourish across a "fence of missiles."[6] Kohl and Genscher sought to put the best face on relations by highlighting economic ties, but Soviet leaders refused to go along. In the run-up to the planned NATO deployments, the Soviet media warned that new missiles on German soil would violate the spirit of the Moscow Treaty. When the last round of INF negotiations failed and the Bundestag approved first deployments in November 1983, Andropov launched a tirade against German militarism and revanchism.[7]

Through the mid-1980s Soviet leaders made good on their pledge to

4. According to Horst Teltschik, Kohl's top foreign policy advisor, Bonn sought a resumption of the superpower dialogue in order to increase German freedom of maneuver in both East and West (interview by author, Gütersloh, July 16, 1992).

5. On inter-German relations during the early 1980s, see A. James McAdams, *Germany Divided: From the Wall to Reunification* (Princeton: Princeton University Press, 1993), 152–64; Matthias Zimmer, *Nationales Interesse und Staatsräson: Zur Deutschlandpolitik der Regierung Kohl, 1982–1989* (Paderborn: Schöningh, 1992), 137–82.

6. On the development of German-Soviet relations during the INF crisis, see Michael J. Sodaro, *Moscow, Germany and the West from Khrushchev to Gorbachev* (Ithaca: Cornell University Press, 1990), 265–316.

7. Soviet leaders appear to have believed that they could prevent deployment with threats and intimidation. Genscher warned Soviet foreign minister Andrei Gromyko in November 1983 that the tough Soviet stance would backfire—a point on which, according to Genscher, Gromyko concurred only much later (Hans-Dietrich Genscher, interview by author, Bonn, August 24, 1992).

punish Bonn for its solidarity with Washington. On several trips to Moscow Genscher tried but failed to enliven the bilateral dialogue. Soviet pressure forced Honecker to cancel his plans to visit Bonn in September 1984. The INF issue even cast a shadow over bilateral ties after Mikhail Gorbachev came to power. During their first meeting in Moscow, in March 1985, for example, Gorbachev berated Kohl for his strong pro-Atlantic orientation. "Where is the federal chancellor's policy drifting?" he pointedly asked.[8] Over the year that followed Gorbachev spurned an invitation to visit Bonn and continued to block Honecker's travel plans. When German-Soviet relations finally began to improve in the summer of 1986, a Kohl blunder created a new furor. In a *Newsweek* interview the chancellor compared Gorbachev's public relations skills with those of Goebbels. The interview—and Kohl's refusal to apologize—sparked an angry Soviet reaction and set back the improvement of bilateral ties until 1987.[9]

While German-Soviet relations suffered through the mid-1980s as a result of the INF struggle, the Federal Republic's ties with its key allies improved. Kohl's public support for Reagan's tough negotiating stance, and his government's success in carrying out first deployments, reinforced ties between Bonn and both Washington and Paris. German support for the Strategic Defense Initiative (SDI), the proposed space-based missile defense system that moved to the top of the East-West arms control agenda after 1983, also met with U.S. approval. Kohl and his advisors backed SDI in the face of strong Soviet opposition, anxiously aware that it might undercut their Ostpolitik.[10] Alongside policy coordination, public symbolism also reinforced the FRG's strong Western orientation. In September 1984 Kohl and Mitterrand held hands on the fields of Verdun, commemorating the furious battle there seventy years earlier. And in May 1985, the fortieth anniversary of the end of World War II, Reagan laid a wreath at the German military cemetery in Bitburg. The Bitburg ceremony proved a public relations fiasco. The presence of Waffen-SS graves at the site, overlooked by Reagan's advance team, overshadowed the effort to dramatize U.S.-German reconciliation. But Reagan's decision to go ahead with the visit at Kohl's behest—and against the fervent pleas of his politi-

8. The Gorbachev statement was cited in a transcript leaked to the press (cited in *Spiegel,* March 25, 1985). According to Jörg Kastl, then German ambassador in Moscow, the transcript was authentic (interview by author, March 30, 1992).

9. Kohl's interview appeared in *Newsweek,* October 27, 1986. According to Teltschik, Kohl knew that the comparison was a foreign policy blunder but did not want to make a public apology shortly before the January 1987 national election (interview).

10. Teltschik, interview. See also Ernst Czempiel, "SDI and NATO: The Case of the Federal Republic of Germany," in *Strategic Defense and the Western Alliance,* ed. Sanford Lakoff and Randy Willoughby (Lexington, Mass.: D.C. Heath, 1987), 147–64.

cal advisors—underscored the robustness of the FRG's key bilateral relationship at a critical juncture.[11]

New Cold War Challenges: Solidarity with the West, Engagement in the East

What explains the German focus on Atlantic solidarity during the new cold war of the early 1980s? Part of the answer can be found at the level of international structure. The gradual shift from detente to confrontation, which began in the 1970s and reached its peak in 1982–83, confronted German leaders with new and difficult policy problems. During the detente of the 1970s the Federal Republic managed to enjoy positive relations with both the Western powers and the Soviet Union. Growing tensions between the superpowers made this combination increasingly difficult to sustain. Given its continued security dependence on the United States, the FRG could not directly oppose Washington's confrontational, anti-Soviet stance. But given the economic and political benefits derived from close ties with the Soviet Union and East Berlin, German leaders also had an interest in continued cooperation with the East. In the early 1980s this general dilemma found its most concrete expression in the INF context. In the run-up to the first deployments in late 1983 German leaders wrestled with how to combine deterrence and dialogue, rearmament and arms control, in their relations with East and West.

These policy challenges had their roots in the gradual, global breakdown of detente that began in the mid-1970s. The October 1973 Arab-Israeli War placed strains on superpower ties, as did proxy wars in Angola and Ethiopia in subsequent years. At the end of the decade the Nicaraguan revolution sharpened U.S. anxiety about Soviet expansionism, while the normalization of U.S.-Chinese relations heightened Soviet concerns about strategic encirclement. Superpower detente did not evaporate altogether. At a June 1979 Vienna meeting—the first superpower summit in almost five years—Brezhnev and Jimmy Carter signed a second Strategic Arms Limitation Treaty (SALT II) and pledged to maintain and deepen their bilateral dialogue. Only six months later, however, the Soviet invasion of Afghanistan marked a clear turn from dialogue to confrontation. Carter adopted a hard line. He suspended SALT II ratification and engineered an anti-Soviet sanctions campaign, including a boycott of the 1980 Moscow

---

11. On the politics of Bitburg, see David B. Morris, "Bitburg Revisited: Germany's Search for Normalcy," *German Politics and Society* 13, no. 4 (winter 1995): 92–109; Geoffrey H. Hartman, ed., *Bitburg in Moral and Political Perspective* (Bloomington: Indiana University Press, 1986).

Summer Olympics. As president, after January 1981, Reagan adopted an even more confrontational approach to ties with the Soviet Union.[12]

The global downturn in U.S.-Soviet relations was also evident in the European context. The Mutual and Balanced Force Reductions talks began in 1973, but made no substantive progress. The NATO and Warsaw Pact participants could not even reach agreement on the relative strength of their existing armed forces. The CSCE process culminated in the Helsinki Final Act in 1975 but then floundered amid clashes over its human rights provisions. From 1980 onward events in Poland generated further tensions. The emergence of Solidarity, an independent trade union, led to Soviet charges of Western interference and to Western warnings against any Soviet military intervention. The Polish government's recognition of Solidarity in August 1980 did not defuse the crisis. Under the leadership of Lech Walesa the union grew into a mass social protest movement directed against the political monopoly of the communist party. In December 1981, with Soviet support, the Polish military declared martial law and disbanded Solidarity. In response, Reagan leveled a series of political and economic sanctions against both Warsaw and Moscow—including measures designed to block the planned German-Soviet natural gas pipeline between Siberia and Western Europe.[13]

Within this broader context the INF issue gradually moved to the center of the new cold war in Europe.[14] From the mid-1970s onward the Soviet deployment of SS-20s—mobile, accurate nuclear missiles targeted at Western Europe—generated growing concerns in NATO about an emerging nuclear imbalance on the continent. In October 1977 Schmidt called for a military and a diplomatic response. Not until a meeting in Guadeloupe in January 1979, however, did U.S., French, and British leaders endorse Schmidt's dual strategy—the combination of an INF modernization plan and an offer of negotiations. During the late 1970s Soviet leaders repeatedly insisted that an INF balance already existed, pointing to French and British arsenals and to U.S. bombers stationed in Western Europe. But their objections were futile. At a summit in December 1979

---

12. On these developments, see Raymond L. Garthoff, *Detente and Confrontation: American-Soviet Relations from Nixon to Reagan* (Washington: Brookings Institution, 1985), chaps. 26–28.

13. On the downturn in detente and the U.S. and Soviet reactions, see Kenneth A. Oye, Robert J. Lieber, and Donald Rothchild, eds., *Eagle Resurgent? The Reagan Era in American Foreign Policy* (Boston: Little, Brown, 1987); Harry Gelman, *The Brezhnev Politburo and the Decline of Detente* (Ithaca: Cornell University Press, 1984), chaps. 4–5.

14. On INF, see Thomas Risse-Kappen, *The Zero Option: INF, West Germany, and Arms Control* (Boulder: Westview, 1988); Lothar Rühl, *Mittelstreckenwaffen in Europa: Ihre Bedeuting in Strategie, Rüstungskontrolle und Bündnispolitik* (Baden-Baden: Nomos, 1987); and Boutwell, *German Nuclear Dilemma*, chaps. 2–5.

NATO leaders officially adopted the Two-Track Decision, a proposal to deploy 472 Pershing II and Cruise missiles from 1983 onward and an immediate offer of INF negotiations.

Just as a reluctant Soviet leadership agreed to such negotiations, Reagan's election in November 1980 set the process back a full year. The new president initiated a comprehensive nuclear and conventional arms buildup, and focused his energies on the deployment half of the Two-Track Decision. In November 1981, at Schmidt's insistence, the United States did finally agree to begin INF negotiations and Strategic Arms Reduction Talks (START). Reagan even adopted Schmidt's idea of a zero option. In contrast to Schmidt, however, who considered the complete elimination of Soviet and Western INF arsenals the optimal solution, but was willing to consider a compromise short of it, Reagan and his advisors made the zero option an all-or-nothing position. Soviet leaders, too, remained intransigent. They continued to insist that an INF balance already existed and offered only to freeze their SS-20 deployments or to reduce them to the level of the French and British arsenals in exchange for a cancelation of the Two-Track Decision. The positions on both sides all but ruled out any substantive progress in the talks. During a July 1982 "Walk in the Woods" the chief negotiators did outline a compromise that would have limited U.S. deployments in exchange for some Soviet reductions. But their governments in Washington and Moscow rejected it in favor of continued adherence to inflexible, incompatible positions.[15]

The year 1983 marked the high point of superpower tensions, internationally and in Europe. In March Reagan publicly branded the Soviet Union an "evil empire" and announced his Strategic Defense Initiative. Both actions met with stinging rebukes from Andropov and the rest of the Soviet leadership. As the INF talks stagnated during the spring and summer of 1983, a growing peace movement, opposed to the planned INF deployments under any circumstances, protested across Western Europe and in the Federal Republic in particular. In September and October, as the date envisioned for first NATO deployments approached, two further developments cast a pall over superpower relations: the U.S. invasion of Grenada and the Soviet downing of a South Korean passenger liner. When first Pershing II deployments began in the Federal Republic, in November 1983, Soviet negotiators left the INF and START talks in Geneva. The walkout marked the climax of the new cold war in Europe.

The crisis in East-West relations, and the evolution of the INF controversy in particular, confronted German leaders with difficult security

---

15. On INF negotiations in the early 1980s, see Strobe Talbott, *Deadly Gambits: The Reagan Administration and the Stalemate in Nuclear Arms Control* (New York: Knopf, 1984). On the origins of the "zero-option" proposal, see Risse-Kappen, *Zero Option,* 78–85.

policy challenges. The Federal Republic found itself at the center of the
INF struggle from the outset. The majority of the new U.S. missiles,
including the more effective 108 Pershing IIs, were earmarked for deployment in the FRG. Capable of hitting targets in the western Soviet Union
with a high degree of accuracy, the Pershing IIs represented a critical link
in the U.S. strategy of extended deterrence. Given this strategic configuration, both the Carter and Reagan administrations considered a united
front with Bonn a top priority. The course of the INF controversy threatened to disrupt, if not unravel, the alliance.[16] At the same time, the
potency of the Pershing IIs, and their centrality for NATO strategy, made
the planned deployments on German soil a central concern of Soviet
diplomacy. German support for deployment, Brezhnev and Andropov
insisted, would lead to counterdeployments that would make the Federal
Republic less, not more secure. In the face of U.S. and Soviet intransigence
on the INF issue the FRG faced tradeoffs between solidarity with the West
and cooperation with the East.

This tradeoff, acute in the case of INF, also characterized the Federal
Republic's overall approach to both superpowers amid the new cold war.
During the early 1970s Brandt managed to combine integration in the
West and active engagement in the East. As chancellor during the second
half of that decade, Schmidt was able to maintain the same policy constellation through the human rights and neutron bomb controversies—
although with considerably more difficulty. With the Soviet invasion of
Afghanistan, the crisis in Poland, and the INF controversy, however, German leaders were forced to redefine their priorities between East and West.
Over the 1980–83 period first Carter and then Reagan sought German support for their confrontational anti-Soviet course. At the same time, Brezhnev and then Andropov made clear that German solidarity with the
United States would undermine any constructive Ostpolitik. Attention to
Western unity promised to undercut detente, while a focus on detente
promised to undercut Western unity. The international configuration presented German leaders with difficult choices.

Institutions and Alternatives: Between Washington and Moscow

During the early 1980s a dense web of international institutions mediated
the policy challenges posed by the East-West constellation. The Federal
Republic had grown more powerful during the 1970s, in both economic
and military terms. Under Schmidt's leadership the German economy

---

16. On divisions within the alliance during the late 1970s and early 1980s, see Robert
W. Tucker and Linda Wrigley, eds., *The Atlantic Alliance and Its Critics* (New York: Praeger,
1983).

weathered the recessions of the 1970s more effectively than did those of its allies. The success of the German social market model generated discussion of "Modell Deutschland" and its particular advantages.[17] At the same time, the strength and reputation of the Bundeswehr translated into growing influence on security matters, as evidenced by Schmidt's role at the Guadeloupe summit. German clout in the West went hand in hand with a greater influence in the East. As the most important Soviet partner in Western Europe—and its largest worldwide trade partner—the Federal Republic assumed a more visible role in East-West relations. On balance the FRG emerged as a more powerful country over the course of the 1970s. At the same time, however, German power unfolded within the constraints posed by international institutions. During the early 1980s both NATO and the EC in the West and the Eastern Treaties and the CSCE in the East framed German approaches to the twin problems of INF policy and relations with both superpowers.

NATO constituted the most prominent institutional context for German foreign policy over this period. By the early 1980s the Federal Republic had emerged as the most influential European member of the alliance. France's departure from NATO's military integration in 1966, together with the Bundeswehr's emergence as its largest conventional force, enhanced the German voice within the alliance. At the same time, however, Bonn remained completely dependent on Washington for its defense and the security of West Berlin. The relative growth of German military power did nothing to erase the Federal Republic's dependence on the U.S. nuclear deterrent. Bonn did gain a seat within NATO's Nuclear Planning Group in the mid-1960s. Without its own general staff, however, and with limited logistical resources, the Bundeswehr continued to rely heavily on U.S. military planning and intelligence. By necessity, German security policy retained its multilateral orientation.[18]

In the context of the INF struggle NATO's Two-Track Decision represented the central institutional constraint on German foreign policy. The decision embodied the twin norms set down in the 1967 Harmel Report: defense and detente. The deployment track of NATO strategy aimed both to counter the Soviet SS-20 buildup and to modernize U.S. forces in Europe, while its negotiations track aimed to create an INF balance at the lowest possible level and to avert an all-out arms race. Both tracks were conceived as self-reinforcing. The determination to deploy was designed to exert pressure on the Soviet Union to negotiate, while a determination to

17. Andrei S. Markovits, ed. *The Political Economy of West Germany: Modell Deutschland* (New York: Praeger, 1982).
18. Helga Haftendorn, *Security and Detente: Conflicting Priorities in German Foreign Policy* (New York: Praeger, 1985), chap. 3.

negotiate was designed to secure the political support necessary to deploy. Once Schmidt endorsed the Two-Track Decision, he and his successors as chancellor were bound to adhere to both its parts—or break with multi-lateralism and risk a major crisis in the alliance.[19]

Amid the INF struggle the European Community was a much less salient institutional framework for German foreign policy. During the 1970s, efforts to transform the EC from a trading bloc into a political union were largely unsuccessful. European Political Cooperation, a multi-lateral forum for foreign policy consultations, did enjoy some success in coordinating EC policy toward the Middle East and the developing world.[20] Yet, in the context of security policy, and the INF controversy in particular, the EC was completely subordinate to NATO. A more significant context for German security policy was the Franco-German Treaty of 1963, with its provisions for regular consultations on security affairs. Although France was not part of NATO's integrated military command, Mitterrand made no secret of his strong support for INF deployments in the event that negotiations should fail. He even used the dramatic occasion of a Bundestag speech on the twentieth anniversary of the treaty to underscore the importance of the FRG's ties with the West.[21] Institutional links with Paris, like the NATO link with the United States, constrained German leaders to cooperate with their allies on major political and security issues.

Of the institutions linking the Federal Republic with the Soviet Union and its allies, the Moscow Treaty of 1970 was the most important. The treaty not only recognized the status quo of the division of Germany and Europe, ending two decades of sharp confrontation around the issue of German unity. It also provided a framework for subsequent bilateral cooperation between Bonn and Moscow. Its first article, for example, called on both sides to make "the maintenance of international peace and the achievement of detente an important objective of their policies."[22] Broader political and security affairs emerged as prominent themes at

---

19. On the arms control dilemmas facing German leaders in the early 1980s, see Wolfram F. Hanrieder, ed., *Arms Control, the FRG and the Future of East-West Relations* (Boulder: Westview, 1987).

20. On the German role in the EC through the 1970s, see Simon Bulmer and William Paterson, *The Federal Republic of Germany and the European Community* (London: Allen and Unwin, 1987).

21. Mitterrand address of January 20, 1983, *Verhandlungen des deutschen Bundestags,* ser. 9, 8978–84.

22. Text in *Außenpolitik der Bundesrepublik Deutschland: Dokumente von 1949 bis 1994* (Cologne: Verlag Wissenschaft und Politik, 1995), 337. On German-Soviet economic ties, see Angela Stent, *From Embargo to Ostpolitik: The Political Economy of West German-Soviet Relations* (Cambridge: Cambridge University Press, 1981).

German-Soviet summits from the early 1970s onward, as did bilateral economic relations. Some major problems persisted, particularly on the subject of Berlin. Soviet leaders, eager to place limits on the Federal Republic's political presence in the former German capital, refused to incorporate West Berlin into a series of cultural and scientific accords with Bonn. In contrast to the 1950s and 1960s, however, Berlin—and the broader question of German unity—did not sour the overall bilateral relationship.

The strength of new institutional links with the East was most evident in the case of inter-German ties. The December 1972 Basic Treaty, which set out a framework for relations between the FRG and the GDR, remained an object of clashing interpretations. East Berlin stressed the GDR's claim to equality and independence, while Bonn continued to articulate the ultimate goal of national unity. FRG leaders highlighted treaty provisions calling for greater interaction among Germans, East and West, while the SED leadership stressed GDR sovereignty and sought to contain that interaction through the restriction of contacts [*Abgrenzung*]. Despite these differences of interpretation, the Basic Treaty and subsequent accords constituted a firm institutional basis for economic cooperation and increased inter-German contacts. Amid the crisis of detente the security provisions of the Basic Treaty became particularly significant. Both German states had pledged to "contribute to security and cooperation in Europe" and to support disarmament. Meeting in the GDR for the first time, in December 1981, Schmidt and Honecker stressed the responsibility of both German states for peace and detente in Europe.[23]

The CSCE and the Four-Power regime represented less salient institutional contexts for German foreign policy in the early 1980s. The CSCE Helsinki Final Act outlined three areas for cooperation between the blocs: economics, security, and humanitarian issues. But clashes over its human rights provisions—a U.S. priority under both Carter and Reagan—prevented substantive progress at follow-up meetings in Belgrade in 1978 and Madrid in 1982.[24] Over the same period the Four-Power regime faded altogether as a context for German foreign policy. During the decade after the 1971 Berlin Treaty the United States and the Soviet Union clashed sharply on many issues, but the division of Germany and its former capi-

23. Text in *Außenpolitik der Bundesrepublik,* 370–72. On the development of inter-German ties on the foundation of the Basic Treaty, see Lawrence L. Whetten, *Germany East and West: Conflicts, Collaboration, and Confrontation* (New York: New York University Press, 1980), chaps. 4–5; Wilhelm Bruns, *Deutsch-deutsche Beziehungen: Prämisse, Probleme, Perspektiven* (Opladen: Leske and Budrich, 1984), chap. 7.

24. See Vojtech Mastny, *Helsinki, Human Rights, and European Security: Analysis and Documentation* (Durham: Duke University Press, 1986).

tal were not among them. While neither the CSCE nor the Four-Power regime figured centrally in the controversies of the early 1980s, both continued to represent constraints on German policy toward the unity issue. Within the framework of the CSCE the Federal Republic made recognition of postwar borders a starting point for Ostpolitik. And the Four-Power regime precluded a unilateral reunification policy. Under these circumstances the combination of East-West tensions and positive inter-German relations did not imply a revival of the German Problem in the early 1980s, despite the concerns of some foreign observers.[25]

In the context of the INF struggle, ambiguity at the heart of NATO and the Eastern Treaties—the two most prominent institutional frameworks during the new cold war of the early 1980s—confronted German leaders with significant foreign policy alternatives. With the Harmel Report of 1967, the cornerstone of NATO strategy into the 1980s, the alliance embraced both deterrence and dialogue as twin components of its policy toward the Soviet Union. The particular mix between the two, however, was left ambiguous, allowing individual member states considerable leeway in their approaches to Moscow. This basic ambiguity was incorporated into the Two-Track Decision, which endorsed both deployments and negotiations, but did not specify their relative importance. NATO policy empowered the United States to conduct the negotiations. And it specified that the missiles, once deployed, would remain under U.S. control. At the same time, however, it allowed individual member states to place more or less emphasis on the deployment and negotiation tracks of NATO policy—both in internal alliance deliberations and in their relations with the Soviet Union and its allies. As the country designated for the most important deployments, the FRG in particular was well-placed to press its own preferences within the framework of the Two-Track Decision. Specifically, Bonn could opt either to support Washington's hard line or to press for greater emphasis on the negotiations half of NATO strategy.

During the INF controversy of the early 1980s the Eastern Treaties were more ambiguous in their prescriptions than the Two-Track Decision. One month before first NATO deployments the Soviet leadership warned that new U.S. missiles on German soil, "would contradict in both word and spirit the Moscow and [Basic] Treaties and seriously damage the FRG's relations with the German Democratic Republic and the Soviet Union."[26] German leaders were not bound by this interpretation. On the

---

25. For a survey of these concerns, see Eberhard Schulz and Peter Danylow, *Bewegung in der deutschen Frage? Die ausländischen Besorgnisse über die Entwicklung in den beiden deutschen Staaten* (Bonn: Europa Union Verlag, 1984).

26. Text of a USSR-GDR communiqué reprinted in the official SED organ, *Neues Deutschland,* October 19, 1983.

one hand, the passages in the Moscow and Basic Treaties on peace and detente were very general. On the other hand, FRG leaders could and did argue that the Soviet SS-20 buildup, not NATO's response, posed the greater threat to detente. The Eastern Treaties certainly did not compel Bonn to reject deployments once INF talks failed. In the years leading up to 1983, however, they did create pressure to emphasize the negotiations rather than the deployment tracks of NATO strategy. Given Soviet concerns, the deployment of new nuclear missiles on German soil threatened to undermine the cooperative ties that had flourished within the context of the Moscow, Basic and other Eastern Treaties.

During the early 1980s both NATO and the Eastern Treaties framed German foreign policy alternatives in the context of the new cold war and the INF crisis. The Two-Track Decision bound the Federal Republic to carry out deployments in the absence of a negotiated settlement. NATO membership all but ruled out a political break with Washington and a German drift into neutrality—the concerns of some observers notwithstanding.[27] At the same time, however, participation in the alliance allowed Bonn considerable leeway in its approach to deployment and negotiations in the years and months leading up to the fall of 1983. The Moscow and Basic Treaties, by contrast, bound the Federal Republic to eschew open confrontation with the Soviet Union and its allies. They did not, however, prevent the Federal Republic from emphasizing solidarity with the United States—and accepting the political consequences—in the context of INF and other divisive issues. Within this configuration Bonn did not face sharply contrasting alternatives between East and West but, instead, different ways to combine cooperation with Washington and dialogue with Moscow.[28] The existence of these alternatives formed the backdrop for the domestic political debate.

Contrasting Priorities amid the New Cold War

The foreign policy controversies of the new cold war played out within a changing German societal context. The cumulative impact of recessions in the 1970s and 1980s—slower growth, higher inflation, and higher unemployment—placed strains on the German welfare state and spawned

---

27. For the argument the Federal Republic might have drifted into neutrality during the INF crisis but ended up resisting Soviet efforts to disrupt the alliance, see Jeffrey Herf, *War by Other Means: Soviet Power, West German Resistance, and the Battle of the Euromissiles* (New York: Free Press, 1991).

28. On tensions between alliance ties with the United States and detente with the Soviet Union, see Josef Joffe, *The Limited Partnership: Europe, the United States, and the Burdens of Alliance* (Cambridge, Mass.: Ballinger, 1987), chap. 1.

greater material insecurity. At the same time, the Green Party, which grew out of the student protests of the 1960s and the New Social Movements of the 1970s, placed new issues on the political agenda—the environment, women's issues, and peace. The party entered the Bundestag for the first time in the March 1983 elections, bouyed by the peace movement's principled opposition to new U.S. missiles on German soil.[29] There was also movement on the other end of the German political spectrum. The German Far Right, which had sunk into relative obscurity during the 1970s, reemerged somewhat during the mid-1980s. The Republican Party, founded in Bavaria in 1983, made inroads into the CSU's electorate and began to articulate its nationalist, anti-immigrant themes at the national level. While far less successful than the Greens—they never received the 5 percent of the vote necessary for representation in the Bundestag—the Republicans benefited from widespread dissatisfaction with the major parties' approach to pressing economic and social problems.[30]

While the INF struggle did not divide German society as had Western integration and the New Ostpolitik, it sparked intense debate about security, peace, and the German role between the superpowers. The Greens and the peace movement rejected INF deployments under any circumstances. Among the major party leaders, however, the range of debate was much narrower. It revolved around different ways to combine the deployment and negotiations tracks of NATO strategy—and, more generally, relations with Washington and Moscow.[31] A dwindling minority within the CDU/CSU continued to reject the Eastern Treaties as central components of German foreign policy. And a growing minority within the SPD shared the peace movement's opposition to new U.S. missiles under any circumstances. In the years before 1983, however, the dominant parties at the federal level—Christian Democratic, Social Democratic, and Liberal—upheld both tracks of NATO policy and underscored the importance of both the Atlantic Alliance and the Eastern Treaties as founda-

---

29. Alice Holmes Cooper, *Paradoxes of Peace: German Peace Movements since 1945* (Ann Arbor: University of Michigan Press, 1996), chaps. 4–5. On the emergence of the peace movement across Europe, see Wilfried von Bredow and Rudolf H. Brocke, *Krise und Protest: Ursprünge und Elemente der Friedensbewegung in Westeuropa* (Opladen: Westdeutscher Verlag, 1987).

30. On this shift in German political culture, see Kurt Sontheimer, *Die verunsicherte Republik: Die Bundesrepublik nach 30 Jahren* (Munich: Piper, 1979); *Zeitenwende? Die Bundesrepublik zwischen alter und alternativer Politik* (Hamburg: Hoffmann and Campe, 1983). On the emergence of the Republikaner, see Hans-Joachim Veen, Norbert Lepszy, and Peter Mnich, *The Republikaner Party in Germany: Right-Wing Menace or Protest Catchall?* (Westport, Conn.: Praeger, 1993).

31. On elements of consensus, see Gebhard Schweigler, *West German Foreign Policy: The Domestic Setting* (New York: Praeger, 1984).

tions of German foreign policy. Differences among them concerned matters of emphasis. Schmidt and Kohl, the leading rivals for the chancellorship during the early 1980s, defined the main contours of the political debate.

The political biographies of Schmidt and Kohl illuminate their broadly comparable foreign policy stances.[32] Schmidt had fought in World War II, studied economics, and began his career in the SPD in Hamburg. As a foreign policy spokesman and head of the SPD parliamentary group in the 1960s, he had established himself as a leading advocate of the party's new pro-Western orientation. Later, as defense and finance minister under Brandt, he combined strong support for the New Ostpolitik with careful attention to relations with the Western powers. Kohl, too young to fight in the war, had studied history and immediately embarked on a successful political career in his native Rhineland-Palatinate. He was elected governor in 1969, before succeeding Rainer Barzel as CDU chairman in 1973. As a centrist with little foreign policy experience, Kohl advocated a pragmatic acceptance of the New Ostpolitik. By the early 1980s both he and Schmidt had arrived by different routes at broadly comparable perspectives—an embrace of both Western integration and the New Ostpolitik as necessary foundations of German foreign policy.

As detente began to unravel in the late 1970s and early 1980s, both Schmidt and Kohl emphasized the importance of strong German links with the Western powers, and the United States in particular. Under growing pressure from the peace movement—and the left wing of his party—to abandon the Two-Track Decision, Schmidt underscored his continued support for strong ties with the West. "Our basic foreign policy orientation is not negotiable," he wrote in a spring 1981 *Foreign Affairs* article, underscoring the importance of the Federal Republic's political and security links with the United States and Western Europe. Schmidt added that he had never "left any doubt about this point in the minds of the Soviet leaders."[33] Kohl, too, left no doubt about what he considered the institutional and political foundations of German foreign policy. In a major November 1980 Bundestag address, for example, he emphasized that "the western alliance and the friendship with the United States" was a "clear priority."[34]

For both Schmidt and Kohl this Western foundation represented a starting point for an active Ostpolitik. In his first government declaration

---

32. For political biographies, see Werner Maser, *Helmut Kohl: Der Deutsche Kanzler* (Frankfurt am Main: Ullstein, 1990); Jonathan Carr, *Helmut Schmidt: Helmsman of Germany* (New York: St. Martin's Press, 1985).

33. Reprinted in Wolfram F. Hanrieder, ed., *Helmut Schmidt: Perspectives on Politics* (Boulder: Westview, 1982), 40.

34. Address of November 26, 1980, *Verhandlungen des deutschen Bundestags,* ser. 9, 50.

as chancellor, in May 1974, Schmidt underscored the importance of Western integration as a basis for "good relations with the Soviet Union and the countries of the Warsaw Pact."[35] Four years later he used the occasion of Brezhnev's first official visit to the Federal Republic to highlight the positive tenor of bilateral relations.[36] And in December 1981 he made a successful first visit to the GDR. Kohl, too, backed dialogue with the East on a solid Western foundation. As early as January 1975, he authorized informal CDU contacts with East Berlin. In September 1975, one year before his first, unsuccessful run for the chancellorship, Kohl traveled to Moscow to assure Soviet leaders of his commitment to a constructive Ostpolitik.[37] And in his October 1982 government declaration, the first of his chancellorship, he promised to pay "particular attention" to relations with Moscow and to support deeper inter-German relations on the basis of the Eastern Treaties.[38]

On this shared foundation, Kohl and Schmidt articulated different approaches to the Federal Republic's role between the superpowers, and the INF issue in particular. From early in his career Schmidt had underlined the twin imperatives of defense alongside the United States and detente with the Soviet Union.[39] With the downturn in detente he construed the Federal Republic as a mediator between East and West, firmly anchored within NATO but actively committed to preserving and deepening dialogue between the blocs. From the late 1970s onward he did not hesitate to criticize what he considered Washington's overly confrontational policies. And in the context of the INF struggle he pressed for the exhaustion of the negotiations track before deployments should begin. By contrast, Kohl stressed the absolute priority of solidarity with the allies—and the United States in particular—as a necessary condition for continued engagement in the East. On a number of difficult transatlantic issues, from human rights and the neutron bomb in the late 1970s to Afghanistan, Poland, and INF in the early 1980s, he aligned himself carefully with U.S. priorities.

Schmidt set out his conception of the Federal Republic as mediator

---

35. Address of May 17, 1974, ibid., ser. 7, 6597–98.

36. For Schmidt's account of his dealings with Soviet leaders, see Schmidt, *Men and Powers: A Political Retrospective* (New York: Random House, 1989), chap. 1.

37. See the internal report by CDU foreign policy spokesman Walther Leisler Kiep on his talks in East Berlin, January 31, 1975, *Archiv für Christlich-Demokratische Politik,* Mertes papers, I-403–070/2. For Kohl's upbeat assessment of his Moscow trip, see *CDU Pressemitteilung,* September 12, 1975.

38. Declaration of October 13, 1982, *Verhandlungen des deutschen Bundestags,* ser. 9, 7222.

39. See, for example, Helmut Schmidt, *The Balance of Power: Germany's Peace Policy and the Super Powers* (London: William Kimber, 1971), chap. 8.

most clearly in a December 1981 Bundestag address. His government, he asserted, was committed to preserving East-West dialogue through continual contacts with both Washington and Moscow. The Federal Republic was engaged in "making sure that the superpowers do not break off their dialogue with each other and that they pursue their interests toward one another with moderation and a sense of proportion." Schmidt did not use the term *mediator* to describe this role, preferring the more modest *translator*. But he clearly envisioned Bonn working with both Washington and Moscow to sustain detente in Europe—an approach that did not rule out public criticism of the United States. In his *Foreign Affairs* article, for example, he emphasized that "the United States must vigorously work toward arms limitation talks between the superpowers."[40]

During the two last years of his chancellorship Schmidt put this mediating role into practice, straining U.S.-German relations in the process. In April 1980 he proposed an INF moratorium as a first step toward a negotiated settlement—to the surprise and frustration of the Carter administration. Two months later he flew to Moscow, where he persuaded Soviet leaders to begin INF talks. Schmidt's trip, only six months after the Soviet invasion of Afghanistan, exasperated Carter and his advisors and sparked a fiery personal confrontation at the June 1980 Venice G-7 Summit.[41] Schmidt continued to play a mediating role once Reagan took office. In early 1981 he successfully pressured the new administration to set a date for the start of INF negotiations. And at a November 1981 summit with Brezhnev in Bonn he tried, without success, to moderate the Soviet negotiating position. Through the end of his chancellorship the following September, Schmidt pressed for a compromise INF settlement, in sharp contrast to the Reagan administration's focus on deployments.[42]

Schmidt's efforts to mediate between the superpowers were evident on other fronts of the new cold war as well. During early 1980 he both implored the Soviet leadership to withdraw from Afghanistan and dis-

---

40. Government declaration of December 3, 1981, *Verhandlungen des deutschen Bundestags,* ser. 9, 4053; Hanrieder, *Helmut Schmidt,* 45. For a discussion of Schmidt's conception of a mediating role, see Avril Pittman, *From Ostpolitik to Reunification: West German–Soviet Political Relations since 1974* (Cambridge: Cambridge University Press, 1992), 101–8.

41. For contrasting accounts of the Venice meeting, see Schmidt, *Men and Powers,* 202–20; Jimmy Carter, *Keeping Faith: Memoirs of a President* (New York: Bantam, 1982), 535–38.

42. On Schmidt's efforts to mediate in the INF context, see Wolfgang Jäger and Werner Link, *Republik im Wandel, 1974–1982: Die Ära Schmidt* (Stuttgart: Deutsche Verlags-Anstalt, 1987), 321–41. On tensions in the U.S.-German relationship during his chancellorship, see *Barbara Heep, Helmut Schmidt und Amerika: Eine schwierige Partnerschaft* (Bonn: Bouvier, 1990), 193–240.

tanced himself from the U.S. sanctions campaign. Only after initial hesitation did Bonn reluctantly join the boycott of the Moscow Olympics. Schmidt also tried not to let the Polish crisis impede Ostpolitik and the overall course of East-West relations in Europe. His reception of Brezhnev in November 1981 took place as the confrontation between Solidarity and the communist regime was reaching its climax. And after the declaration of martial law the following month, Schmidt refused to cut short his first visit to the GDR. In the Polish context, as in the case of Afghanistan, his stance was markedly less confrontational than Reagan's. He condemned the imposition of martial law but also criticized the United States–led sanctions campaign that followed, especially efforts to kill the joint German-Soviet pipeline project. By mid-1982 U.S.-German relations were frayed.[43]

While Schmidt sought to carve out a mediating role for the Federal Republic, Kohl made solidarity with the United States his top priority from the mid-1970s onward. This emphasis was particularly evident on security matters. During the neutron bomb controversy of 1977–78 Kohl sided with Carter against Schmidt. Subsequently, like Carter and Reagan, Kohl placed more emphasis on the deployment half of NATO's emerging Two-Track Strategy than did the chancellor. In a March 1979 Bundestag debate, for example, he excoriated the Soviet SS-20 buildup and called for an increase in NATO's nuclear potential "in order to arrive at a better balance."[44] While Kohl had misgivings about Reagan's uncompromising INF stance in 1982–83, he carefully followed the U.S. lead in public. In his first government declaration as chancellor, in October 1982, he pledged to "free German-American relations from their unfavorable light." While he sought to improve ties with Moscow and hoped for a breakthrough in INF negotiations, Kohl later explicitly rejected Schmidt's role as a "mediator or an interpreter" between the superpowers.[45]

This difference of emphasis was not only evident in the context of INF. It also marked Kohl's different approach to U.S. policy during the Afghanistan and Poland crises. Like Schmidt, Kohl had reservations about the efficacy of economic sanctions; he also feared their negative

---

43. For Schmidt's measured response to martial law, see his government declaration of January 14, 1982, *Verhandlungen des deutschen Bundestags,* ser. 9, 4404–13. On the pipeline dispute, see Bruce W. Jentleson, *Pipeline Politics: The Complex Political Economy of East-West Energy Trade* (Ithaca: Cornell University Press, 1986), chap. 6.

44. Kohl address of March 8, 1979, *Verhandlungen des deutschen Bundestags,* ser. 8, 11150. In the same speech Kohl sharply criticized Schmidt's handling of the neutron bomb controversy (ibid., 11154–55).

45. Declaration of October 13, 1982, ibid., ser. 9, 7220; May 1983 party conference address, *32. Parteitag der CDU Deutschlands. Niederschrift* (Bonn: CDU, 1983), 47.

implications for German industry. Still, he made the imperative of solidarity with the United States a higher priority. His criticism of Soviet policy toward Afghanistan and Poland paralleled Washington's, and he refrained from any public criticism of U.S.-orchestrated sanctions campaigns.[46] Once he became chancellor, Kohl worked behind the scenes to lift certain sanctions, particularly those affecting the German-Soviet pipeline deal. Unlike Schmidt, however, he refused to defy the United States publicly on the issue. While Kohl's Ostpolitik preferences were more conciliatory than either Carter's or Reagan's, he was careful to avoid irritations in relations with Washington. As he put it in the Bundestag in November 1980, "Ostpolitik can only go as far as western unity allows."[47]

The contrasting priorities of Kohl and Schmidt were rooted in divergent perceptions of the international constellation. Schmidt's perception of a Soviet INF threat had informed his support for the Two-Track Decision during the late 1970s. By the early 1980s, however, he also saw confrontational U.S. policies as detrimental to German security. Located at the fault line between the blocs, he argued, the Federal Republic had a vital interest in continued East-West detente. "Precisely in difficult times," Schmidt outlined in a November 1980 government declaration, the FRG "does not want to allow the dialogue with the Soviet Union to be interrupted."[48] For Kohl, by contrast, the Soviet threat, not the threat to detente, remained the dominant feature of the international constellation. He portrayed the SS-20 buildup as an effort to divide the West and the Soviet campaign against the Two-Track Decision as an effort to drive a wedge between the Federal Republic and its Western allies. Kohl's depiction of Soviet "over-armament" and the threat of "political blackmail" made solidarity with the United States essential.[49]

Different views of the past and its lessons also underpinned these contrasting foreign policy priorities. Like Brandt before him, Schmidt argued that Germans were morally bound, against the backdrop of World War II, to work for peace in Europe. In his May 1979 State of the Nation address, for example, he underlined his wish that "no war will ever originate again on German soil"—a theme he repeated on many other occasions. Schmidt's historically grounded "peace policy" informed both his emphasis on the negotiations track of the NATO strategy and his overall approach to detente. Given the legacy of Hitler's war, Schmidt suggested,

46. On Afghanistan, see Kohl address of January 17, 1980, *Verhandlungen des deutschen Bundestags,* ser. 8, 15585–93. On Poland, see his address of January 14, 1982, ibid., ser. 9, 4413–21.

47. Address of November 26, 1980, ibid., ser. 9, 50.

48. Address of November 24, 1980, in Hanrieder, *Helmut Schmidt,* 159.

49. Address of May 4, 1983, *Verhandlungen des deutschen Bundestags,* ser. 10, 69.

the Federal Republic should refrain from harsh condemnations—and sanctions—in response to Soviet policy in Afghanistan and Poland. During his 1980 Moscow visit, for example, Schmidt evoked "vivid memories of the horrors of war" as a foundation for a German foreign policy "aimed at peace."[50]

From Schmidt's perspective, a mediating role not only made sense given the legacy of Hitler's war, it also represented a way to build on the achievements of the New Ostpolitik. Schmidt acknowledged the historical significance of Western integration as a new foundation for postwar German foreign policy. At the same time, however, he placed emphasis on Brandt's achievement of reconciliation with the East. "The Ostpolitik of the social-liberal coalition," he maintained in his November 1980 government declaration, "has become an essential element of West-East relations in the whole of Europe." Schmidt underscored the concrete gains of the New Ostpolitik—less confrontation, greater trade, and more inter-German contacts. And he depicted his international efforts in the context of INF and other issues as attempts to secure and extend Brandt's achievement. The New Ostpolitik, in his view, had not reduced the importance of Western ties. But it had enabled a "treaty partnership" and even "security partnership" with the East—accomplishments worth preserving.[51]

While Schmidt's view of history informed his efforts to mediate between East and West, Kohl's underpinned the absolute priority he accorded Western unity. Like Adenauer, Kohl drew links between the past and both the style and substance of German foreign policy in the present. On the one hand, he called for a respectful, if not reticent, approach to the allies. Schmidt's arrogant tone in dealings with Carter, he argued in November 1980, evoked "unpleasant memories of Wilhelm II."[52] On the other hand, Kohl insisted that solidarity with the Western powers was necessary to prevent a revival of nationalist balance of power politics in Europe. Even before becoming CDU chairman, Kohl expressed anxiety that a failure to maintain and strengthen Western integration could permit a revival of German nationalism, particularly among younger generations.[53] Once he replaced Schmidt as chancellor, he underscored in May 1983 that Germans were not "wanderers between East and West." Commenting on his own pro-Atlantic stance later that month, he expressed

---

50. Addresses of May 17, 1979 and June 30, 1980, in Hanrieder, *Helmut Schmidt*, 146, 68.

51. Addresses of November 24, 1980, and May 17, 1979, ibid., 159, 147.

52. Address of November 26, 1980, *Verhandlungen des deutschen Bundestags*, ser. 6, 50.

53. Memorandum on Kohl's talks with British leaders, February 24, 1972, *Archiv für Christlich-Demokratische Politik*, Mertes papers, I-403–032/2.

relief that "concerns about a possible German special role [*Sonderrolle*] in the East-West relationship have been overcome."[54]

Kohl not only insisted on a break with prewar patterns. He also sought to safeguard Adenauer's postwar achievements. In an address on the centennial of Adenauer's birth in 1976, he contrasted Western integration with the New Ostpolitik. While the former marked a historic break with the destructive, nationalist policies of the past, he argued, the latter represented only a painful coming to terms with postwar realities, the achievement not of peace but of "half-peace." A continued focus on close ties with the West and the cause of European unity, in Kohl's view, constituted "an obligation of Adenauer's legacy."[55] Amid the downturn in detente Kohl did echo some of the historical themes associated with the New Ostpolitik. In 1980, for example, he referred to the responsibility of both German states for peace in Europe. And in a major 1983 policy address he underscored the "historically-conditioned security needs of the Soviet Union." At the same time, however, he construed his policy focus on solidarity with the West as an effort to sustain Adenauer's achievement amid difficult circumstances.[56]

The historical narratives espoused by Schmidt and Kohl, while different in some respects, were broadly similar. Each construed 1945 as a sharp break in German history and described Western integration and the New Ostpolitik as historical achievements of the Federal Republic. A strong identification with the state created by Bismarck, evident during early controversies, was absent. During the cold war of the 1950s Schumacher had stressed the priority of reunification over Western integration. Twenty years later Strauss and other CDU/CSU hard-liners had insisted that the "Reich within its 1937 borders" remain a frame of reference for German foreign policy. For Schmidt and Kohl, by contrast, the Federal Republic, with its domestic institutions and international alignments, was the clear focus of identification. Schmidt exuded pride in "Modell Deutschland," the FRG's particular mix of economic, social and political institutions. And Kohl, eager to foster popular identification with the Federal Republic, sponsored the creation of a *West* German history museum in Bonn.

---

54. Address of May 3, 1983, *Verhandlungen des deutschen Bundestags,* ser. 11, 67; May 1983 party conference address, *32. Parteitag der CDU,* 44–45.

55. Address of January 4, 1976, Helmut Kohl, *Der Kurs der CDU: Reden und Beiträge des Bundesvorsitzenden, 1973–1993* (Stuttgart: Deutsche Verlags-Anstalt, 1993), 144–53.

56. Speech of November 26, 1980, *Verhandlungen des deutschen Bundestags,* ser. 9, 47; address of May 4, 1983, ibid., ser. 10, 69. For a statement of Kohl's view of history and its lessons on the eve of the fortieth anniversary of the end of World War II, see his State of the Nation address of February 27, 1985, ibid., ser. 10, 9009–17.

While some historians and publicists sought to revive the question of German unity during the late 1970s and early 1980s, the major foreign policy debate revolved around the priorities of the Federal Republic, conceived as a modern, Western democracy much like any other.[57]

The outcome of the "Historians' Debate" of 1986–87 underscored the shift away from a national toward a more West German orientation among both historians and politicians. From the late 1970s onward conservative historians including Thomas Nipperdey and Michael Stürmer sought to revive some of the themes of the 1950s. They portrayed the Kaiserreich as a normal nation state within the European balance of power, not an inherently aggressive forerunner of Hitler's Germany. The implication, most clearly articulated by Stürmer, was that the Federal Republic might draw on Bismarck's Reich for elements of a positive German identity.[58] Two national conservative historians, Ernst Nolte and Andreas Hillgruber, went a step further. In the mid-1980s they questioned the uniqueness of the Holocaust. Nolte compared Hitler's genocide with Stalin's Gulag, while Hillgruber drew a parallel between the slaughter of the Jews and the German army's defensive struggle on the Eastern Front. When Jürgen Habermas attacked these arguments as transparent efforts to relativize Hitler's crimes, a lively controversy ensued. Nolte and Hillgruber found themselves under siege in the academy, their arguments dissected and dismissed by most of their colleagues. Moreover, their efforts to downplay the catastrophe of Nazism and forge a positive line of continuity between Bismarck's Reich and the Federal Republic did not resonate at all within the political elite.[59]

---

57. Treatments of the unity theme included Josef von Becker and Andreas Hillgruber, eds., *Die deutsche Frage im 19. und 20. Jahrhundert* (Munich: Vögel, 1983); Arno Klönne, *Zurück zur Nation? Kontroversen zu deutschen Fragen* (Cologne: Diedrichs, 1984); Wolfgang Venrohr, ed., *Die deutsche Einheit kommt bestimmt* (Bergisch Gladbach: Gustav Lübbe Verlag, 1982).

58. Thomas Nipperdey, *Nachdenken über die deutsche Geschichte: Essays* (Munich: Beck, 1986); Michael Stürmer, *Das ruhelose Reich: Deutschland, 1866–1918* (Berlin: Severin and Siedler, 1983). For criticisms, see Wolfgang J. Mommsen, "Gegenwärtige Tendenzen in der Geschichtsschreibung der Bundesrepublik," *Geschichte und Gesellschaft* 7, no. 2 (1981): 149–88; Hans-Jürgen Puhle, "Die neue Ruhelosigkeit: Michael Stürmers nationalpolitischer Revisionismus," ibid., 13, no. 3 (1987): 382–99.

59. Ernst Nolte, "Vergangenheit, die nicht vergehen will: Eine Rede, die geschrieben, aber nicht gehalten werden konnte," *Frankfurter Allgemeine Zeitung,* June 6, 1986; Andreas Hillgruber, *Zweierlei Untergang: Die Zerschlagung des Deutschen Reiches und das Ende des europäischen Judentums* (Berlin: Siedler, 1986). On the controversy, see Charles S. Maier, *The Unmasterable Past: History, Holocaust, and German National Identity* (Cambridge: Harvard University Press, 1988); Geoff Eley, "Nazism, Politics and the Image of the Past: Thoughts on the West German *Historikerstreit*," *Past and Present,* no. 121 (November 1988): 171–208.

While Schmidt and Kohl both rejected a national orientation in favor of a multilateral, supranational one, they advocated different responses to the new cold war of the 1980s. Their contrasting foreign policy priorities, rooted in different perceptions of the international configuration and the lessons of history, represented alternative policy paths during the INF struggle. Had he remained in power after September 1982, Schmidt certainly would have continued to prod the superpowers toward an INF settlement. Schmidt himself made this clear in the decisive November 1983 Bundestag debate on deployment. He leveled a blistering attack on Kohl for not using German leverage to promote an interim INF solution along the lines of the Walk in the Woods compromise formula. When that formula became public in the fall of 1982, Schmidt reminded Kohl, "You made no working visits, first in Washington, and then in Moscow, to discuss the topic." Kohl's diplomacy, he charged, "should have been working full steam." Schmidt, recounting how he had visited Moscow in 1980 against U.S. wishes, underscored that he would have actively sought to promote a negotiated settlement.[60] Schmidt's statements provide no proof that he would have acted differently had he remained chancellor. But his track record during the early 1980s made his claims plausible.

Given the level of hostility between Washington and Moscow in 1983, a more active German diplomacy would not necessarily have facilitated a breakthrough at the INF talks. Had Schmidt remained chancellor, though, he would have been in a good position to edge the superpowers toward compromise: as the target date for first deployments neared, German influence over the Western negotiating position was bound to increase. Had such mediation efforts failed, they still would have transformed the European constellation of the mid-1980s. INF deployments would have taken place. But U.S.-German ties would not have been as positive and German-Soviet relations as negative as they turned out. Divisions within NATO might have persisted, and the Eastern Treaties might have remained a robust framework for an active Ostpolitik. Given the existence of policy alternatives during the early 1980s—and the contrasting priorities at the center of the political debate—the struggle for government power shaped the direction of German foreign policy.

For a collection of sources, including Habermas's response, see James Knowlton and Truett Cates, eds., *Forever in the Shadow of Hitler: Original Documents of the Historikerstreit, the Controversy Concerning the Singularity of the Holocaust* (Atlantic Highlands, N.J.: Humanities Press, 1993).

60. Schmidt address of November 21, 1983, *Verhandlungen des deutschen Bundestags,* ser. 10, 2379–80. See also Schmidt, *Men and Powers,* 277–79.

The Politics of Atlantic Solidarity

Kohl's strong pro-Atlantic stance prevailed not because it better fit the constraints posed by the new cold war and the institutional configuration, but because he proved able to place it on a stable political foundation. In order to implement his foreign policy priorities Kohl had to anchor them at three levels of party politics—in the CDU/CSU, in coalition with the FDP, and in competition with the SPD. During the late 1970s and early 1980s he managed to defeat CSU leader Franz Josef Strauss's claim to Christian Democratic leadership, create and maintain a coalition with Genscher and the Liberals, and outmaneuver Schmidt and the Social Democrats. On each of these levels of party politics, competition for power interacted with conflict over foreign policy priorities in complex ways. The interaction of the different levels, in turn, drove the direction of German foreign policy at the height of the INF crisis.[61]

In order to win CDU/CSU support for his foreign policy priorities Kohl first had to defeat the charismatic Strauss in a drawn-out leadership struggle.[62] The governor of Bavaria espoused a contrasting set of foreign policy views through the 1970s and into the early 1980s. He and Kohl agreed on the importance of solidarity with the United States amid the downturn in East-West relations. But Strauss, unlike Kohl, rejected the Eastern Treaties as the foundation of Ostpolitik. While he recognized the existence of the treaties, he insisted that policy rest on two other documents: the May 1972 Bundestag Declaration, which reiterated traditional positions on Western integration and German unity, and the July 1973 Constitutional Court ruling, which placed strict limits on any recognition of the GDR and referred to "the borders of 1937" as the legal framework for a future German settlement. In effect, Strauss insisted that the CDU/CSU should acknowledge the reality of the Eastern Treaties but break with social-liberal Ostpolitik. As early as 1972, Strauss's position was "pacta sunt servanda"—treaties are to be upheld. The critical question, he insisted in 1983, was: "What is the content of the Pacta, and how does one understand Servanda?"[63]

During the late 1970s when Strauss's position in the CDU/CSU was ascendant, his hard-line views colored the party's foreign policy stance. In May 1977, for example, CSU leaders criticized Alois Mertes, a top Kohl advisor, for having termed the Moscow Treaty a "fundamental compo-

---

61. On the politics of INF, see Risse-Kappen, *Zero Option,* 37–48, 69–78.

62. On this clash, see Clay Clemens, *Reluctant Realists: The Christian Democrats and West German Ostpolitik* (Durham: Duke University Press, 1989).

63. Interview in *Spiegel,* March 28, 1983.

nent" of German foreign policy, and Kohl did not come to his defense.[64] The CDU's 1978 program also reiterated traditional positions, including a commitment to Germany "in all its parts"—a reference to territories East of the Oder-Neisse.[65] With Kohl on the defensive Strauss secured the CDU/CSU chancellor candidacy for the October 1980 elections. But the extent of Strauss's defeat—the worst Christian Democratic showing since 1949—gave Kohl a chance to reassert his authority and bring the party onto his foreign policy line. In a major Bundestag address just one month after the election, Kohl recognized the Eastern Treaties not simply as "valid law to which we adhere" but also as "essential components of German foreign policy." Party hard-liners protested in vain.[66]

As chancellor, after October 1982, Kohl further strengthened his position with respect to Strauss. He first deflected CSU efforts to make a break with the New Ostpolitik part of the new government's program, and then deprived Strauss of the coveted post of foreign minister, which remained secure in Genscher's hands.[67] Strauss, defeated in his efforts to take charge of foreign policy in Bonn, then abandoned his opposition to the New Ostpolitik in stunning fashion. He brokered the government's July 1983 DM 1 billion credit to the GDR, shocking CSU party stalwarts in the process. Faced with an internal party revolt, and the founding of the Far Right Republican Party, Strauss continued to articulate his commitment to national unity and the openness of the Oder-Neisse question.[68] But his sniping at Kohl's foreign policy gradually subsided. With his victory over Strauss in the leadership struggle, Kohl finally managed to

---

64. Address of May 10, 1977, Mertes papers, I-403–070/3. For the CSU objection, see Zimmermann to Kohl, May 13, 1977, ibid.

65. The original program draft, written under the supervision of Richard von Weizsäcker, did not include this phrase. The head of the CDU/CSU expellees, Herbert Hupka, pressed for its inclusion. Herbert Hupka, interview by author, Bonn, January 22, 1992. For the foreign policy passages of the program, see Peter Hintze, ed., *Die CDU-Parteiprogramme: Eine Dokumentation der Ziele und Aufgaben* (Bonn: Bouvier, 1995), 160–67.

66. Address of November 26, 1980, *Verhandlungen des deutschen Bundestags,* ser. 9, 47.

67. As a concession to the CSU, Kohl did not refer to "continuity" with social-liberal policies in his first government declaration. For a draft of the internal September 1982 CDU/CSU coalition paper on foreign policy, see Mertes papers, I-403–043/1.

68. On Strauss's role in inter-German diplomacy, see Franz Josef Strauss, *Die Erinnerungen* (Berlin: Siedler, 1989), 470–98. On the internal CDU/CSU debate in the early 1980s, see Heinrich Potthoff, *Die "Koalition der Vernunft": Deutschlandpolitik in den 80er Jahren* (Munich: Deutscher Taschenbuch Verlag, 1995), 42–47. According to CDU/CSU foreign policy spokeswoman Michaela Geiger, Strauss's uncompromising rhetoric was aimed mainly at expellee groups from beyond the Oder-Neisse Rivers after the war, an important electoral potential in Bavaria (Michaela Geiger, interview by author, Bonn, July 8, 1992).

anchor his foreign policy priorities—a focus on solidarity with the Western allies combined with an endorsement of the New Ostpolitik—within the CDU/CSU.

In order to implement those priorities in government, Kohl also had to embed them at the level of coalition politics. From the mid-1970s onward he embraced a two-part strategy: waiting for the social-liberal coalition to collapse, on the one hand, and finding points of policy consensus with the FDP, on the other. Growing economic and social policy strains within the ruling coalition promoted the first part of his strategy. Through the 1970s the Liberals' free-market tradition coexisted uncomfortably with the Social Democratic commitment to a strong welfare state. During the recession of the early 1980s these domestic policy tensions gradually dissolved the bonds of the coalition. The FDP came out in favor of considerable cuts in social spending, while Schmidt, under pressure from his party's left wing, backed less extensive measures. As the coalition parties fared badly in a series of state elections in 1981–82, more and more FDP politicians pressed for the formation of a new government with the CDU/CSU.[69]

In this context the second part of Kohl's strategy—movement toward policy consensus with the Liberals—proved critical. Agreement on the contours of economic and social policy was not difficult to reach: the CDU/CSU, like the FDP, came out in favor of budget austerity in the 1980s. Foreign policy rapprochement proved more difficult. From the mid-1970s onward Genscher made it clear that a CDU/CSU embrace of the New Ostpolitik was a precondition for any renewal of the governing alliance with the Christian Democrats. For that very reason, Genscher later maintained, Kohl was clearly "interested in moving closer to the Ostpolitik of the FDP."[70] Strauss was determined to prevent any such movement: he favored the pursuit of an absolute CDU/CSU majority over a coalition with the Liberals. While Kohl sought to reduce the policy distance with the social-liberal coalition, Strauss intentionally sought to polarize the foreign policy debate. In a well-known 1974 address to the CSU faithful, the Bavarian leader insisted that the opposition accuse the government of "furthering Soviet hegemony over West Europe."[71]

In this constellation Kohl's victory over Strauss helped not only to anchor his foreign policy priorities in the CDU/CSU but also to win sup-

---

69. On the FDP, see Peter Lösche and Franz Walter, *Die FDP: Richtungsstreit und Zukunftszweifel* (Darmstadt: Wissenschaftliche Buchgesellschaft, 1996), 104–14.

70. Genscher, interview. Kohl authorized contacts between Genscher and his foreign policy advisor Mertes as early as 1974.

71. A passage from Strauss's "Sonthofer speech," in which he also welcomed the country's economic problems as a boon for the opposition (excerpted in *Spiegel,* March 10, 1975).

port for them at the level of coalition politics. Strauss's blanket attacks on the government's policies—and his personal animosity toward Genscher and the FDP—had shored up the social-liberal coalition in both the 1976 and 1980 election campaigns. In the years after 1980, however, Kohl's embrace of the thrust of the New Ostpolitik contributed to the collapse of the ruling coalition. When economic and social policy differences within the government reached the breaking point, Genscher and the FDP left the coalition with Schmidt and helped to elect Kohl chancellor in an October 1982 constructive vote of no confidence. Kohl's patient strategy of waiting for the social-liberal coalition to collapse—and forging foreign policy consensus with the FDP in the meantime—proved successful.[72]

The coalition with Genscher provided the basis for German foreign policy during the critical 1982–83 period. Both Kohl and Genscher aligned the Federal Republic with the United States and its uncompromising stance at the INF negotiations. Genscher, who later gained a reputation for a critical stance toward Washington, placed almost as much emphasis as Kohl on alliance solidarity during the early 1980s—despite the existence of a considerable minority within the FDP opposed to NATO policy.[73] At the same time, both Kohl and Genscher agreed on the importance of an unbroken dialogue with the East. Here Genscher, whose party had contributed to the realization of the New Ostpolitik under Brandt, was more adamant. Together with Kohl, he pressed—behind the scenes and with little success—for a moderation of the U.S. stance on INF in the run-up to deployments. The new government's foreign policy, Genscher later pointed out, rested on a bargain: the FDP came out in favor of the deployment half of the Two-Track Decision and the CDU/CSU accepted Ostpolitik continuity.[74]

During the mid-1980s foreign policy tensions emerged periodically within the coalition. After first deployments Kohl continued to emphasize solidarity with Washington, while Genscher sought to break through Moscow's diplomatic blockade.[75] The foreign minister increasingly distanced himself from the United States SDI program and was skeptical of Reagan's May 1985 visit to Bitburg to celebrate U.S.-German reconciliation forty years after the war. During his first term in office, however, Kohl

72. On the dissolution of the social-liberal coalition, see Klaus Bölling, *Die letzten 30 Tage des Kanzlers Helmut Schmidt. Ein Tagebuch* (Hamburg: Spiegel-Verlag, 1982).

73. At a May 1981 party conference one-third of the delegates refused to back a resolution in favor of the Two-Track Decision (Jäger and Link, *Die Ära Schmidt,* 337).

74. Genscher, interview.

75. On efforts to maintain German-Soviet detente during the mid-1980s, see Hans-Dietrich Genscher, *Rebuilding a House Divided: A Memoir by the Architect of Germany's Reunification* (New York: Broadway Books, 1998), 174–201.

proved strong enough to set the overall tone of German foreign policy. The switch of coalition partners in 1982 unleashed an internal crisis within the FDP: much of the party's social wing had supported continued cooperation with the SPD under Schmidt. Poor election results in a series of state elections led Genscher to resign as party chairman in 1984, although he remained the Liberals' single most influential leader. Through the mid-1980s Kohl's strong position within the coalition served as a foundation for his emphasis on solidarity with the United States.

For Kohl to implement his foreign policy priorities it was not enough to forge a coalition with the Liberals that relegated the Social Democrats to the opposition. He also had to maintain the chancellorship through new elections called for March 1983 and overcome SPD opposition to first deployments in November. The Social Democratic turn against the deployment track of NATO policy had its roots in the late 1970s. An SPD party conference endorsed the Two-Track Decision in December 1979 but underscored the priority of the arms control half of NATO strategy. Over the next several years, as U.S.-Soviet tensions increased, Social Democratic support for nuclear rearmament in the absence of a negotiated settlement began to evaporate.[76] Brandt, who remained SPD chairman through 1987, was more critical than Schmidt of the Reagan administration's INF policy. And growing numbers of younger party leaders and rank-and-file members identified themselves with the swelling peace movement. As long as he was chancellor, Schmidt was able to maintain party support for his foreign policy—for the last time at an April 1982 party conference in Munich. Once the governing coalition with the FDP collapsed, however, Brandt and a majority of the party leadership distanced themselves from the proposed deployment timetable in favor of more time for negotiations.[77]

The widening gulf between the CDU/CSU and SPD foreign policy stances became evident during the campaign for the March 1983 elections. Schmidt, whose economic and foreign policies no longer enjoyed majority support within his party, opted not to run. His successor as chancellor candidate, Hans-Jochen Vogel, placed the INF issue at the center of the Social Democratic campaign. The SPD's chief slogan, "In the German Interest," drew a distinction between the party's support for peace and disarmament and Kohl's strong emphasis on solidarity with the United States. Vogel was critical of Reagan's confrontational anti-Soviet stance. Before and

---

76. On these developments, see Boutwell, *German Nuclear Dilemma,* chap. 3.

77. On the leftward shift of the SPD on foreign policy after October 1982, see the memoirs of Schmidt's defense minister, Hans Apel, *Der Abstieg: Politisches Tagebuch, 1978–1988* (Stuttgart: Deutsche Verlags-Anstalt, 1990), 269–81.

after a January 1983 visit to Moscow he pressed for serious consideration of Andropov's proposal to include British and French forces in the INF talks. Deployments without bona fide negotiations beforehand, so went the official SPD position, would make the Federal Republic less, not more secure. In the end Social Democratic arguments resonated little with an electorate more concerned about economic issues. The CDU/CSU and FDP increased their ruling majority, dealing the SPD a humiliating defeat.

The election proved a turning point in Kohl's efforts to implement his pro-Atlantic course. Still, in the run-up to the first deployments, his government had to cope with fierce opposition to its INF policy both inside and outside the Bundestag. The Green Party, which secured parliamentary representation for the first time in the elections, objected to new U.S. missiles in principle.[78] And SPD parliamentarians, under Vogel's leadership, turned against deployment, charging that the potential for a negotiated settlement had not been adequately explored. A wave of peace demonstrations swept over German cities in the months before the climactic November Bundestag vote, including a gathering of 350,000 citizens in Bonn. After a fiery debate marked by sharp mutual recriminations between government and opposition, the governing parties approved first INF deployments by a solid margin.[79]

Enduring Effects of Atlantic Solidarity

The gradual dissolution of detente in the late 1970s and early 1980s—and the INF struggle that marked its climax—constituted a final critical juncture in the foreign policy of the old Federal Republic. Embedded within a dense web of institutions, East and West, German leaders faced difficult choices. Their alternatives revolved not around whether to work with the United States and talk with the Soviet Union but around how to combine both pursuits under difficult circumstances. Within this constellation Schmidt and Kohl articulated contrasting foreign policy priorities. Schmidt envisioned a mediating role for the Federal Republic—active German efforts to arbitrate a compromise INF solution. Kohl, by contrast, made solidarity with the United States his overriding foreign policy priority during the early 1980s. Ultimately, Kohl, not Schmidt, proved able to embed his priorities on a stable political foundation. During the early 1980s he defeated Strauss in the CDU/CSU leadership struggle,

---

78. On the Greens, see Eva Kolinsky, ed., *The Greens in West Germany: Organisation and Policy Making* (Oxford: Berg, 1989).

79. See the Bundestag debate of November 21, 1983, *Verhandlungen des deutschen Bundestags,* ser. 10, 2321–456.

secured a partnership with Genscher and the FDP, and relegated the SPD to the opposition.

In the years after 1983 Kohl's pro-Atlantic orientation during the INF crisis had enduring institutional and political effects. In institutional terms Kohl's policies contributed to the cohesion of Western institutions at an important juncture. NATO, riven by internal divisions amid the Afghanistan, Poland, and INF crises, emerged stronger in the mid-1980s. The tensions that had surrounded U.S. sanctions policy and the handling of arms control negotiations several years earlier faded. The FRG contribution to alliance unity led to a rapid improvement in U.S.-German ties during the years after 1982—relations that contrasted markedly with those of the final Schmidt years. A first effort to underscore this shift, Reagan's Bitburg visit in May 1985, proved a public relations fiasco. But close bilateral cooperation continued in the years that followed. In May 1989, during his first trip to Bonn as president, George Bush emphasized the positive state of relations, calling the Federal Republic and the United States "partners in leadership."[80]

Kohl's strong emphasis on Western unity also improved Franco-German ties at a critical juncture. His government's unequivocal support for INF deployments—a vital concern for Mitterrand and other French leaders worried about the strength of the Federal Republic's commitment to the West—improved bilateral relations that had suffered during the final years of Schmidt's chancellorship. In addition to improved bilateral security cooperation, symbolized by the creation of a Franco-German brigade, both governments worked to resurrect the WEU as a meaningful framework for West European security cooperation. Most significant in institutional terms was the drive to complete the European market. The Single European Act of 1987, a commitment to eliminate intra-EC trade barriers by 1992, derived in large part from Franco-German initiative, as did discussions in the late 1980s about a renewed drive for monetary union. The European diplomacy of the early 1980s ultimately strengthened the EC, as well as NATO, as an institutional foundation for German foreign policy.[81]

The implementation of the Two-Track Decision and the cohesion of the Atlantic Alliance also laid the groundwork for stronger East-West institutions in the late 1980s. Both NATO's successful deployments and

---

80. *New York Times,* June 4, 1989.

81. On SEA, see Andrew Moravcsik, "Negotiating the Single European Act: National Interests and Conventional Statecraft in the European Community," *International Organization* 45, no. 1 (winter 1991): 19–56. On the FRG and the EC in the late 1980s, see Simon Bulmer and William E. Paterson, "West Germany's Role in Europe: 'Man-Mountain' or 'Semi-Gulliver'?" *Journal of Common Market Studies* 28, no. 2 (December 1989): 95–117.

Gorbachev's opening to the West made possible the resolution of the INF issue. The reality of deployments in the Federal Republic—and the collapse of the German peace movement—helped to bring Soviet leaders back to the INF talks in January 1985, two months before Gorbachev took office. But only with Gorbachev's reform drive at home and embrace of arms control abroad did an INF breakthrough become possible. Following extended negotiations, during which the German government agreed to include shorter-range Pershing IA's within a "double-zero" formula, the United States and the Soviet Union signed the December 1987 INF Treaty, eliminating their arsenals worldwide.[82] Treaties reducing strategic arsenals (START I) and ending the war in Afghanistan followed the next year. And the CSCE process revived at a meeting in Vienna in 1988–89. While the implementation of the deployment track of NATO strategy shored up the Western alliance in the early 1980s, the realization of its negotiations track sparked a breakthrough in East-West relations at the end of the decade. A new web of arms control accords added to the institutional context of Ostpolitik.

During the late 1980s Western unity and more robust East-West institutions served as a foundation for improved bilateral relations with Moscow and East Berlin. In 1986–87, as the contours of an INF accord began to materialize, Gorbachev gradually abandoned his criticisms of German militarism and gave up his opposition to Honecker's travel plans, allowing an inter-German summit to take place in Bonn in September 1987.[83] At that summit Kohl reiterated the Federal Republic's constitutional commitment to national unity. But he also signed a number of accords designed to intensify inter-German cooperation on the basis of the territorial and political status quo. The dramatic rapprochement with East Berlin took place just before a breakthrough in relations with Moscow. Kohl's visit to the Soviet capital in October 1988, his first since the height of the INF crisis five years earlier, marked the crucial turning point. Kohl announced a DM 3 billion credit in support of Soviet reforms, and he and Gorbachev endorsed several further economic and cultural accords. Their subsequent meeting in Bonn in June 1989 marked the high point for postwar German-Soviet reconciliation, a qualitative shift not only from the

---

82. On the German role in the resolution of the INF issue, see Risse-Kappen, *Zero Option,* 124–43.

83. During his first official visit to the GDR, in April 1986, Gorbachev had leveled a blast against "revanchism" in the FRG and continued to oppose Honecker's plans to visit Bonn. See the memoir by a member of the SED leadership, Günter Schabowski, *Das Politbüro: Ende eines Mythos* (Hamburg: Rowohlt, 1990), 35–36. Kohl was careful to reiterate his commitment to German unity during the Honecker visit. Address of September 7, 1987, *Bulletin des Presse-und Informationsamtes der Bundesregierung,* September 10, 1987.

cold war atmosphere of the early 1980s but also from the detente of the early 1970s. Kohl and Gorbachev signed eleven further accords and endorsed a joint declaration outlining principles for the construction of a "Common European Home." This more dynamic Ostpolitik, on a solid Western foundation, aroused only isolated concerns about German reliability in Paris, London, and Washington. On the eve of the collapse of the GDR the Federal Republic was embedded in a web of institutions, East and West, more dense than at any previous juncture.[84]

The outcome of the INF struggle not only altered the configuration of international institutions in Europe. It also spawned movement toward greater foreign policy consensus at the level of German domestic politics. During the second half of the 1980s Kohl proved able to maintain his position atop the CDU/CSU and to anchor his combination of solidarity with the West and engagement with the East within the party. With Strauss's reluctant backing Kohl secured the chancellor candidacy for the January 1987 elections. After winning reelection, Kohl's support for U.S. efforts to reach an INF settlement, and his readiness to include German Pershing IA's in the December 1987 treaty, aroused the opposition of party hardliners skeptical about arms control.[85] Kohl also faced some internal party opposition to his reception for Honecker in Bonn in September 1987 and his enthusiastic embrace of Gorbachev over the next two years. Opposition to de facto recognition of the GDR, however, had all but disappeared in the years after Strauss's first 1983 visit to East Berlin.[86] And, after Strauss's highly publicized visit to Moscow in December 1987—the first in his forty-year career—CDU/CSU skepticism about Gorbachev subsided. For the first time since World War II the entire Christian Democratic leadership rallied around both Western integration *and* an active Ostpolitik as the core of German foreign policy.[87]

---

84. On the declaration and the visit, see Fred Oldenbourg, *Sowjetische Deutschland-Politik nach den Treffen von Moskau und Bonn, 1988–89* (Cologne: Bundesinstitut für ostwissenschaftliche und internationale Studien, 1989), 11–50.

85. See Clay Clemens, "Beyond INF: West Germany's Centre-Right Party and Arms Control in the 1990s," *International Affairs* (London) 65, no. 1 (winter 1988–89): 55–74.

86. On the persistence of reunification as a theme on the Far Right of the CDU/CSU, see Jürgen Todenhöfer, *Ich denke deutsch: Abrechnung mit dem Zeitgeist* (Erlangen: Straube, 1989); Bernhard Friedmann, *Einheit statt Raketen: Thesen zur Wiedervereinigung als Sicherheitskonzept* (Herford: Busse Seewald, 1987).

87. Strauss had maintained as late as September 1987 that Gorbachev "had not yet sworn off the revolutionary geostrategic goals of the Soviet Union." See his notes for a campaign speech in Schleswig Hollstein, September 10, 1987, *Archiv für Christlich-Soziale Politik,* Strauss papers, RA 87 (118 e1). For his account of the trip, see Strauss, *Die Erinnerungen,* 552–65.

During the years after the INF crisis the FDP under Genscher also articulated this basic foreign policy orientation. Toward the end of the 1980s the foreign minister's particular mix of priorities contrasted somewhat with Kohl's. Genscher's alignment with the United States was not as enthusiastic as the chancellor's, as evidenced in his skepticism about SDI. And his embrace of Gorbachev took place earlier and was more complete. As early as February 1987, before the completion of the INF Treaty, Genscher argued that the West should take Gorbachev "at his word."[88] At the time, Genscher's emphasis on an active Ostpolitik, which helped the FDP at the polls in the 1987 elections, raised some concerns in Western capitals about his commitment to the alliance. But *Genscherism,* defined as a nationally oriented Ostpolitik, never really existed.[89] Like the CDU/CSU, the FDP remained firmly committed to Western institutions as the foundation for relations with the East. Genscher did initially irritate Kohl and Bush with his opposition to the modernization of short-range nuclear forces (SNF) in 1988–89. But Kohl's embrace of Gorbachev—and his eventual support for Genscher's position on SNF—again created a solid foreign policy consensus within the coalition.

By the end of the 1980s the consensus around Western solidarity and Eastern engagement extended to the SPD as well. The Social Democratic opposition to INF first deployments and campaign against SDI created a major rift with the governing parties—and with the United States—in the years after 1983. After meeting with Gorbachev in Moscow in June 1985, for example, Brandt charged that Kohl's lack of independence with respect to Washington had undermined German influence in both East and West.[90] Gradually, however, both the reality of INF deployments and the success of negotiations to remove them drove a shift in the SPD position. During the 1987 campaign the party moderated its call for a unilateral withdrawal of U.S. missiles. And after the INF Treaty party leaders moved to mend ties with Washington. Social Democrats continued to push harder than either Christian Democrats or Liberals for a "second phase of Ostpolitik" and even engaged the SED leadership in a dialogue about European security.[91] The SPD was also vehemently opposed to SNF modernization in 1988–89. Amid the renewed detente of the late 1980s, however, major differences with the ruling parties evaporated. The depth of

---

88. Genscher, *Rebuilding a House Divided,* 201.

89. See Emil J. Kirchner, "Genscher and What Lies behind 'Genscherism,'" *West European Politics* 13, no. 2 (April 1990): 159–77.

90. See Brandt's interview in *Spiegel,* June 3, 1985.

91. On the "Second Phase of Ostpolitik," see Timothy Garton Ash, *In Europe's Name: Germany and the Divided Continent* (New York: Random House, 1993), 312–42.

consensus was particularly evident during the Bundestag debate that followed Gorbachev's June 1989 visit. Leaders of the major parties all underscored the absolute necessity of a German foreign policy both anchored in the West and open to the East.[92]

On the eve of reunification the Federal Republic was firmly embedded in NATO and engaged in an active dialogue with the Soviet Union and its allies. With the INF controversy the alliance weathered its final cold war crisis. German links with the United States, troubled during the final years of Schmidt's chancellorship, improved significantly by the mid-1980s. And German-Soviet relations, which worsened over the same period, flourished after the successful implementation of the Two-Track Decision and Gorbachev's new foreign policy departure. Ironically, Kohl and Gorbachev celebrated the end of the cold war between the blocs in Bonn in June 1989—just months before the Soviet bloc collapsed. For, while Gorbachev's diplomacy enabled unprecedented East-West detente, his domestic reforms unleashed revolutionary forces in Central and Eastern Europe. The unexpected collapse of the GDR and the subsequent rush to reunification in 1989–90 marked a further critical juncture for postwar German foreign policy.

---

92. See the debate of June 16, 1989, *Verhandlungen des deutschen Bundestags,* ser. 11, 11185–211.

CHAPTER 5

Post-Reunification Foreign Policy

The collapse of the Soviet bloc and reunification transformed the context of German foreign policy, but not its direction. The breakdown of the postwar bipolar order in Europe left the Federal Republic more powerful than ever before. At the same time, it confronted the FRG, more than its allies, with pressing policy challenges in the East—the maintenance of economic, political, and security stability in Russia and Central and Eastern Europe. In the five years after reunification, however, these momentous international shifts did not spark a reorientation of German foreign policy. Bonn did not move to redefine its national interests or embrace a more independent Ostpolitik. As chancellor, Helmut Kohl continued to embrace a strong Western orientation; his government pressed both for deeper European integration and the assumption of greater German responsibility within NATO. Engagement in the East did continue. The FRG pursued active cooperation with Russia and backed the expansion of the European Community and the Atlantic Alliance to Central and Eastern Europe. But a strong pro-Western, multilateral, supranational orientation persisted across the 1990 divide.[1]

This basic continuity was already evident during the reunification process itself.[2] In the summer of 1989 democratic reforms in Poland and Hungary—and Soviet leader Mikhail Gorbachev's reluctance to stop them

---

1. On German foreign policy during the early 1990s, see Karl Kaiser and Hanns W. Maull, eds., *Deutschlands neue Außenpolitik,* 3 vols. (Munich: R. Oldenbourg: 1994); Christian Hacke, *Weltmacht wider Willen: Die Außenpolitik der Bundesrepublik Deutschland* (Frankfurt am Main: Ullstein, 1993), chap. 9; Arnulf Baring, ed., *Germany's New Position in Europe: Problems and Perspectives* (Oxford: Berg, 1994).
2. On the diplomacy of reunification, see Philip Zelikow and Condoleezza Rice, *Germany Unified and Europe Transformed: A Study in Statecraft* (Cambridge: Harvard University Press, 1995); Stephen F. Szabo, *The Diplomacy of German Unification* (New York: St. Martin's Press, 1992); Elizabeth Pond, *Beyond the Wall: Germany's Road to Unification* (Washington, D.C.: Brookings Institution, 1993); Konrad H. Jarausch, *The Rush to German Unity* (New York: Oxford University Press, 1994).

with force—undermined the hardline GDR leadership under Erich Honecker. During the month of September thousands of East Germans fled to the FRG over the newly opened Hungarian-Austrian border and thousands more began to demonstrate for democratic reforms within the GDR itself. Under pressure from Gorbachev and increasingly isolated within the SED, Honecker stepped down in October 1989. Faced with an ongoing outflux and swelling protests, SED reformers sought to stabilize their rule by dropping travel restrictions and calling for free elections. But in the weeks after the fall of the Berlin Wall, on November 9, growing support for reunification transformed the democratic revolution in the GDR into a national one. Without any prompting from Bonn, German unity moved onto the European agenda—for the first time since the early 1950s.[3]

Faced with the crisis in the GDR, Kohl seized the initiative in late November with a Ten-Point Plan on German unity—without first consulting the Four Powers, the SPD in opposition, or even his own foreign minister.[4] The plan envisioned a transition from an inter-German "treaty community" to "confederative structures" and, ultimately, unity in a single state. At the same time, it reiterated the continued centrality of NATO, the EC, the Eastern Treaties, and the CSCE as foundations for German foreign policy.[5] While the Bush administration was generally supportive of the initiative, the French, British, and Soviet governments expressed varying degrees of irritation. Four-Power representatives met in Berlin in early December—a clear reminder of where ultimate legal responsibility for the unity issue lay. Later that month and in early January, however, the rapid collapse of the East German regime rendered both Kohl's plan and international reservations about it increasingly irrelevant. Worsening economic dislocation in the GDR, an ongoing flight of refugees to the West and a pro-unity consensus among the new East German democratic parties created inexorable momentum for reunification. In early February the Four

---

3. For notable absences of any initiatives on the unity issue, see Kohl's State of the Nation address, November 8, 1989, *Verhandlungen des deutschen Bundestags. Stenographischer Bericht,* ser. 11, 13010–18; and his press conference after a meeting of EC heads of state on November 18, *Bundespresseamt News Files,* November 20, 1989.

4. On the origins of the Ten-Point Plan, conceived in secret for maximum diplomatic and political effect, see Helmut Kohl, *"Ich wollte Deutschlands Einheit"* (Berlin: Ullstein, 1996), 157–211; and the account of his top foreign policy advisor, Horst Teltschik, *329 Tage: Innenansichten der Einigung* (Berlin: Siedler, 1991), 11–58.

5. As Kohl put it, "The future architecture of Germany must fit into the future all-European architecture" in an "organic" development. For the speech of November 28, 1989, see *Bulletin des Presse- und Informationsamtes der Bundesregierung,* November 29, 1989, 1145–48.

Powers and both German states set up the Two-Plus-Four Talks, a forum to negotiate the international terms of a settlement. And in March the CDU-East and its allies won the first free GDR elections on a platform calling for rapid unity.[6]

Within the Two-Plus-Four framework the Kohl government sought to bind the new Federal Republic as closely to the West as the old. After a controversy surrounding the Oder-Neisse line in February 1990—Kohl initially argued that its final recognition would have to await the completion of the reunification process but then relented under tremendous international pressure—both German states and Four Powers took up the question of the new Germany's institutional affiliations.[7] Gorbachev did not object to the EC but initially "absolutely ruled out" NATO membership.[8] During the first half of 1990 Kohl and Foreign Minister Hans-Dietrich Genscher worked closely with the allies—and the Bush administration in particular—to win over Gorbachev for German membership in the Western alliance. Only after Western leaders agreed to redefine NATO's anti-Soviet stance, strengthen the CSCE, limit the size of the German army, and support Soviet economic reforms, did Gorbachev abandon his opposition. During a dramatic July 1990 Caucasus summit with Kohl he agreed to NATO membership in exchange for financial support for the Soviet troop withdrawal from Eastern Germany. The Two-Plus-Four talks concluded successfully in September and reunification took place on October 3, 1990.[9]

In the years after reunification the pattern of 1989–90—a strong Western orientation combined with multilateral engagement in the East—continued to characterize German foreign policy. Kohl's emphasis on Western ties was particularly evident in his drive for deeper European integration. In late 1989 and early 1990 he and French president François Mitterrand pressed for intergovernmental conferences on monetary and polit-

---

6. On the collapse of the GDR, see Charles S. Maier, *Dissolution: The Crisis of Communism and the End of East Germany* (Princeton: Princeton University Press, 1997); A. James McAdams, *Germany Divided: From the Wall to Reunification* (Princeton: Princeton University Press, 1993), chap. 6.

7. According to Teltschik, Kohl's hesitation was rooted in an eagerness not to alienate the expellees, an important clientele, during an election year. See Teltschik, *329 Tage,* 164.

8. Gorbachev interview, in *Frankfurter Allgemeine Zeitung,* March 8, 1990.

9. For firsthand accounts of the Caucasus meeting, see Kohl, *Ich wollte Deutschlands Einheit,* 421–44; Teltschik, *329 Tage,* 313–45; Hans Klein, *Es begann im Kaukasus: Der entscheidende Schritt in die Einheit Deutschlands* (Berlin: Ullstein, 1991). On the intricate diplomacy that led to the shift in Gorbachev's position, see Hans-Dietrich Genscher, *Rebuilding a House Divided: A Memoir by the Architect of Germany's Reunification* (New York: Broadway Books, 1998), 384–431.

ical union that culminated in the February 1992 Maastricht Treaty on European Union (EU). Over the next several years the German government emerged as the most vocal and influential backer of the treaty's central provisions: monetary union by 1999, the establishment of a Common Foreign and Security Policy, and stronger European institutions. Divisive ratification struggles in Denmark, France, and Britain and successive crises of the European Monetary System in 1992–93 did not temper Bonn's support for deeper integration. Amid the sluggish growth of the mid-1990s the Federal Republic raised taxes and cut spending in an effort to meet the economic criteria for monetary union. And Kohl pressed for further progress toward political union during the follow-up "Maastricht II" conference in 1996–97.[10]

The new Germany combined this strong support for deeper European integration with an active Ostpolitik. During the late 1980s and early 1990s the Federal Republic extended more economic aid to the Soviet Union and Central and Eastern Europe than all of its allies combined.[11] In 1990–92 Bonn also negotiated a series of new Eastern Treaties, bilateral accords with Moscow, Warsaw, and other capitals outlining areas for economic, political, and security cooperation. In addition, both before and after the collapse of the Soviet Union in 1991, the German government pressed for a stronger CSCE and an expanded NATO as the core of a new all-European security structure. Increasingly, however, Kohl and Klaus Kinkel, Genscher's successor as foreign minister after May 1992, focused their attention on Germany's immediate eastern neighbors, particularly Poland, Hungary, and the Czech Republic. With strong German support the June 1993 European Summit in Copenhagen approved the prospect of eventual EU membership for Central and Eastern Europe. A half-year later the FRG greeted NATO's January 1994 endorsement of the possibility of alliance expansion to the region.

While the Federal Republic had a full Ostpolitik agenda through the mid-1990s, it continued to focus its energies on relations with the Western allies. On those few occasions when Bonn's approach to the former Soviet bloc raised concerns in Washington and Paris, Kohl demonstrated the absolute priority of solidarity with the West. For example, when U.S.

---

10. On German policy toward the EU, see Lily Gardner Feldman, "Germany and the EC: Realism and Responsibility," *Annals of the American Academy of Political and Social Science* 531 (January 1994): 25–43; Jeffrey J. Anderson, "Hard Interests, Soft Power, and Germany's Changing Role in Europe," in *Tamed Power: Germany in Europe,* ed. Peter J. Katzenstein (Ithaca: Cornell University Press, 1997), 80–107.

11. On the new Germany's economic links with the East, see Jeffrey J. Anderson and Celeste A. Wallander, "Interests and the Wall of Ideas: Germany's Eastern Trade Policy after Unification," *Comparative Political Studies* 30, no. 6 (December 1997): 675–98.

officials objected to Genscher's March 1990 suggestion that the CSCE might eventually displace NATO as a framework for all-European security, Kohl distanced himself from his foreign minister.[12] And when Defense Minister Volker Rühe irritated Washington in 1993 with his demands for more rapid progress on NATO expansion, Kohl did not support him. The absolute priority of Western unity was also evident in relations with Paris. Kohl did not criticize French efforts to delay EU association accords with Central and Eastern Europe in 1991–93. Moreover, partly in response to French concerns about an eastward shift in the EU center of gravity, he dropped plans to press for a timetable for expansion at the December 1994 European Summit in Essen. Negotiations on accession were put off until the completion of Maastricht II in June 1997.[13]

During the five years after reunification security controversies also established a continued pattern of German solidarity with the West.[14] This solidarity was not immediately evident in 1991, the year of both the Gulf War and the escalation of civil war in Yugoslavia. Despite their generous financial support for the anti-Iraq coalition, German leaders faced a barrage of international criticism for failing to commit troops to the multilateral effort. If the Gulf War raised the specter of German isolationism, the Yugoslav conflict provided an example of German unilateralism. When Croatia and Slovenia declared their independence in June 1991, EU foreign ministers refused to grant them diplomatic recognition. As the war with Serbian forces escalated, however, Kohl and Genscher pressed for recognition of the breakaway republics as the best means to halt the conflict. In December 1991 Bonn unilaterally announced its intention to recognize Croatia and Slovenia. Paris and London, concerned that recognition might provoke a further intensification of the fighting, went along only reluctantly, preserving a veneer of Western unity. The Federal Republic's initiative in the Balkan War, like its abstinence during the Gulf War, raised concerns about a more independent, national post-reunification orientation.[15]

---

12. Genscher before the West European Union (WEU) assembly, March 23, 1990, *Bulletin des Presse- und Informationsamtes,* March 27, 1990, 309–13. Kohl's reaction is described in Teltschik, *329 Tage,* 182.

13. On Kohl's decision not to press for decisive steps toward EU expansion in Essen, see *Deutsche-Presse Agentur,* December 6, 1994. On German policy toward the twin imperatives of deepening and widening, see Christian Deubner, *Deutsche Europapolitik: Von Maastricht nach Kerneuropa?* (Baden-Baden: Nomos, 1995).

14. For an overview, see Phillip H. Gordon, "The Normalization of German Foreign Policy," *Orbis* 38, no. 2 (spring 1994): 225–43.

15. On this, see Beverly Crawford, "Germany's Unilateral Recognition of Croatia and Slovenia: A Case of Defection from Multilateral Cooperation," *World Politics* 48, no. 4 (July 1996): 482–521. An editorial in *Le Monde* warned of the "the return of the German Question," and officials in Paris and London expressed similar concerns—off the record. See *Le Monde,* December 23, 1991. On concerns in Western capitals, see *New York Times,* December 29, 1991.

These concerns proved unfounded. Over the next several years German leaders were careful to align their security policies with those of the United States, France, and Britain. On the one hand, Bonn refrained from any unilateral initiatives. As the war in former Yugoslavia shifted to Bosnia, for example, Kohl favored lifting the embargo against the besieged Muslim-controlled Bosnian government. But he did not press the issue in his dealings with Paris and London.[16] On the other hand, the German government began to take part in multilateral military operations outside NATO territory. This started modestly in 1991–92 with the dispatch of support units as part of UN-sponsored peacekeeping efforts in Cambodia and Somalia. In 1992 the FRG then deployed naval and air force units to the Adriatic to help monitor the arms embargo in the former Yugoslavia. Later, when UN peacekeepers took up positions in Bosnia in 1993–94, German flight crews helped to monitor the no-fly-zone over the area. The major breakthroughs in German security policy took place in 1994 and 1995. In July 1994 the Constitutional Court approved the participation of German armed forces in out-of-area operations. And when the November 1995 Dayton Accord ended fighting in Bosnia, the Federal Republic agreed to station ground units in the region as part of a NATO peacekeeping effort.[17]

The German commitment to multilateral military operations outside NATO's defensive perimeter marked a break with forty years of security policy. Five years after reunification German troops were deployed abroad—and in a region once occupied by the *Wehrmacht.* This represented a significant change at the level of foreign policy instruments. In the context of the new Germany's overall foreign policy orientation, however, the new approach to security matters demonstrated not change but continuity. Through its participation in multilateral operations after the end of the cold war, the Federal Republic strengthened its ties with the Western powers amid new circumstances. By 1995 the concerns about German unilateralism that had surfaced in the immediate aftermath of reunification had all but disappeared. In the case of security policy, as in the context of efforts to strengthen and expand NATO and the EU, unity with the Western powers remained a leitmotif of German foreign policy.

---

16. In November 1994 Kohl assured Mitterrand that he would continue to restrain his "moral" sympathy for the Bosnian Muslims in the interest of maintaining European unity behind the arms embargo. Kohl had supported a CDU/CSU resolution calling for a lifting of the embargo. See *Financial Times,* December 1, 1994.

17. On post-1990 security policy, see Jeffrey S. Lantis, "Rising to the Challenge: German Security Policy in the Post–Cold War Era," *German Politics and Society* 14, no. 2 (summer 1996): 19–35.

Post–Cold War Challenges: Fostering Peace and Stability to the East

Post-reunification German foreign policy was a response to dramatic and ongoing changes at the level of international structure. The GDR revolution and reunification transformed what had been an external problem, inter-German relations, into an internal one. At the same time, the collapse of the Warsaw Pact, the break-up of the Soviet Union, and the dissolution of Yugloslavia presented German leaders with stark new policy challenges to the East. The division of Europe into blocs, the starting point for an active Ostpolitik in the 1970s and 1980s, came to an end. A rival political and ideological system collapsed and the threat of military assault across the Central European plain, a constant of German foreign policy for over forty years, all but vanished. In its place a new constellation emerged, confronting Germany and its allies with problems of economic, political, and security stability in Russia and Central and Eastern Europe.

This new constellation, with its roots in the 1980s, crystallized in 1989–91. In the years after he took office in 1985, Gorbachev dropped the traditional Soviet ideological hostility toward the West. His "New Thinking" on foreign policy did not entail a repudiation of socialism or the postwar bipolar order in Europe. In encouraging reform throughout the Warsaw Pact, Gorbachev insisted on the leading role of communist parties throughout the region and on the division of Germany as a fact of European life.[18] Once democratic and nationalist revolutions swept through Central and Eastern Europe, however, his reluctance to intervene with force enabled a revolutionary transformation. The collapse of the GDR and reunification destroyed the political substance of the Warsaw Pact, which quietly disbanded in March 1991. Around the same time, national conflicts and economic and political crises sparked the dissolution of the multinational Soviet Union. A conservative communist coup against Gorbachev in August 1991 failed, but he proved unable to hold the country together in the months that followed. In December 1991 the Soviet Union dissolved into its constituent republics and Russia, under President Boris Yeltsin, assumed its international legal obligations. Six new East European states materialized: Lithuania, Latvia, Estonia, Ukraine, Belarus, and Moldavia. Around the same time, the breakup of Yugoslavia added several more: Croatia, Slovenia, and Bosnia.

These revolutionary changes not only increased the number of Ger-

---

18. The clearest exposition of that vision is Mikhail Gorbachev, *Perestroika: New Thinking for Our Country and the World* (New York: Harper and Row, 1987). For his conceptualization of the division of Germany as the outcome of World War II, see 199–201.

many's neighbors to the East. They also confronted the Federal Republic with pressing new policy challenges. The overthrow of state socialism brought with it sometimes intractable domestic problems: the creation of stable democratic institutions, the transition to market economies, and the eruption of ethnic conflicts. And these problems, in turn, had an international dimension. On the one hand, Russia and East and Central Europe turned to the West, and to Germany in particular, for support in mastering the political and economic transition. To different degrees they pressed for cooperation with—and membership in—both NATO and the EU. On the other hand, national and ethnic tensions in the former Soviet Union, and particularly in the former Yugoslavia, precipitated armed conflict with broader implications for European security. Under the auspices of the UN, both NATO and EU members sought to end the fighting through a combination of diplomatic and military means. Given its geographical position as the East of the West, the new Germany had to come to terms with these policy challenges.

During the early 1990s both these policy challenges—reform throughout the Soviet bloc and containment of national and ethnic conflict—confronted German leaders with two difficult tradeoffs. The first concerned the relationship between an active Ostpolitik and unity with the Western allies. Given its geography and its traditional economic links, Bonn had more to gain from the success of economic reform and political stability in the East than its Western allies—and more to lose from its failure. "Because of its geography," as Hans-Dietrich Genscher put it in the summer of 1992, "Germany will be affected earlier by instability in the East."[19] As the controversy surrounding the recognition of Croatia and Slovenia demonstrated, however, any unilateral German policies toward the East risked evoking old fears about German nationalism and seesaw policies between East and West. Within this configuration Germans had to press their allies to join them in multilateral actions designed to stabilize Central and Eastern Europe, while being careful not to strain Western unity in the process. During the early 1990s, for example, U.S. and French leaders supported NATO and EU expansion in principle but were less enthusiastic than their German counterparts. For Bonn, adopting a cautious approach to the expansion of both institutions risked exacerbating problems to the East, while pressing assertively for expansion risked political irritations with the West.

A second major tradeoff facing German leaders in the early 1990s concerned the use of military force. The outbreak of national and ethnic

---

19. Hans-Dietrich Genscher, interview by author, Bonn, August 24, 1992.

conflict in the East, and in the former Yugoslavia in particular, placed the issue squarely on the German foreign policy agenda. The escalation of the Balkan War—and the increasing involvement of the Western allies in efforts to stop it—created cross-cutting pressures for German diplomacy. On the one hand, memories of German military aggression abroad necessitated a cautious approach to a more active military role, particularly in those regions once occupied by German forces. The Serbs objected most vehemently to any Bundeswehr presence. On the other hand, in the years after the Gulf War, German leaders faced allied demands for more active participation in multilateral operations. Abstention from peacekeeping efforts in the Balkans threatened to undermine relations with the Western powers. In the aftermath of reunification the war in former Yugoslavia confronted German leaders with a difficult policy challenge: the adjustment of military security policy to new circumstances without the revival of old fears.[20]

Institutions and Alternatives: Western Foundations for Eastern Engagement

Within this new international constellation the foreign policy of the Federal Republic remained bound within a dense web of institutions.[21] It is certainly true that German power increased in both absolute and relative terms as a result of reunification. The FRG's population and economic potential outstripped that of its most important West European allies, France and Britain. Moreover, the retreat of the Soviet army and reductions in U.S. forces left Germany with the largest conventional armed forces in Central Europe. These greater capabilities did not, however, translate directly into more influence or freedom of action. With the exception of the Four-Power regime, the institutions linking the old Federal Republic with both East and West persisted after 1990. Those institutions—NATO and the EU, the CSCE, and the Eastern Treaties—went through important changes after the end of the cold war. But they contin-

---

20. On security dilemmas, see Lothar Gutjahr, *German Foreign and Defence Policy after Unification* (London: Pinter, 1994); Christoph Bertram, "The Power and the Past: Germany's New International Loneliness," in Baring, *Germany's New Position in Europe,* 91–105.

21. On the salience of international institutions for German foreign policy, see Peter J. Katzenstein, ed., *Tamed Power: Germany in Europe* (Ithaca: Cornell University Press, 1997). On the European institutional constellation after 1989, see Robert O. Keohane, Joseph S. Nye, and Stanley Hoffmann, eds. *After the Cold War: International Institutions and State Strategies in Europe, 1989–1991* (Cambridge: Harvard University Press, 1993); Richard H. Ullman, *Securing Europe* (Princeton: Princeton University Press, 1991).

ued to constrain German power and to frame German choices in the face of new policy challenges.[22]

The end of the Four-Power regime in 1990–91 marked the most dramatic change in the institutional context of German foreign policy.[23] The Western powers and the Soviet Union had insisted on shared sovereignty in Berlin and responsibility for the unity issue through all the changes of the previous decades—the cold war of the 1950s, the detente of the 1970s, and the new cold war of the 1980s. After reunification and the ratification of the Two-Plus-Four accord, the members of the wartime anti-Hitler coalition finally withdrew their armed forces from the former Reich capital in early 1991. With the end of the Four-Power regime the Federal Republic was free to move its capital from Bonn to Berlin—a step approved by the Bundestag in a close June 1991 vote. Germany finally secured sovereignty over its own affairs. It did not, however, exercise full external sovereignty as a matter of practice. The new FRG, like the old, remained anchored in Western institutions, its policy concerns interwoven with those of its allies.

Continued restrictions on German sovereignty were most evident in the context of the European Union. The new Germany emerged an even more powerful force within the EU, but remained fully embedded within its institutions. The momentum for deeper integration, which originated in the mid-1980s, continued into the early 1990s. Plans for a single market, set down in the Single European Act of 1987, were realized in 1992, the year the Maastricht Treaty committed European leaders to the further goal of a single currency. The objective of a European foreign policy, also reiterated in the Single European Act, moved one step closer to fruition with the Maastricht Treaty's provisions for a Common Foreign and Security Policy. European leaders committed themselves to more active foreign policy cooperation and consultation and placed the West European Union, a regional alliance long overshadowed by NATO, within the institutional fold of the EU. Overall, European integration emerged a more significant framework for German foreign policy than it had been in the 1980s.[24]

---

22. On the resilience of institutions across the 1990 divide, see Harald Müller, "German Foreign Policy after Reunification," in *The New Germany and the New Europe,* ed. Paul B. Stares (Washington: Brookings Institution, 1992), 126–73.

23. See Christoph-Matthias Brand, *Souveränität für Deutschland* (Cologne: Verlag Wissenschaft und Politik, 1993).

24. On the EU as a context for German foreign policy, see Carl F. Lankowski, ed., *Germany and the European Community: Beyond Hegemony and Containment?* (New York: St. Martin's Press, 1993); Simon Bulmer and William E. Paterson, "Germany in the European Union: Gentle Giant or Emergent Leader?" *International Affairs* (London) 72, no. 1 (1996): 9–32; Peter H. Merkl, *German Unification in the European Context* (University Park: Pennsylvania State University Press, 1993).

The salience of the European Union was particularly evident with respect to new policy challenges in the East. The collapse of the Soviet bloc, by putting the issue of expansion on the agenda, transformed the European Union into an increasingly important international actor. A *West* European institution for four decades, it began to take on an all-European character. The German pursuit of expansion, a hoped-for means of stabilizing East and Central Europe, could only be pursued within a multilateral European framework. At the same time, the German approach to national and ethnic conflict in the Balkans unfolded within the context of the CFSP. Confronted with the Bush and Clinton administrations' initial reluctance to become involved in the conflict, European leaders handled it poorly. Divisions on the question of recognition for Croatia and Slovenia were followed by unsuccessful efforts to mediate a solution to the war in Bosnia. The failure of CFSP to bring peace to the region did not signify its complete bankruptcy. While Europeans had few concrete results to show for their efforts, their level of foreign policy cooperation and coordination was probably greater than at any previous juncture.[25]

On security matters NATO remained the more salient institutional constraint on German foreign policy. As part of the Two-Plus-Four accord that made NATO membership possible for the new Federal Republic, German leaders accepted a ceiling of 370,000 on the Bundeswehr and confirmed the 1954 renunciation of the production of atomic, biological, and chemical weapons. German forces remained directly integrated into the alliance's command structure without an intervening national general staff. In the years after 1990 major organizational reforms, both in NATO and in the Bundeswehr, loosened German dependence on the United States. The reduction of foreign forces stationed in the Federal Republic and the shift in allied planning away from coordinated defense against an attack from the East made the smaller Bundeswehr a more independent force than it had been in previous decades. Still, alliance membership continued to preclude the development of a nationally oriented, unilateral security policy. NATO remained the central institutional framework for German security policy.

The centrality of NATO as a framework for German foreign policy was particularly evident in the context of Ostpolitik. At their November 1991 Rome summit NATO foreign ministers moved beyond the 1967 Harmel Report formula of deterrence and detente to make cooperation the centerpiece of alliance policy toward the East. And the inauguration of NATO's Partnership for Peace program in 1994, an offer of increased

---

25. On the emergence of the CFSP, see Reinhardt Rummel, ed., *Toward Political Union: Planning a Common Foreign and Security Policy in the European Community* (Baden-Baden: Nomos, 1992).

security cooperation with former Warsaw Pact countries as a possible first step toward NATO membership, provided a framework for the subsequent expansion discussion.[26] German security policy toward the Balkan War also unfolded in the NATO context. In the wake of the Gulf War the alliance set up a Rapid Reaction Force designed to address out-of-area problems. After the failure of EU mediation efforts in Bosnia, the force was assigned to protect UN peacekeeping efforts in the region. And in late 1995 NATO troops moved into the Balkans to oversee the implementation of the Dayton Accord. As a member of the multilateral alliance, Germany faced institutional pressure to participate in these unfolding peacekeeping efforts.

Like NATO and the EU, the CSCE also survived the collapse of bipolarity as an institutional context for German foreign policy. During the Two-Plus-Four negotiations Gorbachev insisted on—and Western leaders agreed to—a strengthening of the CSCE as a framework for European security. The Paris Charter, signed amid fanfare in November 1990, committed member states to democracy, civil liberties, minority rights, and economic freedoms. European leaders also endorsed far-reaching arms control and confidence-building measures, annual foreign ministers meetings, and regular high-level contacts. Despite these changes the CSCE, redubbed the Organization on Cooperation and Security in Europe (OSCE), did not emerge as a prominent institutional framework for postreunification German foreign policy. The incorporation of former Soviet republics made the organization increasingly unwieldy, while the outbreak of ethnic conflict in Yugoslavia and the former Soviet Union demonstrated its ineffectiveness. By the mid-1990s NATO and the EU—not the OSCE—were clearly the central institutional sites for all-European economic, political, and security cooperation.[27]

The Eastern Treaties, like the OSCE, lost much of their salience after 1990. Reunification made the Basic Treaty between the FRG and the GDR superfluous and the crux of the Moscow and Warsaw Treaties—the recognition of the status quo of the division of Europe and Germany—irrelevant. A revised set of bilateral accords, however, incorporated many of the earlier treaties' core provisions: the renunciation of force; respect for existing borders; support for bilateral economic, political and cultural

---

26. Rome Declaration, November 8, 1991, *Außenpolitik der Bundesrepublik Deutschland: Dokumente von 1949 bis 1994* (Cologne: Verlag Wissenschaft und Politik), 830–41.

27. See Michael R. Lucas, ed., *The CSCE in the 1990s: Constructing European Security and Cooperation* (Baden-Baden: Nomos, 1993); Vojtech Mastny, *The Helsinki Process and the Reintegration of Europe, 1986–1991: Analysis and Documentation* (New York: New York University Press, 1992).

cooperation; and joint efforts to promote European security. The two most important of these accords—treaties with the Soviet Union in November 1990 and Poland in June 1991—also included new commitments. Most significant in the case of the German-Soviet Treaty—later a foundation for German-Russian relations—were provisions for regular foreign policy contacts and consultations on security issues. And in the German-Polish Treaty the Federal Republic committed itself to support Warsaw's membership in the European Union as soon as possible. Taken together, these treaties—along with similar accords with Hungary and the Czech and Slovak Republics—provided a framework for Germany's ties with its most important Eastern neighbors.[28]

Overall, this configuration of institutions, East and West, constituted a set of constraints on German foreign policy comparable to that of the 1980s. German absolute and relative power grew as a result of reunification. The collapse of the Soviet bloc created an opportunity for the Federal Republic to extend its influence eastward. At the same time, however, membership in the EU and NATO continued to rule out a strictly unilateral foreign or security policy. Furthermore, the new Eastern Treaties and the OSCE still provided a framework for a peaceful, cooperative Ostpolitik. Taken together, these institutions constituted considerable constraints on the foreign policy of the new Germany. NATO and the EU, in particular, were contexts for both major post-1990 challenges—the promotion of economic reform and political stability in Russia and Central and Eastern Europe, and the cessation of armed conflict in the Balkans.[29] The institutional configuration framed German efforts to combine an active Ostpolitik and Western unity and to adopt a new security stance without provoking old fears.

This constellation did not, however, deprive Germans of significant choices. In certain respects the EU was an ambiguous context, both for Ostpolitik and for German efforts to address the war in former Yugoslavia. In the case of Ostpolitik the key ambiguity concerned the relative priority of widening and deepening. The Maastricht Treaty did not bind the Federal Republic to put the consolidation of integration in the West ahead of its expansion to the East. It did commit leaders to the goal of monetary union and an effective European foreign policy. At the same time, however, it was vague about the pursuit of both goals. The exact timing of the introduction of a single currency, its precise institutional

---

28. For the text of the new treaties with Moscow and Warsaw, see *Außenpolitik der Bundesrepublik Deutschland,* 738–44, 800–810.

29. For a discussion of the dilemmas posed by this constellation, see Bertel Heurlin, ed. *Germany in Europe in the Nineties* (New York: St. Martin's Press, 1996).

arrangements, and the identity of the participating countries, were not specified in advance. Moreover, the posited convergence criteria for membership were open to interpretation. In the context of the Balkan War, too, the EU was an ambiguous framework in certain respects. The CFSP organized EU foreign policy on an intergovernmental basis, leaving members free to pursue their own foreign policy priorities when vital interests were deemed at stake. And the exact nature of its relationship with the WEU and NATO, the much more important security institution, was left unclear. Given the ambiguities in the Maastricht Treaty, the Federal Republic was in a position to make deepening less of a priority than widening and to stake out its own position on the war in former Yugoslavia.

The constraints posed by NATO, in the Ostpolitik and Balkan contexts, were also somewhat ambiguous. With its 1991 Rome summit the alliance embarked on internal reforms, increased security cooperation with the former Warsaw Pact, and began to consider the question of expansion eastward. In subsequent years, the multilateral structure of the alliance allowed individual member states leeway in their approach to these issues. Both the Rome Declaration and the Partnership for Peace Program permitted different emphases on the consolidation of the alliance and its expansion. This ambiguity gave German leaders, eager to create a "zone of stability" to their East—and bound by the Paris Charter to work toward an "all-European security system"—the opportunity to press the expansion issue more than their allies. In the context of the war in former Yugoslavia, too, German leaders had some room for maneuver. The United States, Britain, and France pressed for German participation in joint operations in the region. The norm of multilateralism created pressure to adjust the Federal Republic's traditional rejection of any out-of-area role. At the same time, however, decisions to commit troops remained national ones in the NATO context, and the Western allies expressed some understanding for Germany's historically informed caution about deploying the Bundeswehr abroad. Institutional constraints compelled German leaders to reconsider their reticent approach to military instruments of foreign policy but left them with freedom as to how.

Overall, the intersection of policy problems and institutional context left German leaders with circumscribed freedom of action. The institutional changes of the 1950s and the 1970s, which bound Germany to the West and created a framework for cooperative ties with the East, persisted through the mid-1990s. Despite revolutionary changes in the external context of German foreign policy, core European institutions—NATO, the EU, the Eastern Treaties, and the OSCE—continued to constrain the Federal Republic's choices. At the same time, however, those institutions left

German leaders with significant alternatives in the face of policy challenges to the East. Within the multilateral framework of EU and NATO
they could place different degrees of emphasis on the consolidation of
established institutions and their extension eastward, and adopt different
approaches to Western efforts to end the war in former Yugoslavia. How
German leaders situated themselves with respect to the alternatives posed
by the international constellation was determined at the level of domestic
politics.

Defining Post-Reunification Priorities

In the years after 1990 the *internal* challenges of reunification absorbed
most of Germany's political energy. At the level of state structures few
changes took place. Under Article 23 of the Basic Law five new federal
states—the old GDR—became part of an enlarged Federal Republic. In
economic, social, and cultural terms, however, reunification brought
about extensive changes, mainly in the East. The collapse of the East German state-run economy led to chronic unemployment, an explosion of federal social spending, and high budget deficits. Cultural differences compounded economic and social problems. Germans in the old and new
federal states, separated for four decades, often viewed one another with
suspicion and resentment. The period 1992–93 marked a low point: the
onset of recession in the West and continued dislocation in the East went
hand in hand with a rash of violence against foreigners living in Germany.
Against this backdrop it is perhaps not surprising that no foreign policy
debate engulfed German society.[30]

Political parties dominated the foreign policy discussion—the same
parties that controlled German politics before 1990, with many of the
same arguments. The Christian Democrats, Social Democrats, and Liberals continued to manage German politics at the federal level. And they
continued to articulate the foreign policy consensus that had emerged by
the late 1980s: support for both integration in the West and engagement in
the East. The Greens, who participated in several state-level governments
during the early 1990s, sometimes called for the dismantling of NATO and
the creation of an all-European security system in its place. And the Party
of Democratic Socialism—the reformed SED, with solid representation in

---

30. On reunification and its impact, see Michael G. Huelshoff, Andrei S. Markovits,
and Simon Reich, eds., *From Bundesrepublik to Deutschland: German Politics after
Reunification* (Ann Arbor: University of Michigan Press, 1993). On the absence of a foreign
policy debate, see Elisabeth Noelle-Neumann, "Öffentliche Meinung und Außenpolitik: Die
fehlende Debatte in Deutschland," *Internationale Politik* 50, no. 8 (August 1995): 3–12.

the new federal states—combined similar criticism of NATO with attacks on the EU.[31] While they enjoyed some representation in the Bundestag, however, neither party could exert any real influence on German foreign policy. This was even more true of the Republicans and other Far Right parties, who remained unrepresented at the national level. Their national opposition to EMU appeared to resonate with much of German public opinion, but did not translate effectively into votes.[32] The major government and opposition parties, the CDU/CSU and the SPD, articulated the contours of the foreign policy debate. On the basis of a broad consensus their leaders espoused somewhat contrasting approaches to the external challenges facing the Federal Republic.

During the years after reunification, Kohl's foreign priorities overlapped considerably with those of successive SPD leaders, Bjorn Engholm (1991–93) and Rudolf Scharping (1993–95). The focus here is on Scharping, Kohl's challenger in the 1994 elections and the more important of two. Both Scharping and Kohl hailed from Rhineland-Palatinate, where they had served as governor before taking over the leadership of their national parties. Their formative political experiences, however, were very different. As a teenager at the end of World War II, Kohl had witnessed postwar reconstruction and begun his political career under Konrad Adenauer's chancellorship. For Scharping, born after the war, the student movement, the New Ostpolitik, and the INF struggle were formative experiences. While Kohl considered himself Adenauer's heir, Scharping did not shun the label "Brandt's grandson." These contrasting political biographies shed some light on both men's somewhat different approaches to Western integration and engagement in the East.[33]

Most striking, however, were broad points of agreement.[34] During the early 1990s both Kohl and Scharping pressed for stronger Western institutions and an active Ostpolitik. They backed efforts to deepen the European Union and to make NATO less of a military and more of a political alliance. They called for the expansion of both institutions eastward, particularly to encompass Germany's immediate eastern neighbors.

---

31. On the evolution of the left end of the German political spectrum from the 1960s through the 1990s, see Andrei S. Markovits and Philip S. Gorski, *The German Left: Red, Green and Beyond* (New York: Oxford University Press, 1993).

32. Manfred Brunner, a former German official in Brussels, left the FDP to form an anti-Maastricht party, the League of Free Citizens, with little success. For an argument against Maastricht, see Hermann Lübbe, *Abschied vom Superstaat. Vereinigte Staaten von Europa wird es nicht geben* (Berlin: Siedler, 1994).

33. For biographical background, see Werner Maser, *Helmut Kohl: Der deutsche Kanzler* (Berlin: Ullstein, 1990); Ulrich Rosenbaum, *Rudolf Scharping* (Berlin: Ullstein, 1993).

34. For an overview of foreign policy stances, see Kohl, *"Ich wollte Deutschlands Einheit"*; Rudolf Scharping, *Was jetzt zu tun ist* (Munich: Piper, 1994), 211–26.

And they advocated a German role in efforts to end the Bosnian civil war. At the same time, however, differences in emphasis distinguished their stances. For Kohl solidarity with the West constituted an absolute priority. The deepening of Western institutions should precede their expansion eastward, he insisted, and Bonn should participate fully in multilateral military efforts outside NATO territory. Scharping was more willing to countenance some friction with the allies. He was less enthusiastic about Maastricht and more supportive of an active Ostpolitik. And he advocated only partial changes in Germany's reticent approach to the use of the Bundeswehr.

In articulating his foreign policy priorities, Kohl continually underscored the importance of solidarity with the West, particularly the United States and France. Reunification, he insisted, should not mark a new departure for German foreign policy. Kohl acknowledged the existence of pressing new challenges in the East—the importance of economic and political stability in the former Soviet bloc. And he called for active multilateral efforts—and the expansion of the EU and NATO—to meet them. At the same time, however, he was careful not to make the extension of Western institutions eastward a priority over their consolidation. In the context of the EU, for example, he argued that the Europeans would "only really be able to bring East and West Europe together" if they first moved to "deepen the existing Community and make it into an anchor for stability for all of Europe in the future." A similar logic infused Kohl's approach to NATO's role in the East. He insisted that Germany move cautiously on the expansion issue, not only to prevent confrontation with Russia, but also to preserve alliance unity. The bond with the United States through the Atlantic Alliance, he insisted, remained one of existential importance for the Federal Republic, even after 1990.[35]

Kohl's emphasis on solidarity with the allies was also evident in his approach to the use of the military. Caught off guard by the Gulf War, which broke out only months after reunification, Kohl initially held to the FRG's established position—that the provision for participation in "collective security," set down in Article 24 of the Basic Law, ruled out German military activities outside NATO's defensive perimeter. Partly in response to Western pressures, he modified that stance in the years that followed. First, he insisted that the Federal Republic could take part in UN peacekeeping missions worldwide without a constitutional change. And then, as the war in Bosnia escalated, he embraced the view that no constitutional change was necessary for any out-of-area deployments, as

---

35. Kohl address before the Bertelsmann Forum on April 3, 1992, *Bulletin des Presse- und Informationsamtes,* April 8, 1992, 354; Bundestag address on the Partnership for Peace, January 13, 1994, *Verhandlungen des deutschen Bundestags,* ser. 12, 17412–15.

long as they took place within a multilateral framework. His support for German participation in the 1994–95 NATO effort in the region was grounded first and foremost in a determination to avoid the new Germany's isolation in the Western alliance. "The word 'isolation'," he told a CDU party conference in February 1994, "can never again be a motto of German policy."[36]

In articulating his foreign policy priorities, Scharping stressed unity with the West less than did Kohl. While supportive of NATO's internal reforms and plans to expand, he placed greater emphasis than Kohl—and the Bush and Clinton administrations—on the OSCE as a core component of any all-European security system. Moreover, Scharping did not match Kohl's enthusiasm for deeper European integration. While he backed moves toward greater political union and supported EMU in principle, Scharping also expressed concern about the economic and social consequences of a single European currency. He warned that EMU without a corresponding European social policy might undermine the German social welfare system. And in October 1995 he stated that the stability of the Deutschmark should not be sacrificed to the "idea" of European unity.[37] This more cautious approach to deepening went hand in hand with somewhat stronger support for widening. Scharping pressed the government to provide more assistance for reform in Central and Eastern Europe. "The greatness of the words about the beginning of a new era in 1989/90," he argued in May 1994, "have often clearly contradicted the smallness of the deeds that followed." After the December 1994 Essen summit, Scharping chided Kohl and other European leaders for not having set a timetable for EU expansion.[38]

Differences in emphasis between Kohl and Scharping were also evident on security issues. From the Gulf War onward the SPD resisted any major shift away from the traditional German culture of reticence. At party conferences in 1992 and 1993 Scharping and other Social Democratic Party leaders won support for changes in the Basic Law to accommodate UN peacekeeping missions. But the party continued to oppose the use of German troops in potential combat situations outside the NATO area—and to insist that any such deployment required a constitutional change. Scharping backed some kind of German supportive role in the Bosnian war. But he rejected Kohl's view

---

36. Address of February 20, 1994, in Helmut Kohl, *Wir setzen auf Sieg* (Bonn: CDU, 1994), 3.

37. Scharping cited in *Frankfurter Rundschau,* October 27, 1995.

38. Address of May 27, 1994, *Verhandlungen des deutschen Bundestags,* ser. 12, 20126. Remarks on Essen summit cited in *Süddeutsche Zeitung,* December 16, 1994.

that membership in NATO obliged the German government to follow the allied lead in military actions in the Balkans and elsewhere. Germany, he argued, would sometimes have to decide for itself on security matters. "The capacity to form alliances and partnerships," he told the Bundestag in July 1994, "is an important perspective, but it is not the only one."[39]

These somewhat different approaches to unity with the West and engagement in the East rested in part on different assessments of the international situation. Both Kohl and Scharping perceived the potential for economic, political, and security instability throughout the former Soviet bloc—not just in the Balkans. But Kohl, unlike Scharping, was also very concerned about the prospect of national divisions within the West. At the CDU's February 1994 party conference, for example, he asked the delegates whether they really believed "that the terrible examples of racial hatred, 'ethnic cleansing', religious animosity, and chauvinism of the worst kind in the Balkans—that these evil spirits only live there and could never move elsewhere?" For Kohl the end of the cold war made Western solidarity more, not less, imperative. In the absence of a clear external threat the maintenance of NATO and EU unity required a concerted effort. "NATO remains our anchor of security and stability," he insisted in June 1994, and "Europe needs an America that assumes a central role in questions of European security."[40]

Scharping's slightly different priorities—his somewhat less emphasis on unity with the West—rested on different perceptions of post-1990 circumstances. Scharping did not, like Kohl, express deep concern about the cohesion of Western institutions after the collapse of the Soviet threat. He viewed German participation in NATO and the EU as vital and backed the further development of both institutions. At the same time, however, he placed marginally more emphasis than Kohl on the policy problems that Germany faced in the East: the challenge of political and economic reform in former Soviet bloc states and the creation of all-European security institutions. In view of these challenges Scharping suggested in July 1994 that Germany and its allies develop a "new Ostpolitik." The states of Central and Eastern Europe, he argued, deserved "a clearer prospect of

---

39. Address of July 22, 1994, *Verhandlungen des deutschen Bundestags,* ser. 12, 21170. For the SPD's reticent approach to military security instruments, see the resolutions of the November 1993 party conference in Wiesbaden, *Perspektiven einer neuen Außen-und Sicherheitspolitik* (Bonn: Vorstand der SPD, 1993).

40. Addresses of February 20, 1994, Kohl, *Wir setzen auf Sieg,* 23; and upon reception of the Konrad Adenauer Prize, June 19, 1994, Helmut Kohl, "Für uns Deutsche ist Europa eine Schicksalsfrage," *CDU-Dokumentation,* no. 21 (1994): 7.

belonging to Europe than is the case today—as participants in its security architecture but also its cultural, social, and economic cooperation."[41]

During the early 1990s different views of the past and its lessons also underpinned these somewhat different foreign policy priorities. After the end of the cold war Kohl construed Western integration as the best guarantee against a return to the destructive, nationalist policies of the prewar era. In April 1992, for example, he argued that the only alternative to the pursuit of European unity was a reversion to the "petty international fragmentation [*Kleinstaaterei*] and rivalries of yesterday or the day before yesterday." He also drew a link between historical experience and the importance of solidarity with Washington. "In view of the lessons of this century," he contended in June 1993, "the United States should continue to play a central role in questions of European security." For Kohl the experience of two world wars not only necessitated further strong institutional links with the West. It also required that Germans make solidarity with the allies on issues like the war in Bosnia an absolute priority. As he reminded a party conference audience in February 1994, "During this century, we have paid bitterly whenever our country fell into isolation."[42]

From Kohl's perspective not only prewar disasters but also the positive postwar legacies of European integration and Atlantic solidarity made continued unity with the West vital. Adenauer and other founders of the European Community, Kohl maintained, had "drawn the consequences" from a history of suffering. The postwar integration process, which had "helped to overcome centuries-old rivalries and conflicts among the participating nations" should continue under new, uncertain post cold war circumstances. From Kohl's perspective the new Germany should also draw on the positive legacy of Atlantic solidarity. The alliance with the United States and Western Europe—a cornerstone of Adenauer's policy of Western integration—had secured the Federal Republic's postwar recovery and made reunification possible. It should therefore not be disrupted under any circumstances. "Since Konrad Adenauer," Kohl insisted at the CDU's 1994 party conference, "our most important goal has been to remain dependable friends and partners."[43]

Scharping's view of the past and its implications differed from Kohl's

---

41. Address of July 22, 1994, *Verhandlungen des deutschen Bundestags,* ser. 12, 21170.

42. Bertelsmann-Forum speech, April 3, 1992, *Bulletin des Presse- und Informationsamtes,* April 8, 1992, 354; address before a security conference in Munich, February 6, 1993, ibid., February 10, 1993, 103; Kohl, *Wir setzen auf Sieg,* 3.

43. Kohl before the Bundestag, December 2, 1992, *Verhandlungen des deutschen Bundestags,* ser. 12, 10824; address in Schwäbisch Hall, 4 May 1994, *Bulletin des Presse- und Informationsamtes,* May 10, 1994, 366. On these themes, see also Kohl's before the European Parliament, February 2, 1993, ibid., February 5, 1993.

only on the margins. He, too, underscored the lessons of Germany's catastrophic prewar experience. The new Germany, he insisted, must remain firmly anchored in NATO and the EU, not least in order to prevent a reversion to the destructive balance of power policies of the past. It should support deeper European integration and a continued U.S. presence in Europe. At the same time, however, Scharping drew somewhat different conclusions than Kohl from the legacy of the militarist past. He did not, like Willy Brandt and Helmut Schmidt before him, posit a clear link between the memory of the German war of aggression in the East and the importance of an active Ostpolitik. On the other hand, he argued that the legacy of German militarism required a reticent approach to the use of armed forces outside the NATO area, particularly in those regions once occupied by the *Wehrmacht*. As Scharping underlined before an SPD conference in Essen in June 1993, "the Bundeswehr cannot become a freely available army of intervention!" In positing a connection between the German past and the necessity of an active "peace policy," Scharping did draw on themes previously articulated by Brandt and Schmidt.[44]

Scharping not only invoked the historical themes of former Social Democratic leaders in setting out his foreign policy priorities. He also pointed to their concrete achievements. While Kohl posited a link between Western integration and reunification, Scharping and other SPD leaders insisted that the New Ostpolitik had contributed decisively to German unity. And while Kohl insisted on building on Adenauer's legacy amid new circumstances, Scharping explicitly called for a second New Ostpolitik.[45] Oskar Lafontaine, another key Social Democratic figure during the early 1990s, made the link even more obvious. "After the detente policy of Willy Brandt," he stated at a November 1995 party conference, "we have a special responsibility to forge a new security architecture in Europe that includes East European states and Russia."[46] The differences between the historical perspectives articulated atop the CDU/CSU and SPD should not be overdrawn. Scharping acknowledged Adenauer's achievements, while Kohl recognized Brandt's. But the different emphasis accorded each postwar legacy underpinned somewhat different priorities after 1990.

Controversies about the past and its lessons also revived among his-

---

44. Address of June 25, 1993, *Protokoll vom außerordentlichen Parteitag Essen 25 Juni 1993* (Bonn: Vorstand der SPD, 1993), 92. See also his Bundestag address of July 22, 1994, *Verhandlungen des deutschen Bundestags*, ser. 12, 21174.

45. See, for example, Scharping's addresses of November 24, 1993 and July 22, 1994, *Verhandlungen des deutschen Bundestags*, ser. 12, 16573, 21170.

46. Lafontaine address of November 15, 1995, *Presseservice der SPD: Parteitag Mannheim. 14.–17. November 1995*, 8.

torians and political scientists during the early 1990s. In the wake of reunification there were renewed efforts to portray the first German nation state as a point of reference for the second—a development analyzed in the concluding chapter. Academics also contributed to the controversy surrounding the relative contribution of Western integration and the New Ostpolitik to reunification. Armed with new sources, scholars again debated whether Adenauer had missed an opportunity to achieve reunification in the early 1950s.[47] The most vociferous controversy, however, surrounded the New Ostpolitik, and whether it had solidified the division of Europe and Germany or promoted its dissolution. Jens Hacker and other conservative academics singled out the SPD's "second Ostpolitik" during the 1980s, which encompassed dialogue with the SED on security matters and talk of recognizing GDR citizenship, as a particularly blatant example of national betrayal. Peter Bender and other scholars sympathetic to the New Ostpolitik underscored the degree to which Kohl, too, had come to terms with the division of Germany by the mid-1980s. And they suggested that detente, not the strength and unity of the West, had brought about the dissolution of the Soviet bloc. Most scholars adopted a less polemical perspective, one that acknowledged the roles of both Adenauer and Brandt making reunification possible. Their agreement on the historical achievements of both Western integration and the New Ostpolitik—and the importance of preserving them under post-1990 circumstances—mirrored the narrative broadly shared by Kohl, Scharping, and most other party leaders.[48]

The somewhat different foreign policy priorities articulated by Kohl and Scharping did not represent two sharply divergent potential paths for the FRG foreign policy. Given the configuration of international constraints, any chancellor would most probably have sought to deepen the European integration process and to align German security policy more with that of the Western allies. The institutional constellation did allow for different emphases—for more or less attention to Western integration and Eastern engagement and for different approaches to the use of German armed forces in the former Yugoslavia. In their assessment of that constellation and their interpretations of history and its policy implications, Kohl

---

47. See, for example, Wilfried Loth, ed., *Die deutsche Frage in der Nachkriegszeit* (Berlin: Akademie Verlag, 1994); Rudolf Morsey, *Die Deutschlandpolitik Adenauers: Alte Thesen und neue Fakten* (Opladen: Westdeutscher Verlag, 1991).

48. Jens Hacker, *Deutsche Irrtümer: Schönfärber und Helfershelfer der SED-Diktatur im Westen* (Berlin: Ullstein, 1992); Peter Bender, "Der goldene Angelhaken: Entspannungspolitik und Systemwandel," *Aus Politik und Zeitgeschichte,* no. 14 (April 8, 1994): 11–15; A. James McAdams and John Torpey, eds., "The Past as Arsenal: Debating German Unification," *German Politics and Society* no. 30 (fall 1993).

and Scharping differed only on the margins. For Kohl's stronger emphasis on Western solidarity to prevail in practice, it first had to secure the necessary domestic political backing.

The Politics of German Foreign Policy after 1990

Kohl's political strength after 1990 made the implementation of his foreign policy priorities possible. His continued predominance in German
politics appeared doubtful on the eve of reunification. His position within
the CDU/CSU was weaker than it had ever been; relations with the FDP
in the coalition were strained; and the SPD appeared poised to win the
next election, scheduled for late 1990. When the GDR collapsed, however,
Kohl was able to consolidate his position during the reunification process
and retain the chancellorship in the December 1990 all-German elections.
Despite the tremendous economic and social problems associated with the
reconstruction of the new federal states, he managed to hold his government together in the years that followed. Only when he defeated Scharping
in the 1994 elections and again relegated the SPD to the opposition, was he
able to secure his post-reunification foreign policy course, with its strong
emphasis on deeper European integration and Atlantic solidarity.

In the summer of 1989 Kohl's mastery of the CDU/CSU did not
appear likely to continue into the 1990s. Declining Christian Democratic
fortunes in regional elections during the late 1980s, combined with growing tensions between the conservative and moderate wings of the
CDU/CSU, undercut Kohl's authority as party leader. At a September
1989 party conference he only barely foiled an attempt to replace him as
CDU chairman.[49] Kohl's seizure of the unity issue at the same conference
helped to cement his authority atop the party. As late as January 1989, he
had reminded conservatives of Gorbachev's commitment to the GDR.
Now, against the backdrop of a mass exodus of East Germans and
swelling protests against SED rule, he suggested that Gorbachev's recognition of the "right of self-determination" made the issue of German unity
again relevant.[50] After the fall of the Berlin Wall in November, some isolated CDU/CSU voices initially criticized Kohl's rush to reunification. His
success, however, in securing Gorbachev's approval for a united Germany's NATO membership in the summer of 1990, strengthened his posi-

---

49. Ernst Albrecht, interview by author, Bonn, June 23, 1992. On the struggle within
the CDU/CSU, see Friedrich Zimmermann, *Kabinettstücke: Politik mit Strauß und Kohl,
1976–91* (Munich: Herbig, 1991), 298–305.

50. For Kohl's position in January, see *Bundespresseamt News Files,* January 13, 1989.
For his September 1989 address, see *37. Parteitag der CDU. Niederschrift* (Bonn: CDU,
1989), 29.

tion within the party. Embattled only a year earlier, Kohl emerged as the almost unassailable "chancellor of unity."[51]

Kohl's unchallenged authority atop the CDU/CSU in the years after 1990 allowed him to implement his strong pro-Western orientation.[52] After the death of Franz Josef Strauss, in 1988, the CSU no longer posed a challenge to Kohl's foreign policy authority. As finance minister and CSU chairman, Theo Waigel participated actively in the negotiation and implementation phases of the Maastricht Treaty. Edmund Stoiber, Waigel's intraparty rival and governor of Bavaria, set different foreign policy accents. He combined support for EU and NATO expansion eastward with a skepticism of the deepening agenda set out in Maastricht. In sharp contrast to Kohl, Stoiber dismissed the goal of a federal Europe and held up the nation state as a resilient and successful form of political organization. Through the mid-1990s Kohl made some cosmetic concessions to the small, national conservative wing of the CDU/CSU. In 1992, for example, he dropped references to the goal of a "United States of Europe" from his speeches. With his authority atop the party unchallenged, however, he was able to make support for deeper integration one of the main themes of the CDU's new party program, officially adopted in 1994.[53]

Within the CDU the two figures most often mentioned as possible successors to Kohl—Wolfgang Schäuble and Volker Rühe—only rarely articulated divergent foreign policy views. As head of the CDU/CSU parliamentary group Schäuble occasionally espoused a more assertive foreign policy stance. In September 1994, for example, he coauthored a position paper that included an impassioned plea for both deepening *and* widening the EU. If West European countries failed to work together to foster stability in the East, the paper suggested, "Germany might be called upon, or tempted by its own security constraints, to try to effect the stabilization of

---

51. Party moderates like Heiner Geissler, the former CDU general-secretary, echoed President Richard von Weizsäcker's concerns about the pace of unity. For Weizsäcker's admonition that Germany should grow together and not be "thrown together," see his GDR television interview, December 13, 1989, *Bulletin des Presse- und Informationsamtes,* December 15, 1989, 1215.

52. Wolfgang Schäuble acknowledged that the reunification process fostered greater CDU/CSU unity but was quick to add that it was not one of the motivations behind Kohl's policy. Wolfgang Schäuble, interview by author, Bonn, July 15, 1992. For his account of reunification, see Wolfgang Schäuble, *Der Vertrag: Wie ich über die deutsche Einheit verhandelte* (Stuttgart: Deutsche Verlags-Anstalt, 1991).

53. *Freiheit in Verantwortung: Grundsatzprogramm der Christlich Demokratischen Union Deutschlands* (Bonn: CDU, 1994), 87–91. For Stoiber on Europe, see his address of November 11, 1993, *Verhandlungen des deutschen Bundestags,* ser. 12, 16295–300. Peter Gauweiler, Bavarian minister for environmental affairs, used the term *Esperanto Money* to mock the proposed European Currency (cited in *Süddeutsche Zeitung,* February 3, 1992).

Eastern Europe on its own and in the traditional way."[54] When the French government objected to both the tone and content of the paper, Kohl distanced himself from it. As defense minister, Rühe initially pressed more assertively than Kohl for the expansion of NATO eastward. In January 1994 he welcomed the Partnership for Peace program but called it "no substitute for the opening of the alliance."[55] Kohl did not openly differ with Rühe. Given reservations in Washington—and Moscow—at the time, however, he was more cautious than his defense minister.

While Schäuble and Rühe sometimes set somewhat different foreign policy accents, neither posed a challenge to Kohl's leadership during the early 1990s. Kohl's standing with voters fell precipitously in 1991, when he broke his campaign promise not to raise taxes to pay for reunification. And amid recession, unemployment, and a wave of violence against foreigners, the CDU fared badly in local and regional elections in 1992–93. Still, Kohl faced no opposition within the party leadership to his renewed chancellor candidacy for the 1994 elections. Stoiber, Schäuble, Rühe, and other CDU/CSU leaders all supported him without reservations. On the eve of reunification Kohl had survived a direct assault on his position as party leader. Five years later his foreign policy priorities rested on a solid internal party foundation.

During the early 1990s Kohl's authority within the ruling coalition with the Liberals was also impressive. Here, too, the contrast with the late 1980s was striking. Then, faced with declining electoral fortunes, Genscher and the FDP had considered the possibility of a renewed social-liberal coalition after the 1990 election. During early 1989 differences with the CDU/CSU over the modernization of short-range nuclear forces and the legal status of the Oder-Neisse line revealed the fragile state of the coalition. Genscher had threatened to resign as part of a successful effort to put off SNF modernization and had criticized Kohl's failure to endorse the Oder-Neisse border as legally binding on any future, united Germany.[56] The revolution in the GDR and the rush to reunification, however, brought Kohl and Genscher closer together. With the Ten-Point Plan,

---

54. CDU/CSU-Fraktion des Deutschen Bundestages, "Reflections on European Policy," September 1, 1994, 3. For his policy views, see also Wolfgang Schäuble, *Und der Zukunft zugewandt* (Berlin: Siedler, 1994).

55. Rühe address of January 13, 1994, *Verhandlungen des deutschen Bundestags,* ser. 12, 17431. For Rühe's basic foreign policy approach see Volker Rühe, *Deutschlands Verantwortung: Perspektiven für das neue Europa* (Frankfurt am Main: Ullstein, 1994).

56. On Genscher's successful efforts to win an independent foreign policy profile in the late 1980s, see Emil J. Kirchner, "Genscher and What Lies behind 'Genscherism,'" *West European Politics* 13, no. 2 (April 1990): 159–77; and Genscher's own account of the SNF controversy in Genscher, *Rebuilding a House Divided,* 232–59.

Kohl seized the unity issue. Genscher, not even informed about the plan in advance, hewed close to Kohl's line in the weeks that followed. During the first half of 1990 close cooperation between the CDU/CSU and FDP in resolving the international and domestic problems associated with the reunification process all but ruled out a Liberal switch back to a coalition with the SPD after the December elections.

Both before and after those elections, which the ruling coalition won handily, Genscher did continue to set slightly different foreign policy accents than Kohl. Overall he was less concerned than the chancellor about Western unity and more insistent on addressing the concerns of Eastern neighbors and Gorbachev's Soviet Union in particular. Genscher's March 1990 suggestion that *both* alliances might eventually dissolve into a new European security architecture, for example, provoked an angry response from Kohl. Through his resignation in May 1992, moreover, Genscher continued to press more forcefully than Kohl for a stronger CSCE. As it happened, his vision of the latter as a "stability framework from the Atlantic to the Urals" gradually lost relevance after the dissolution of Yugoslavia and the Soviet Union.[57] Kohl's stronger emphasis on NATO shaped the direction of post-reunification foreign policy.

Genscher's successor as foreign minister and FDP chairman, Klaus Kinkel, presented less of a challenge to Kohl's foreign policy authority. Like Genscher, Kinkel originally placed more stress on the CSCE than Kohl. But the ineffectiveness of the CSCE in managing ethnic conflicts in the Balkans and the former Soviet Union led him, from 1993 onward, to focus on NATO as the nexus of a future European security architecture. In the EU context Kinkel's stance paralleled Kohl's. While a vocal advocate of expansion eastward, Kinkel also shared Kohl's concern with deepening and the absolute priority of Franco-German partnership.[58] More serious differences emerged in the context of security issues. Kinkel and the Liberals were more cautious in carving out a more active German security role in the Balkans. In 1992 the FDP even questioned the constitutionality of German participation in the enforcement of the no-fly-zone over Bosnia. Yet in practice Liberal reservations did not hamper Kohl's efforts to increase German involvement in peacekeeping efforts in the region.

Kohl's strength within the coalition of the early 1990s was in part a function of the broader political configuration. The 1990 elections

---

57. In describing his vision, Genscher stated: "The unity of Europe is now a reality; the zone of democracy will inevitably expand even further. Here the CSCE can serve as a model" (interview).

58. For Kinkel's approach to these issues, see his Bundestag address of November 24, 1993, *Verhandlungen des deutschen Bundestags,* ser. 12, 16587–92.

strengthened the CDU/CSU's strategic position: the FDP and SPD together lacked a majority in the Bundestag, denying Liberals the opportunity of switching coalition partners before the 1994 elections. Moreover, the policy differences between the Liberals and the Social Democrats, on both foreign and domestic matters, remained considerable. In this context friction between CDU/CSU and FDP approaches to domestic economic and social problems in 1992–93—together with the foreign policy differences that were minor by comparison—did not seriously threaten to unravel the coalition. Kohl, who had faced the possibility of a Liberal defection in 1989, enjoyed the solid backing of the FDP in the run-up to the 1994 elections five years later. His post-reunification foreign policy priorities were firmly anchored at the level of coalition politics.

The implementation of Kohl's foreign policy priorities during and after reunification also depended on his continued capacity to isolate the Social Democrats in opposition. In the summer of 1989 the CDU/CSU was running behind the SPD in the polls going into the 1990 national election campaign. The revolution in the GDR and the rush to reunification, however, gave Kohl an opportunity to improve his position and that of his party. After the fall of the Berlin Wall, in early November 1989, Kohl spurned Social Democratic calls for bipartisan efforts to address the challenge of national unity. His Ten-Point Plan, sprung upon the opposition at the end of the month, seized the national issue for the CDU/CSU. Kohl was not only anxious to stabilize the revolutionary situation in the GDR. He reportedly also told CDU leaders it was crucial that the SPD not be allowed to steal the unity issue.[59]

Over the following year the rush to reunification divided the Social Democrats. Willy Brandt, honorary party chairman after his retirement in 1987, backed Kohl's Ten-Point Plan and the drive for unity. Many younger party leaders, more comfortable with the existence of two German states, were ambivalent.[60] Lafontaine, the party's chancellor candidate for the 1990 election, came out in favor of reunification in principle. But he called Kohl's Ten-Point Plan a failure, expressed skepticism of the

59. Teltschik, *329 Tage,* 53. According to Hans Klein, then minister for press and information, Kohl already thought in mid-August 1989 that unequivocal support for the goal of national unity would be a key to victory in the December 1990 elections. See Klein, *Es begann im Kaukasus,* 50–51. SPD chairman Hans-Jochen Vogel later argued that, had it not been an election year, Kohl would have been more likely to accept the SPD's offer of bipartisan cooperation (interview by author, Bonn, June 3, 1992).

60. The new SPD party program, approved in December 1989, was marked by ambiguity on the national issue. It called for German national unity but placed greater emphasis on both German states' interest in the promotion of European security. See *Grundsatzprogramm der Sozialdemokratischen Partei Deutschlands* (Bonn: Vorstand der SPD, 1989), 14.

government's efforts to win Gorbachev for NATO membership, and warned of the economic and social costs of unity.[61] In electoral terms these divisions within the SPD proved disastrous. The Social Democrats lost the first free elections in the GDR in March 1990, overrun by the CDU-East's promise of quick unity. The SPD fared better in May 1990 in two key elections in Western states, where uncertainty about the consequences of reunification abounded. After the breakthrough on NATO membership in the Caucasus in July, however, the ruling coalition amassed an insurmountable lead in the polls. Kohl ran a campaign around the historic achievement of unity and won reelection easily.[62]

The demoralizing SPD loss unleashed a prolonged leadership transition within the party. Engholm, elected chairman in April 1991, resigned two years later in connection with a scandal in his native Schleswig-Holstein. Scharping then defeated Gerhard Schröder, his main rival at the time, for the position of SPD chairman and chancellor candidate. Despite this leadership turmoil—and the status of opposition party—the SPD was able to challenge aspects of Kohl's foreign policy in the Bundesrat. With its majority in the Federal Chamber the SPD attached stringent conditions to the 1992 ratification of the Maastricht Treaty. Together with his colleagues—and over government objections—Scharping, then governor of Rhineland-Palatinate, insisted that German entry into a future monetary union require Bundesrat approval. The SPD also applauded aspects of the October 1993 Constitutional Court decision on Maastricht. The court ruled the treaty compatible with the Basic Law, as long as the EU was considered a confederation of states [*Staatenverbund*] and not a federal state [*Bundesstaat*] in its own right. The ruling further stipulated that both federal legislative organs, as the legitimate representatives of the German people, be empowered to accept or reject future transfers of sovereignty to European institutions.[63]

The sharpest conflict between government and opposition unfolded in the context of security policy. Scharping and other Social Democratic leaders insisted that any out-of-area military activity required a change in the Basic Law. In 1992 the SPD joined the FDP in a suit to determine the

---

61. Remarks on the Ten-Point Plan cited in *Bundespresseamt News Files,* December 4, 1989. In another interview Lafontaine charged that "Kohl's policy ran counter to the goal of reunification" (interview in *Bild,* December 4, 1989). On Lafontaine's warnings about the costs of unity, see his Bundestag address of September 20, 1990, *Verhandlungen des deutschen Bundestags,* ser. 11, 17808–16.

62. On the campaign and its outcome, see Herbert Kitschelt, "The 1990 German Federal Election and the National Unification: A Watershed in German Electoral History?" *West European Politics* 14, no. 4 (October 1991): 121–48.

63. Text of the decision of October 12, 1993, *Außenpolitik der Bundesrepublik Deutschland,* 967–71.

constitutionality of German participation in the enforcement of the weapons embargo and no-fly-zone in Bosnia. And at a November 1993 party conference the Social Democrats backed constitutional changes that would only allow for noncombat peacekeeping missions under UN auspices. In the end the Constitutional Court decision of July 1994 repudiated the thrust of the Social Democratic position. The ruling held that the reference to "collective security" as a framework for German armed forces in Article 24 of the Basic Law permitted out-of-area deployments within a multilateral framework. On one important point, however, the court sided with the SPD. The ruling required that all such deployments secure majority approval in the Bundestag.[64]

As he consolidated his position within the SPD in the run-up to the October 1994 elections, Scharping centered the campaign mainly around economic and social issues. He emphasized points of foreign policy agreement and sought to address Western concerns about SPD reliability—concerns still active a decade after the INF struggle. At a Munich security conference in February 1994, for example, Scharping called the alliance "indispensable." Once in government, he insisted, Social Democrats would be "reliable partners and not loose cannons."[65] Nevertheless, as the year wore on, Scharping did articulate somewhat contrasting priorities—his calls for a second New Ostpolitik and for a more reticent approach to German involvement in Bosnia.[66] As it happened, economic and social issues ultimately decided the election in favor of the CDU/CSU. With the help of an economic recovery Kohl's government secured reelection in October 1994, if only by a small margin. With the SPD still isolated in opposition, Kohl's foreign policy course retained the necessary political backing.

Taken together, then, political trends in the early 1990s favored the implementation of Kohl's foreign policy priorities. Authority atop the CDU/CSU, domination of the coalition with the FDP, and isolation of the SPD, anchored the absolute priority of Western unity at the level of domestic politics. Overall the political conflict over foreign policy was muted in the years after 1990—partly because of the greater salience of other issues, and partly because of the persistence of the broad consensus

---

64. Text of July 12, 1994 court decision in ibid., 1071–80. See Manfred H. Wiegandt, "Germany's International Integration: The Rulings of the German Federal Constitutional Court on the Maastricht Treaty and the Out-of-Area Deployment of German Troops," *American University Journal of International Law and Policy* 10 (winter 1995): 889–916.

65. Scharping cited in *Washington Post,* February 7, 1994.

66. On the party's call for a "new Ostpolitik" and opposition to combat missions abroad, see the resolutions of the SPD party conference of November 1993, *Perspektiven einer neuen Außen- und Sicherheitspolitik,* 5–6, 10–15.

forged by the late 1980s. The differences between Kohl and Scharping were differences of emphasis. Nevertheless, Kohl's dominance of German domestic politics still had important foreign policy consequences. It assured a high degree of continuity in the direction of FRG foreign policy across the 1990 divide and dispelled allied concerns that Germany might embrace a more national stance or more independent Ostpolitik in the wake of reunification.

Enduring Effects of Post-Reunification Choices

Reunification and the end of the cold war dramatically altered the context of German foreign policy. The collapse of the Soviet bloc confronted German leaders with the challenge of fostering economic, political, and security stability to its East. The German response to the challenge was framed by a dense web of institutions: NATO and the EU in the West and the Eastern Treaties and the OSCE in the East. The Federal Republic faced different ways to combine Western unity and Eastern engagement—the consolidation of NATO and the EU and their extension to the former Soviet bloc. And Germans faced different ways to adapt a traditionally reticent approach to security policy in the context of the war in the Balkans. Through the mid-1990s Kohl proved an ardent supporter of both deeper European integration and of German participation in multilateral efforts to end the war in Bosnia. Scharping, too, stressed the importance of unity with the West. At the same time, however, he was less enthusiastic about Maastricht, more committed to an active Ostpolitik, and wary of placing German armed forces in potential combat situations abroad. Kohl's strong position in German domestic politics in the aftermath of reunification made the implementation of his foreign policy priorities possible.

Kohl's focus on solidarity with the Western powers had important institutional and political consequences through the mid-1990s. Reunification within both the Atlantic Alliance and the European Union helped to secure the survival of both institutions after the collapse of the bipolar order within which they had emerged. In addition, German efforts to strengthen NATO and the EU in the years after 1990 contributed to their continued prominence as a framework for FRG foreign policy. In 1996–97 slow economic growth across Europe complicated the drive for a single European currency by the end of the decade. And the Maastricht II conference, completed in Amsterdam in June 1997, did not bring about major political reforms or progress toward a robust Common Foreign and Security Policy. Nevertheless, the German government's clear pro-European orientation continued to sustain efforts to deepen integration. In the NATO context controversy about the division of rights and responsibilities between the United States and its European partners periodically strained alliance unity. At the Madrid Summit of July 1997, for example, conflict between Washington and Paris over the distribution of command posts derailed efforts to bring France back into NATO's military integration. At the same time, however, strong German ties with both the United States and France, unbroken in the years after reunification, helped to preserve the alliance as a central framework for the new Federal Republic's foreign and security policy.[67]

Nowhere was this centrality more evident than in the context of Ostpolitik. While the new Eastern Treaties and the OSCE remained important frameworks for Germany's ties with its eastern neighbors, the EU and NATO came to overshadow them. The internal cohesion of both institutions across the 1990 divide, a top German foreign policy priority, facilitated their gradual transformation from Western into all-European institutions. In June 1997 the EU announced that accession negotiations with six Central and Eastern European states would begin the following year. Almost simultaneously, NATO announced plans for accession negotiations with Poland, Hungary, and the Czech Republic—Germany's top three candidates—and further institutionalized its political and security cooperation with Russia. Five years earlier Hans-Dietrich Genscher had underscored that Germans did not "want to monopolize relations with Russia and the other states of Central and Eastern Europe."[68] With EU and NATO expansion finally under way the Ostpolitik of the new Germany remained securely embedded within a multilateral framework.

German choices during the early 1990s not only embedded the new Federal Republic within strengthened institutions. They also helped to preserve a far-reaching domestic political consensus around a multilateral, supranational orientation. Within the governing coalition Rühe and Schäuble, who emerged as Kohl's probable successor as CDU leader by the mid-1990s, acknowledged the continued salience of NATO and the EU as a framework for German foreign policy. Schäuble did refer openly to problems of national identity and national interests after 1990. Like both Kohl and Rühe, however, he made Atlantic solidarity and European unity starting points for FRG foreign policy.[69] Stoiber and the CSU continued to snipe at Kohl's European policy from Munich. But their skepticism of

---

67. Philip H. Gordon, *France, Germany, and the Western Alliance* (Boulder: Westview, 1995), chap. 2; Gunther Hellmann, "Eine Flucht nach vorn ohne Ende? Die deutsch-französische Achse und die Vertiefung der europäischen Integration," *Aus Politik und Zeitgeschichte,* no. 30 (July 21, 1995): 19–27.

68. Genscher added: "Therefore, we asked our partners not to leave us alone in this policy, because it is one we have to conduct in any case" (interview).

69. See, for example, Rühe, *Deutschlands Verantwortung;* Wolfgang Schäuble and Rudolf Seiters, eds., *Außenpolitik im 21. Jahrhundert: Die Thesen der jungen Außenpolitiker* (Bonn: Bouvier, 1996), 11–27. For objections to the label "nationalist," see Schäuble's interview in *Die Woche,* September 9, 1994.

deeper political integration and monetary union reflected less a nationalist streak than concerns about Bavaria's role in the new Europe and the CSU's efforts to maintain its predominance in Bavarian politics. In Bonn, Waigel—finance minister and CSU chairman—supported Kohl's strong pro-integration stance.[70] Finally, Kinkel and the FDP continued to rally around Kohl's priorities. While economic and social policy differences periodically threatened to unravel the coalition in 1996–97, foreign policy remained an area of harmony.

A high degree of consensus was also evident in relations with the two main opposition parties, the SPD and the Greens. Lafontaine, who replaced Scharping as Social Democratic chairman in November 1995, was a veteran of the peace movement and an opponent of German military deployments abroad. He nevertheless continued Scharping's efforts to move the SPD toward a pragmatic acceptance of the Bundeswehr's new role. Most of the Social Democratic parliamentary group voted in December 1995 to support a German peacekeeping role in the Balkans. On the EU, too, differences between the CDU/CSU and SPD remained minimal. Gerhard Schröder, governor of Lower Saxony and the SPD's chancellor candidate in 1998, raised the possibility of a delay of monetary union. But he and other Social Democratic leaders underscored their continued support for the project in principle.[71] Support for a greater security role and deeper European integration was even evident among the Greens, who reentered the Bundestag after the 1994 elections. The chairman of the Green parliamentary group, Joschka Fischer, led a successful drive to moderate the party's opposition to military deployments abroad. And by the mid-1990s most Green leaders had abandoned their traditional opposition to NATO and skepticism of the EU. With the exception of the formerly communist PDS, the foreign policy consensus among the Bundestag parties remained robust.[72]

The course of German foreign policy in the early 1990s had important institutional and domestic political consequences. On the one hand, the Kohl government managed to anchor increased German power within established Western institutions. The new Germany remained embedded

---

70. Monetary union was not popular among most Germans inside and outside Bavaria. See Hans Rattinger, "Public Attitudes to European Integration in Germany after Maastricht: Inventory and Typology," *Journal of Common Market Studies* 32, no. 4 (December 1994): 525–40.

71. On the SPD and monetary union, see Michael J. Baun, "The SPD and EMU: An End to Germany's All-Party Consensus on European Integration?" *German Politics and Society* 15, no. 3 (autumn 1997): 1–23.

72. See Hans-Peter Hubert, ed., *Grüne Außenpolitik: Aspekte einer Debatte* (Göttingen: Die Werkstatt, 1993); Joschka Fischer, *Risiko Deutschland: Krise und Zukunft der deutschen Politik* (Köln: Kiepenheuer und Witsch, 1994).

within the EU and NATO, its Ostpolitik firmly grounded on a multilateral foundation. Concerns in 1990–91 about the possibility of a more nationally oriented German foreign policy faded in the years that followed. On the other hand, Kohl's policies helped to reinforce the broad domestic consensus around foreign policy that had emerged by the late 1980s. The CDU/CSU and the FDP—but also the SPD and the Greens—rallied around the view that solidarity with the West should guide the German response to new foreign policy problems in Russia and East and Central Europe. In 1995, five years after reunification and fifty years after the end of World War II, the Federal Republic remained anchored in the West and engaged in the East.

CHAPTER 6

History and German
Foreign Policy

The years after reunification attested to the enduring transformation of the German Problem. The collapse of superpower bipolarity and the emergence of pressing policy challenges in the East did not provoke a reorientation of German foreign policy. The contours of the pre-1945 German Problem—the dilemmas posed by German power and national interests—did not reemerge. On the one hand, Germany did not again find itself at the center of a fluid European balance of power. NATO, the EU, and other European institutions remained starting points for its foreign policy. On the other hand, no concerted efforts to define and pursue specifically *national* interests took place. A political consensus persisted around a strong multilateral, supranational foreign policy orientation. The continuity of this institutional and political configuration across the 1990 divide showed the enduring effects of postwar choices. At successive critical junctures chancellors from Konrad Adenauer through Helmut Kohl managed to embed German power within institutions and on a broad political foundation. Postwar legacies, not prewar parallels, best illuminate the dynamics of post-reunification foreign policy.

This argument about historical legacies and their effects is one of path dependence. German choices at postwar turning points—the cold war, detente, new cold war, and post–cold war periods—shaped institutional and political constellations, which in turn constrained subsequent choices. This trajectory does not imply determinism. There was nothing inevitable about the development of German foreign policy along this particular path. At each juncture complex international and domestic forces interacted to shape German choices. Faced with new policy problems and particular arrays of institutions, rivals for the chancellorship articulated contrasting foreign policy priorities and sought to anchor them within parties. A multidimensional analysis attentive to the effects of structure and institutions, ideas and politics, underscores the element of openness and contingency at each turning point. German foreign policy could have gone in different directions, less multilateral and less supranational. Only a detailed examination of its development from one period to the next—a task undertaken in the preceding chapters—can explain its enduring transformation in the decades after 1945.

This chapter is divided into two parts. Part 1 sets out the book's argument about path dependence. Through a comparison of the findings of the individual chapters, it traces the evolution of the institutional and political context of German foreign policy—before and after reunification. Part 2 sets out a related argument about historical memory. The institutional constellation created at successive critical junctures did not constitute a clear, cumulative constraint on German leaders. A particular historical narrative—a story linking power politics and nationalism with war and disaster, and international institutions with peace and prosperity—reinforced the strong German commitment to multilateralism and supranationalism. That narrative, originally contested within and across the parties, became an object of consensus by the late 1980s and early 1990s. Both before and after reunification, however, it generated opposition from more nationally oriented historians and political scientists. Whether or not the postwar transformation of German foreign policy persists will depend not only on changes in structure, institutions, and politics, but also on future German leaders' ideas about the lessons of the past.

The Institutional and Political Transformation

A comparison of the chapters immediately reveals a clear trend—a continual increase in German economic and military power over the postwar decades. Through the rapid economic growth of the 1950s and 1960s the Federal Republic established itself as the leading economic force in Europe, a position sustained through bouts of recession in the 1970s and 1980s. Reunification further increased its relative weight within the EU. The integration of the former GDR in the early 1990s did place tremendous strains on German resources. But it also added to the FRG's overall economic potential. The growth in German military power over the same period, though less dramatic, was also extensive. Rearmament in the 1950s made the Federal Republic the crucial European ally of the United States, a role it maintained over the subsequent decades. Bonn renounced the production of nuclear weapons, but its modern conventional forces played a crucial in NATO's defensive strategy. With the end of the cold war and the withdrawal of Russian and most allied troops from Germany, the Bundeswehr—even with its numbers reduced—remained the most potent army in Central Europe.

Despite its impressive economic and military capabilities, the new Germany was not in a position to dominate its neighbors. There was no return to the pre-1945 system of sovereign states balancing against one another in pursuit of strictly national interests. A focus on power and interests obscures far-reaching changes in the international and domestic contexts of German foreign policy. Over the postwar decades German power unfolded within NATO, the EC, and other institutions designed to reduce conflict and promote cooperation. The Federal Republic, a "tamed power" (Katzenstein), did not threaten its neighbors, East and West. Over the same period domestic politics transformed German interests. The leaders of the Federal Republic, like their counterparts elsewhere, pursued military security and economic prosperity. But they did so, willingly, through European institutions. By the 1980s a broad political consensus emerged around a multilateral, supranational foreign policy, anchored in the West and open to the East—a consensus that persisted after reunification. The leaders of the new Federal Republic, like those of the old, continued to conceive of German interests in European as well as national terms.

A comparison of the institutional context of German foreign policy at critical junctures reveals the emergence of an intricate web of institutional constraints over time. During the cold war of the early 1950s the institutions that framed German foreign policy into the 1990s—NATO and the EC, the Eastern Treaties and the CSCE—were not yet in place. The consolidation of opposing blocs, which later removed the unity issue from the top of the European agenda for decades, had yet to take shape. The young Federal Republic did find itself embedded in two important institutions: the Three- and Four-Power regimes that emerged out of World War II. The former restricted German sovereignty and ruled out a foreign policy directed against the Western powers, while the latter placed formal responsibility for the question of German unity in the hands of the victors. In some respects, though, this institutional configuration was less restrictive than those that followed. With the questions of rearmament and reunification still at the top of the European agenda, FRG leaders faced a choice subsequently denied them: whether to press for integration within Western security institutions or first insist that the allies intensify their efforts to reach a German settlement with the Soviet Union.

Adenauer's option for the former alternative—German membership in the Atlantic Alliance and the European Community—altered the institutional constellation facing his successors. Western integration brought with it external sovereignty and the dissolution of the Three-Power regime. But participation in NATO and the nascent EC also constrained the subsequent exercise of German military and economic power. Adenauer sanctioned limitations on German armed forces, including a renunciation of nuclear weapons, and integrated the Federal Republic's expanding economy with those of its neighbors. Western integration made multilateralism within NATO and supranationalism within the EC new points of departure for German foreign policy. This new institutional configuration not only ruled out a return to the unilateral seesaw policies of the past, but also undermined prospects for German unity in the near term. In response to German rearmament within NATO, the Soviet Union integrated the GDR into the Warsaw Pact. From the mid-1950s onward Moscow underscored the existence of two sovereign German states, while the Western allies showed little inclination to place the unity issue on the European agenda.

The onset of detente in the 1960s and the 1970s demonstrated the enduring effects of this new institutional constellation. As the superpowers moved toward political and security dialogue on the basis of the status quo of the division of Germany—particularly after the 1961 construction of the Berlin Wall—integration within NATO forced German leaders to adjust to the trend toward detente or face growing diplomatic isolation. The reduction in superpower hostility, most evident in the success of arms control talks, created pressure for abandonment of Adenauer's confrontational Ostpolitik. At the same time, however, the overall institutional context allowed for choices that were later precluded: whether or not to recognize the GDR as a second German state and engage Moscow in an active dialogue. Adenauer's successors had to decide whether to embrace a new Ostpolitik on the basis of the status quo or to press for better ties with the Soviet Union and its allies by downplaying, but not dropping, established positions on nonrecognition of the GDR and the Oder-Neisse border.

Willy Brandt's option for the first alternative anchored German power within a denser web of international institutions. His recognition of the existence of "two states in Germany" in October 1969 made possible both the bilateral Eastern Treaties and the multilateral CSCE, institutions predicated upon the division of Europe into blocs. From one perspective these new institutions increased German power and influence in Europe. They provided a framework for increased economic ties with the East and for the Federal Republic's emergence as the most important European partner of the Soviet Union. From another perspective, however, the treaties represented a further institutional constraint on the exercise of German power. Adenauer had argued that German economic and military strength—together with that of the allies—would ultimately compel the Soviet Union to agree to reunification on Western terms. Ludwig Erhard and Kurt Georg Kiesinger, while less confrontational in their approach to Moscow, nevertheless insisted on progress toward unity as a necessary condition for strong bilateral ties. While still committed to the goal of national unity, Brandt broke with this approach. After his recognition of the political and territorial status quo, no chancellor could make reunification an operative part of Ostpolitik.

The demise of detente in the late 1970s and early 1980s revealed the density of the institutional constellation of which the Federal Republic was a part. During the INF struggle, which reached its height in 1982–83, the prominence of both the Western alliance and the Eastern Treaties framed the policy alternatives confronting German leaders. In the run-up to first Pershing II deployments on German soil, membership in NATO constrained Bonn to accept new U.S. missiles or risk a major crisis in relations with its allies. At the same time, the Eastern Treaties—and the web of cooperative ties that had grown up around them—created an incentive for the FRG to continue the political and security dialogue with the Soviet Union, the GDR, and the rest of the Warsaw Pact. Bonn could neither break with the Western powers nor return to the confrontational Ostpolitik of the 1950s. In this context German leaders did not face a stark choice between solidarity with Washington and cooperation with Moscow. The institutional configuration allowed, instead, for alternative ways to strike a balance between the two.

Kohl's emphasis on solidarity with the United States, evident in his support for the Reagan administration's tough stance in INF talks, had institutional consequences. German approval of first missile deployments in late 1983 fostered the cohesion of the Western alliance, which had been badly strained during the early 1980s. Concerns about a possible German drift away toward neutrality proved unfounded. Although the economic power and military clout of the FRG continued to grow during the 1980s, its foreign policy remained firmly anchored within multilateral Western institutions. The Eastern Treaties, too, continued to serve as a framework for Ostpolitik. German-Soviet ties stagnated through the mid-1980s, as Moscow sought to punish Bonn for its Atlantic solidarity, but then improved rapidly in the wake of the 1987 INF Treaty. On the eve of reunification the Federal Republic was anchored in European institutions, East and West, more securely than at any previous juncture.

This overall institutional constellation proved crucial once the GDR unexpectedly collapsed. In 1989–90 the strength of the Western alliance, in combination with ongoing institutional links with the Soviet Union, facilitated a rush to reunification. Together with the Western allies, and ultimately with Soviet approval, the Kohl government secured the new Federal Republic's membership within NATO, the EC, and a stronger CSCE. With the "Two-Plus-Four" accord Germans finally achieved full sovereignty over their internal affairs and assumed control in Berlin. At the same time, however, their foreign policy remained entwined within a robust multilateral and supranational framework. That framework allowed for different approaches to the pressing policy challenges of the early 1990s—economic and political stability in Central and Eastern Europe and the former Soviet Union and the war in the former Yugoslavia. But it also all but ruled out a return to a strictly national foreign policy orientation or an independent Ostpolitik. European institutions persisted as a framework for German foreign policy after the cold war.

A comparison of German policy at four key postwar turning points reveals not only the persistence of international institutions as a context for FRG foreign policy, but also their increasing salience through time. As the Federal Republic grew stronger economically and militarily, its leaders embedded it within an ever more intricate institutional framework. Successive layers of international institutions—the Three- and Four-Power regimes, NATO and the EC, and the Eastern Treaties and the CSCE—ruled out unilateral, aggressive foreign policies and made German economic and military strength less threatening to its neighbors. Multilateralism within NATO and supranationalism within the EC were most critical; German security policy became inseparable from that of its allies, while more and more of its economic policies were brokered at the European level. Both patterns held after reunification.

The German case convincingly demonstrates that the logic of path dependence can be applied to international politics. Most efforts to demonstrate the persistence of institutions and their effects through time have focused on domestic policies.[1] At first glance such a focus makes sense given the greater density of institutions at the national level and the authority of executive, legislative, and judicial branches of government. International relations, with its absence of final sovereign authority, is marked by less institutional density and stability. As the German case illustrates, however, international institutions can have important foreign policy effects through time. Over the course of its history the Federal Republic became embedded within a set of overlapping European institutions. Those institutions, created at critical junctures, constrained subse-

---

1. See, for example, Sven Steinmo, Kathleen Thelen, and Frank Longstreth, eds., *Structuring Politics: Historical Institutionalism in Comparative Analysis* (Cambridge: Cambridge University Press, 1992); Theda Skocpol, *Protecting Soldiers and Mothers: The Political Origins of Social Policy in the United States* (Cambridge: Harvard University Press, 1992). For an application to EU social policy, see Paul Pierson, "The Path to European Integration: A Historical Institutionalist Analysis," *Comparative Political Studies* 29, no. 2 (April 1996): 123–63.

quent German choices even in the face of a revolutionary structural change: the collapse of the bipolar European order. The Federal Republic's strong multilateral, supranational orientation after reunification is only explainable against a historical backdrop.

Over the postwar decades changes in the institutional context of German foreign policy went hand in hand with the emergence of a broad domestic political consensus around a shared foreign policy orientation. In the face of an increasingly intricate institutional constellation, the policy priorities espoused by rivals for the chancellorship gradually converged. Every critical postwar juncture gave rise to a political conflict over the direction of foreign policy. But the outcome of those struggles—and the policies they produced—generated greater domestic consensus and support for international institutions at the next juncture. As a result, the polarization of the debate declined over time. Successive chancellors had less and less difficulty anchoring their particular policy priorities on a political foundation—in their parties, in coalitions, and in competition with the opposition. On the eve of reunification a broad consensus had emerged around a multilateral, supranational foreign policy, firmly anchored in the West and engaged in the East. That consensus continued to shape German foreign policy in the wake of reunification.

The political struggle over German foreign policy was most intense during the early 1950s. Within a still inchoate set of institutions Adenauer and Kurt Schumacher clashed over fundamental foreign policy priorities. Both supported close ties with the Western powers. But they espoused different approaches to the central issues still on the German foreign policy agenda—rearmament and reunification. Schumacher charged that rapid rearmament in the Western alliance threatened to deepen the German division, while Adenauer insisted it was necessary to meet the Soviet threat. The bitterness of the foreign policy debate, reinforced by the sensitivity of the national issues involved, complicated Adenauer's efforts to secure sufficient political support for his foreign policy priorities. In the CDU/CSU Adenauer's course met with resistance from Jakob Kaiser and his allies. At the level of coalition politics he had to overcome the skepticism of nationally minded Liberals like Thomas Dehler. And Adenauer only finally realized his priority of Western integration after consecutive electoral victories over the SPD in 1949 and 1953.

Adenauer's success in anchoring the Federal Republic within NATO and the EC had domestic political consequences. Faced with the status quo of integration within Western institutions, his opponents gradually embraced the outlines of his foreign policy. By the late 1950s the reality of two emergent blocs, Soviet insistence on the existence of two sovereign

German states, and Western reluctance to place the unity issue on the European agenda deflected domestic political demands for an active reunification policy. The move from the ECSC to the Treaty of Rome and the creation of the Bundeswehr within NATO helped to reconcile Adenauer's opponents to the new institutional status quo. Just as important, the chancellor's crushing electoral victories in 1953 and 1957 indicated growing societal acceptance of Western integration. By 1955 Adenauer's foreign policy became an object of consensus within the CDU/CSU. And by 1960 both the Free Democrats and the Social Democrats embraced NATO and the EC as a new point of departure for German foreign policy.

The political struggle over the Eastern Treaties was only slightly less polarized. Brandt and Kiesinger, rivals for the chancellorship in the late 1960s, differed over the appropriate German response to East-West detente. As in the 1950s, the national issue was central to the controversy. From Brandt's perspective an active Ostpolitik on the basis of the status quo of the German division promised to increase ties between Germans in the FRG and the GDR and preserve the cultural unity of the German nation. Kiesinger, while generally supportive of detente, countered that recognition of the GDR and the Oder-Neisse border would only solidify the German division. On balance Brandt faced fewer political obstacles to the realization of his foreign policy than had Adenauer. Opposition to the New Ostpolitik within the SPD was less pronounced than opposition to Western integration in the CDU/CSU had been. Brandt's alliance with the FDP was initially unstable, but Foreign Minister Walter Scheel managed to rally the Liberals behind the government's foreign policy stance. Competition with the opposition, however, proved just as fierce as it had been during the early 1950s. The clash with the CDU/CSU over the Eastern Treaties was comparable to the bitter controversies surrounding Adenauer's policy of Western integration.

As it had during the 1950s, institutional change in the 1970s altered the subsequent domestic political landscape. The emergence of German cooperation with Moscow, Warsaw, and East Berlin on the basis of the status quo contributed to a growing consensus around the Eastern Treaties as an institutional foundation of German foreign policy. So, too, did the repeated successes of the SPD at the polls. In 1972 and again with Helmut Schmidt as the party's chancellor candidate in 1976 and 1980, the New Ostpolitik and Social Democratic "peace policy" contributed to government victories. In the face of both institutional constraints and political logic the CDU/CSU came to embrace the Eastern Treaties as a central component of Ostpolitik. Social Democrats and Christian Democrats continued to clash over the interpretation of the Eastern Treaties and their relative importance alongside NATO and the EC. Among CDU/CSU hard-liners, harsh anti-Soviet rhetoric and an insistence on reunification as a core component of Ostpolitik persisted into the early 1980s. But the outlines of a consensus began to emerge around the imperatives of strong alignment with the West *and* active engagement in the East.

The INF struggle of the early 1980s, while bitter, was not as divisive as the two previous major foreign policy controversies. The peace movement, opposed to INF deployments on German soil under any circumstances and skeptical of the NATO alliance, injected polarization into the political debate. But the major rivals for the chancellorship, Kohl and Schmidt, articulated broadly convergent foreign policy approaches. Neither considered breaking with the United States or NATO over the INF issue, and both were committed to a continuation of the thrust of the New Ostpolitik. Kohl faced less resistance than Adenauer and Brandt in anchoring his main foreign policy priority—solidarity with the United States—on a firm political basis. Once he defeated Franz Josef Strauss in a drawn-out CDU/CSU leadership struggle, Kohl was able to form a coalition with the FDP in 1982 based on a core bargain—Christian Democratic support for the New Ostpolitik in exchange for Liberal support of Atlantic solidarity. The new coalition then defeated the SPD in the 1983 national elections, making possible Bundestag approval of first INF deployments that same year.

Kohl's success in carrying out NATO policy at the height of the INF struggle ultimately contributed to an even stronger domestic political consensus. In the context of the downturn in detente and the confrontational anti-Soviet stance of the Reagan administration, the SPD broke with the United States on the INF issue. After the social-liberal coalition collapsed in the summer of 1982, Social Democrats came out against the proposed deployments—and isolated themselves within the alliance. By the mid-1980s, however, the reality of the new missiles and the continued cohesion of NATO sparked a slow reorientation of the SPD stance. More important, the INF Treaty of 1987 and NATO's embrace of arms control during the renewed detente of the late 1980s reduced the dissonance between the SPD and the Western allies. By 1989 the centrality of German ties with NATO was again the object of a broad agreement within the party. In the meantime, CDU/CSU hard-liners around Strauss, charmed by Gorbachev, had given up their last objections to an active Ostpolitik based on the political reality of Germany's division. On the eve of reunification the political consensus around both Western integration and Eastern engagement was more robust than at any previous juncture.

German foreign policy during and after reunification illustrated the resilience of this consensus. When the GDR collapsed in 1989–90, all three of the major parties supported reunification within NATO and the EC and strong institutional links between the new Germany and its eastern neighbors. In the years that followed, Kohl and a succession of SPD leaders backed efforts to strengthen the Atlantic Alliance and the integration process and to address new policy challenges in the East. On balance Kohl placed greater emphasis on solidarity with the Western powers than did Rudolf Scharping and other Social Democratic leaders—on a more active role for the German military and the crucial importance of European Monetary Union. But overall policy differences were minor. Kohl had fewer problems placing his foreign policy on a domestic political foundation in the early 1990s than he had a decade earlier. His authority within the CDU/CSU and in the coalition with the FDP was unchallenged in the years after reunification. And by the mid-1990s the Greens and the SPD in opposition overcame most of their initial reservations about a more active role for the Bundeswehr in NATO's out-of-area operations and the introduction of a European currency by the end of the decade. Kohl's focus on solidarity with the West amid new circumstances came to be shared across the political spectrum.

A comparison of the four critical postwar junctures reveals the gradual emergence of a robust German foreign policy consensus. As successive chancellors won support for new policy departures—and changes in international institutions generated additional foreign policy constraints—the polarization of the foreign policy debate declined. In the early 1950s, when rearmament and reunification were still on the agenda and NATO and the EC were not yet in place as frameworks for German foreign policy, the political struggle was most intense. First Western integration and then the New Ostpolitik created overlapping institutional constraints that dampened subsequent controversies. As a result of this dynamic, the major parties converged by the late 1980s in support of a multilateral, supranational foreign policy, anchored in the West and open to the East. During the early 1990s no political contest over German national interests or a more independent Ostpolitik erupted.

The evolution of the domestic political context of German foreign policy highlights an important characteristic of path-dependent development—the tendency of coalitions to form around existing institutions, reinforcing their effects through time. In the context of domestic policy, interest groups and parts of the bureaucracy with a material stake in a given policy tend to dominate such coalition politics. This is also true of certain aspects of foreign economic policy. Where international issues have broader political salience, however, as they did in the case of successive German controversies around issues like national unity and military security, major parties tend to drive the coalition dynamics in support of institutions. Confronted with a shifting international constellation, successive Christian and Social Democratic leaders backed stronger bonds with international institutions—and won the necessary party and electoral support to implement them. Only in conjunction with domestic politics did European institutions shape the direction of foreign policy through time. The norms of multilateralism, supranationalism, and cooperation were not simply imposed from above; they shaped German foreign policy to the extent they did because Germans made them their own.

Historical Memory and the Future of German Foreign Policy

Both these postwar trends, the institutional and the political, underscore the enduring transformation of the German Problem. The Federal Republic still must cope with an international balance of power and formulate its interests. In contrast to the pre-1945 decades, however, German power is embedded in a dense web of institutions while avowed German interests in a peaceful, multilateral, and supranational foreign policy rest upon a democratic political consensus. The problems facing German leaders after 1990, like those facing their counterparts across Europe, revolve around choices at the intersection of international institutions and domestic politics. How should the new Germany combine integration in the West with engagement in the East? Should it make a deeper or a wider EU its top priority? To what degree should it participate in multilateral military operations outside NATO's defensive perimeter? Will patterns of domestic politics permit, or encourage, a greater focus on relations with Germany's Eastern neighbors, a less enthusiastic stance toward European integration, or a still less reticent approach to the use of the Bundeswehr? The traditional German Problem has faded, leaving myriad smaller, less momentous German problems in its place.

Will the postwar transformation of the German Problem persist into the future? Could Germany once again find itself at the center of a fluid balance of power? Might it once again assertively pursue exclusively national interests? It is difficult to imagine a repeat of the prewar past. A stable democracy with limited military capabilities, the new Germany is unlikely ever again to threaten its neighbors. The specific content of the old German Problem—how to protect Europe against German aggression—will likely remain irrelevant. Its contours, however, the centrality of German power and German national interests, could again become salient. Several developments, alone or in combination, could create an opening for a more power-centered, nationally oriented policy: a revived Russian military threat, an outbreak of instability in Central and Eastern Europe, a U.S. withdrawal from Europe, or renewed Franco-German rivalry. Each of these developments is unlikely in the short or medium term, given the continued robustness of European institutions, their gradual extension to the East, and their ongoing role as a framework for political and military cooperation in the West. Still, a crisis or even collapse of major European institutions—NATO, the EU, or the OSCE—cannot be ruled out altogether.

Ultimately, however, whether a reorientation of German foreign policy takes place will depend not only on the international configuration, but also on the German response to it. At critical postwar junctures external constraints did not dictate the course of German foreign policy. The Federal Republic's embrace of multilateralism and supranationalism also reflected particular perceptions of the international constellation and interpretations of the past and its lessons. Future perceptions cannot be predicted with any accuracy, given the different directions in which Europe and the world might move in the coming decades. Established views of history and its lessons, however, may persist well into the next century and continue to underpin a multilateral, supranational foreign policy orientation. The decades after 1945 saw the emergence of a dominant historical narrative that contrasted prewar disasters with postwar achievements. A comparison of the chapters illustrates its development through successive policy controversies and its resilience in the wake of reunification. Some historians and political scientists have articulated alternative views of history, less critical of Bismarck's Reich and more critical of the old Federal Republic. For both political and substantive reasons, however, these counter-narratives, and the more national orientation they support, are unlikely to shape the evolution of German foreign policy in the foreseeable future.

The dominant postwar narrative emerged only gradually. At critical postwar junctures rivals for the chancellorship clashed over historical memory and its foreign policy implications. Their divergent accounts of the pre- and post-1945 periods underpinned different historical lessons and informed contrasting policy priorities. During the transition from the cold war to detente to the new cold war, however, a convergence of historical perspectives took place. The consensus narrative, articulated by the leaders of the major parties in the wake of reunification, contrasted prewar disasters (nationalism, seesaw policy, power politics, and war) with postwar achievements (supranational integration, multilateralism, cooperation, and peace). It construed the new Germany's multilateral, supranational orientation both as a necessary break with pre-1945 precedent and as a constructive extension of post-1945 experience.

The repudiation of the Nazi past was a major theme of German foreign policy controversy from the founding of the Federal Republic. Adenauer and Schumacher interpreted Hitler's negative legacy in different ways. For Adenauer, past German nationalism necessitated solidarity with the allies and supranational integration in the present. German leaders, he insisted, should slowly win back the trust of allied leaders and move to anchor German economic and military potential within Western institutions. For Schumacher, the Nazi catastrophe made necessary the repudiation of nationalism but not of national interests. A failure to press those interests, he argued, would result in the continued subordination of Western Germany and its separation from the East. And such a constellation, he warned, might spark a nationalist reaction within Germany like that between the wars—with disastrous consequences. Adenauer drew narrative links between the Nazi period and his policy of Western integration, while Schumacher buttressed his more national orientation by positing different connections between the pre- and postwar periods.

Once Western integration took effect the SPD leadership gradually abandoned Schumacher's narrative for Adenauer's. Social Democratic leaders acknowledged German integration within NATO and the EC as important breaks with a destructive nationalist legacy. During the struggle over the New Ostpolitik, however, a new set of historical differences emerged. In the context of detente Brandt and Kiesinger drew contrasting links between the prewar period and its postwar implications. Brandt insisted that Hitler's brutal war in the East necessitated recognition of the postwar status quo, while Kiesinger and others warned that an active Ostpolitik might evoke memories of seesaw policies between the wars. In the 1960s and 1970s controversy also extended to conflicting interpretations of postwar FRG foreign policy. Kiesinger stressed Adenauer's achievement of Western integration and voiced concern that the New Ostpolitik might undermine it. Brandt, for his part, praised Western integration as a historic accomplishment but insisted that Adenauer and his successors had not done enough to promote reconciliation with the East and address the painful separation of Germans in the FRG and the GDR. While the leaders of both major parties continued to support Western integration as a necessary break with a disastrous past, they differed over the lessons of history for policy amid detente.

Once the New Ostpolitik took effect, CDU/CSU leaders slowly assimilated aspects of Brandt's narrative. Kohl and other top Christian

Democrats continued to stress Adenauer's achievements but also gradually embraced Brandt's link between World War II and the imperative of reconciliation with the East. During the new cold war of the early 1980s, however, some dissonance persisted. The major parties clashed over the relative importance of postwar achievements—Western integration and the Eastern Treaties—as backdrops for German foreign policy. Kohl insisted on the absolute priority of ties with the United States in order to safeguard the historic accomplishment of Western integration under difficult circumstances. And Schmidt justified his efforts to mediate between the superpowers as a way to secure and expand the positive legacy of the New Ostpolitik. After the end of the INF crisis the renewed detente of the late 1980s sparked greater convergence around a shared narrative— one that construed unity with the West and engagement in the East as both a break with prewar catastrophe and an extension of postwar success.

Both components of this dominant narrative, the negative and the positive, persisted in the wake of reunification. CDU/CSU and SPD leaders did clash over the relative contribution of Western integration and the New Ostpolitik to the realization of national unity. And while Kohl drew links between Adenauer's strong pro-Western stance and his own, SPD leaders called for a second New Ostpolitik to address problems in the East. These differences of emphasis, however, did not displace broad agreement around history and its foreign policy implications. Leaders from both major parties drew links between the legacy of nationalism and support for deeper European integration and between the legacy of war and the importance of security policy anchored firmly within NATO. At the same time, CDU/CSU and SPD leaders—together with their Liberal and Green counterparts—construed both Western integration and the New Ostpolitik as positive legacies of the old Federal Republic to be preserved under new circumstances.

The persistence of this narrative suggests the robustness of the post-1990 consensus around a multilateral, supranational foreign policy. With their negative assessment of pre-1945 foreign policy and their positive construal of what followed, the major parties effectively narrowed the range of the post-reunification foreign policy debate. On those few occasions when politicians like Gerhard Schröder and Edmund Stoiber questioned the consensus, they provoked a barrage of historically grounded criticism. For example, Schröder's October 1995 suggestion that EMU be postponed—and that Social Democrats might be able to take advantage of the "national issue"—engendered warnings against any revival of nationalist thinking, both inside and outside the SPD. Schröder subsequently changed his tone. He underscored his commitment to deeper European integration—while insisting that Germany not suffer economically through the introduction of EMU. His reversal and the SPD's decision not to make EMU a national issue during the 1990s attested to the resilience of the postwar narrative. Political elites continued to define German foreign policy as a sharp break with a destructive, nationalist past.

This consensus view of history and its lessons will not necessarily persist into the future. The core of the dominant narrative—the sharp contrast between prewar disasters and postwar accomplishments—has never been the object of consensus outside the political elite. Over the postwar period, and with renewed vigor after reunification, many prominent historians and political scientists have cast pre-1945 experience in a less negative light and post-1945 experience in a less positive one. With very few exceptions politicians and academics alike have condemned Nazism as a catastrophe and praised the postwar transition to democracy and peace. At the same time, however, their assessments of German foreign policy before and after World War II have diverged in important respects. Were they ever to inform the political debate, more favorable assessments of the Kaiserreich and more critical stances toward the old Federal Republic could legitimate a more national German foreign policy orientation.

Contemporary controversy around the Kaiserreich and its foreign policy can be traced to the postwar decades. The leading historian of the 1950s, Gerhard Ritter, construed the German empire as a normal nation and the outbreak of World War I as the result of mismanagement of the European balance of power. During the 1960s Fritz Fischer and his allies portrayed the Reich as an aggressive autocracy that plunged Europe into World War I and suggested lines of continuity between Bismarck and Hitler—Germany's negative "special path" [*Sonderweg*]. While it shattered the postwar consensus, the Fischer controversy did not replace one orthodoxy with another. Through the 1980s sympathetic portrayals of the Kaiserreich persisted. Their more positive construal of the prewar balance of power system—and Germany's position within it—suggested the possibility of a more national, less multilateral and supranational orientation for the Federal Republic. While a major representative of this approach, Michael Stürmer, espoused a pro-Atlantic orientation, two other influential conservatives, Ernst Nolte and Andreas Hillgruber, advocated a more nationalist stance. By questioning the unique horror of the Holocaust, they aimed to create a positive line of continuity between Bismarck's Reich and the Federal Republic. The ensuing debate, Charles Maier pointed out at the time, "revealed more potential national orientations" and "weakened inhibitions on thinking through national options openly."[2]

---

2. Charles S. Maier, *The Unmasterable Past: History, Holocaust, and German National Identity* (Cambridge: Harvard University Press, 1988), 8.

Efforts to construct a "usable Kaiserreich" as a point of reference for German foreign policy continued in the wake of reunification.[3] In new books Stürmer and Gregor Schöllgen posited broad continuities in the dynamics of German foreign policy, before and after 1945. In the "primacy of foreign policy" tradition both authors used the same categories of power, interest, and geography to analyze the broad sweep of German foreign policy from before 1871 to after 1990. Along the same lines Arnulf Baring and Hans-Peter Schwarz—both political scientists—maintained that Germany had returned to its traditional role as Europe's central power. These authors all acknowledged Bonn's postwar foreign policy as a break with destructive nationalist and militarist traditions. And they underscored the different nature of power and interests in the late nineteenth and late twentieth centuries. At the same time, however, they did not dismiss Bismarck's Reich as a model for the new Federal Republic. They insisted that the reunified Germany, like its unified predecessor, acknowledge the reality of its power and define and pursue its own independent national interests in the new Europe.[4]

The years after 1990 saw the emergence of a second, complementary historical interpretation: a more critical appraisal of the foreign policy of West Germany. Some scholars were critical of postwar FRG policy for its lack of attention to national interests. Rainer Zitelmann, Karlheinz Weissmann, and others, self-consciously national in outlook, focused critical attention on Adenauer's drive for Western integration. While acknowledging integration into Western institutions as a positive break with autocratic and militarist traditions, they also lamented the loss of national identity and orientation that it entailed. Within this narrative, already prefigured in some of the conservative historiography of the 1980s, the end of the war marked not only liberation from dictatorship but also subordination under the Western powers and the United States in particular. For the most part the "New Right" intellectuals who articulated this narrative did not advocate abandoning NATO and the EU or embracing neutrality. But

---

3. On this general theme, see Roger Chickering, "The Quest for a Usable Kaiserreich," in *Imperial Germany: A Historiographical Companion,* ed. Roger Chickering (Westport, Conn.: Greenwood Press, 1996), 1–12 ; Stefan Berger, *The Search for Normality: National Identity and Historical Consciousness in Germany since 1800* (Providence: Berghahn, 1997), chap. 9; Konrad H. Jarausch, "Normalisierung oder Re-Nationalisierung: Zur Umdeutung der deutschen Vergangenheit," *Geschichte und Gesellschaft* 21, no. 4 (1995): 571–84.

4. Michael Stürmer, *Die Grenzen der Macht: Begegnung der Deutschen mit der Geschichte* (Berlin: Siedler, 1992); Gregor Schöllgen, *Die Macht in der Mitte Europas: Stationen deutscher Außenpolitik von Friedrich dem Großen bis zur Gegenwart* (Munich: Beck, 1992); Arnulf Baring, ed., *Germany's New Position in Europe: Problems and Perspectives* (Oxford: Berg, 1994); Hans-Peter Schwarz, *Die Zentralmacht Europas. Deutschlands Rückkehr auf die Weltbühne* (Berlin: Siedler, 1994).

they coupled their critique of Western integration, and their positive portrayal of Adenauer's more nationally minded opponents, with a call for a
more assertive defense of German interests after reunification.[5]

Other scholars criticized the foreign policy of the old Federal Republic for its lack of attention to power. Schöllgen, for example, argued that
postwar German foreign policy exhibited an almost pathological anxiety
about power and its exercise. After reunification, he insisted, the new Germany should overcome its historically grounded fears and assume responsible leadership in the new Europe. Schwarz also pursued this line of argument. As early as 1985, he had criticized German foreign policy for its
"power amnesia" [*Machtvergessenheit*]. Traumatized by the past, he
argued, German leaders had opted to reject the categories of power and
interest and hide instead behind international institutions and idealistic
rhetoric. Schwarz reiterated his critique of power amnesia after
reunification. With its continued obsession with the Nazi past, he argued,
the new Germany threatened to abdicate its leadership role in the new
Europe. As Schwarz put it, "traumatized giants must reflect on their
future, even when their lazy spirit always mulls over the recent and distant
past."[6]

Taken together, the more positive portrayal of the Kaiserreich and
less positive assessment of the Federal Republic clashed sharply with the
foreign policy narrative espoused across the leading parties. While the
dominant narrative stressed continuities across the 1990 divide, the
counter-narrative stressed discontinuities. It construed the old Federal
Republic less as a stable, prosperous member of an international democratic community than as part of a divided nation, subordinate to the superpowers and paralyzed by the catastrophe of Nazism, war, and genocide.
And it portrayed the new FRG less as an extension of the old than as a
German nation state in the pre-1945 mold: united and sovereign, again
Europe's leading power. The policy implications of this contrasting narra-
tive were clear: the new Germany should define and pursue its national

---

5. See, for example, Rainer Zitelmann, Michael Großheim, and Karlheinz Weißmann,
eds., *Westbindung: Chancen und Risiken für Deutschland* (Frankfurt am Main: Ullstein,
1993); Rainer Zitelmann, *Adenauers Gegner: Streiter für die Einheit* (Erlangen: Straube,
1991); Karlheinz Weißmann, *Rückruf in die Geschichte: Die deutsche Herausforderung*
(Berlin: Ullstein, 1992). For the articulation of these historical themes before 1990, see Hellmut Diwald, *Geschichte der Deutschen* (Frankfurt am Main: Ullstein, 1978), 83–135. For a
critique, see Hans-Ulrich Wehler, *Die Gegenwart als Geschichte: Essays* (Munich: Beck,
1995), 138–43.

6. Gregor Schöllgen, *Angst vor der Macht: Die Deutschen und ihre Außenpolitik* (Berlin:
Ullstein, 1992); Hans-Peter Schwarz, *Die gezähmten Deutschen: Von der Machtbessessenheit
zur Machtvergessenheit* (Stuttgart: Deutsche Verlags-Anstalt, 1985); Schwarz, *Die Zentralmacht Europas*, 13. For a critique, see Wehler, *Die Gegenwart als Geschichte*, 254–62.

interests unburdened by a disastrous past. It should break with the exaggerated multilateral, supranational orientation of the old Federal Republic—the product of exceptional, abnormal postwar circumstances—and assume an active leadership role in Europe and the world. Jürgen Habermas and other critics construed this as an effort to finally free Germans "from the trauma of mass crimes" and give them back their "national innocence."[7]

Were this narrative to gain adherents within the political elite, it could come to inform a more national foreign policy orientation. Through the mid-1990s, however, its impact outside certain academic and journalistic circles was minimal. The June 1991 Bundestag debate on whether to move the capital of the new Federal Republic from Bonn to Berlin was an important watershed. The vote was narrowly decided in favor of the old Reich capital. But the arguments put forward in support of Berlin centered on the importance of overcoming the East-West divide and the heroic story of West Berlin's perseverance during the postwar decades—not historical continuities with the Kaiserreich.[8] The New Right did make some inroads in the ranks of the CDU/CSU and among those fringe groups still unreconciled to the Oder-Neisse border. And it enjoyed the sympathies of some of the editors of the influential conservative *Frankfurter Allgemeine Zeitung*. But the overall impact of its efforts to project a "self-confident nation" and transform the political culture of the old Federal Republic and its foreign policy orientation was extremely modest. The dominant postwar narrative, and the foreign policy orientation it reinforced, endured.[9]

Historical perspectives conducive to a new foreign policy departure not only exercised little political appeal through the mid-1990s; they were also inherently flawed. There was nothing inherently problematic about sympathetic appraisals of the Kaiserreich and its domestic and foreign policies. The historical evidence has allowed for divergent assessments of Germany's pre-1945 historical trajectory—and will continue to do so in the future. At the same time, however, historical parallels between the foreign policy of the reunified Germany and its unified predecessor a century ear-

---

7. Jürgen Habermas, *Vergangenheit als Zukunft* (Zürich: Pendo-Verlag, 1991), 42.

8. Debate of June 21, 1991, *Verhandlungen des deutschen Bundestags: Stenographischer Bericht,* ser. 12, 2735–926.

9. Friedbert Pflüger, *Deutschland driftet: Die konservative Revolution entdeckt ihre Kinder* (Düsseldorf: Econ-Verlag, 1994); John Ely, "The *Frankfurter Allgemeiner Zeitung* and Contemporary National Conservatism," *German Politics and Society* 13, no. 2 (summer 1995): 81–121. On the theme of a "self-confident nation," see Heimo Schwilk and Ulrich Schacht, eds., *Die selbstbewußte Nation* (Frankfurt am Main: Ullstein, 1995).

lier are unsustainable. Yes, the new Germany, like Bismarck's Reich after 1871, is a powerful country at the heart of Europe. But the international and domestic contexts of its foreign policy are different in fundamental respects. A web of international institutions and a broad consensus in favor of multilateral, supranational foreign policy—the product of four decades of postwar development—separate the new Germany from its pre-1945 predecessor. The image of a sovereign Germany adrift in a shifting balance of power—the thrust of the old German Problem—does not reflect European reality at the end of the twentieth century.

Critical portrayals of the old Federal Republic as inattentive to interests or prone to power amnesia also distort the historical record. German leaders from Adenauer through Kohl did not abjure the pursuit of German interests or ignore international power realities. Against the backdrop of World War II, the rise of the superpowers, and the onset of European integration, they refused to conceptualize those interests in strictly national terms. They deliberately sought to anchor the exercise of German power within a multilateral, supranational framework—and were able to secure political support for their efforts. Given the legacy of German aggression this century, an independent, power-centered foreign policy would almost certainly have sparked anxieties abroad and threatened the Federal Republic with political isolation. The new German Problem—multiple foreign policy challenges at the intersection of international institutions and domestic politics—is one that Germans and their neighbors can live with in peace. There is no need for politicians or scholars to conjure up the old one.

The GDR and the German Problem

The course of GDR foreign policy reinforces this book's central argument about the transformation of the German Problem. In East as well as West Germany a determination to break with nationalist, militarist traditions informed official foreign policy from the outset. The GDR, like the Federal Republic, was embedded within a robust set of international institutions, its basic foreign policy orientation the object of domestic political consensus. At first glance such parallels seem superficial and misleading. While officially opposed to militarism, East German leaders loyally supported Soviet military interventions in Hungary and Czechoslovakia. The SED regime's key institutional affiliation was membership in the Soviet-dominated Warsaw Pact, and its one-party dictatorship precluded any open foreign policy debate. Despite these sharp contrasts, certain parallels between postwar East and West German foreign policy development are significant—particularly in the wake of reunification. After 1990, differences between both parts of the country, compounded by forty years of separation, complicated the political, economic, and social dimensions of reunification. In the foreign policy context, however, the legacy of both German states' official repudiation of a nationalist and militarist past—though articulated in very different idioms—reinforced continuity in the foreign policy of the new Federal Republic.

In the case of the GDR, like that of the FRG, that repudiation rested on a particular view of history and its consequences.[1] From the late 1940s onward East German leaders conceived of the GDR as a break with

---

1. On the general theme of contrasting historical perspectives in East and West Germany and their implications for domestic politics, see Jeffrey Herf, *Divided Memory: The Nazi Past in the Two Germanys* (Cambridge: Harvard University Press, 1997); Jane Kramer, *The Politics of Memory: Looking for Germany in the New Germany* (New York: Random House, 1996).

nationalist, militarist German traditions. Within the context of Marxist-Leninist ideology the East German state represented a more complete break than its Western counterpart. The FRG was ruled by the same capitalist elites who had dominated Wilhelmine Germany, maintained their grip through the Weimar Republic, and helped Hitler to power. With the support of an imperialist United States, they were determined to swallow East Germany, if necessary by force. The GDR, by contrast, had placed power in the hands of a working-class party, creating the first truly democratic German state. As an ally of the Soviet Union, which had borne the brunt of Hitler's aggression and secured allied victory in World War II, East Germany represented a force for peace in Europe. This ideological perspective on the German Problem, sharply different from that of the Federal Republic, informed GDR foreign policy discourse, to one degree or another, over the entire postwar period. Amid the transition from cold war in the 1950s to detente in the 1960s and 1970s and the new cold war of the 1980s, however, East Berlin's approach to nationalism, militarism, and the lessons of history also converged with Bonn's in significant respects.

During the cold war of the early 1950s GDR leaders, like their counterparts in the FRG, openly articulated to the goal of reunification. Walter Ulbricht and the other German communists who assumed leadership positions in the Soviet zone of occupation did not envision themselves as the architects of a separate East German state. Even as they erected a one-party dictatorship, they underscored their commitment to a peaceful, united, and socialist Germany. They attacked the combination of the Western zones into the FRG and construed the founding of the GDR in October 1949 as a reluctant response. In his first address as the president of the new state Wilhelm Pieck underscored its "provisional" status and urged Germans to "apply all their powers to overcoming the division of Germany."[2] The GDR leadership subsequently made several reunification proposals and came out in support of Stalin's 1952 offer of unity in exchange for German neutrality. Only after the June 1953 workers' uprising in East Berlin and Soviet intervention to crush it did East German leaders make the construction of socialism in the GDR their top priority.

For East Berlin, as for Bonn, the shift in emphasis away from the pursuit of national unity toward internal consolidation dovetailed with integration into international institutions. The GDR became part of the Warsaw Pact in 1956, a year after the Federal Republic joined NATO. A

---

2. Address of October 11, 1949, *Dokumente zur Außenpolitik der Regierung der Deutschen Demokratischen Republik* vol. 1 (East Berlin: Rürren and Loening, 1954), 12–19. See also Pieck's address in support of the Stalin Note, March 11, 1952, ibid., 398–403. A classic account of the establishment of SED rule is Wolfgang Leonhard, *Child of the Revolution* (Chicago: Regnery, 1958).

member of the Soviet-sponsored Council of Mutual Economic Assistance, it increasingly enmeshed its economy with that of its eastern neighbors, while maintaining some trade links with the Federal Republic and the West. The GDR's integration into the Soviet bloc, and the more international orientation that accompanied it, did not signify a clear break with established national goals. Ulbricht continued to call for reunification, and the SED floated several plans for an all-German confederation in the late 1950s and early 1960s. But these initiatives, like GDR and Soviet diplomacy in general, were predicated on the separate existence of two German states. They rejected free all-German elections as a first step in any reunification process—a long-standing West German demand—and insisted instead on full diplomatic recognition of the GDR as a precondition for any negotiations. The consolidation of the SED regime at home and stronger institutional links with the Soviet Union and its allies assumed clear priority over any pursuit of reunification.[3]

The shift to detente in the 1960s and early 1970s reinforced this trend. The construction of the Berlin Wall in 1961 proved a milestone. The flight of Germans from the GDR capital, East Berlin, to the Western sectors of the city threatened the survival of the communist regime and contributed to the Berlin Crisis. The Soviet ultimatum of November 1958, designed to drive the Western allies from Berlin, ultimately failed. But the resolution of the crisis—the construction of the Wall—provided a new starting point for East German domestic and foreign policy. With the flight of its citizens curtailed, the SED regime could finally embark on a full-fledged effort to construct a socialist economy. Moreover, the detente that followed the Berlin Crisis improved its prospects for greater international recognition. The Western powers proved more willing to pursue dialogue with Moscow on the basis of the status quo of the German division, and several developing countries exchanged ambassadors with East Berlin, provoking Bonn's wrath. Within this context the East German leadership played down national goals even further. A new constitution in 1968 did refer to the "German nation." But Ulbricht's diplomacy focused almost exclusively on full diplomatic recognition for the GDR.[4]

The onset of detente forced East German leaders—like their counterparts in Bonn—to rethink relations between both German states. While the Federal Republic struggled to come to terms with the existence of the

---

3. See, for example, Prime Minister Otto Grotewohl's address on the GDR's tenth anniversary, October 6, 1959, *Dokumente zur Außenpolitik,* vol. 7 (East Berlin: Rürren and Loening, 1960), 128–37.

4. See, for example, Ulbricht's address of October 6, 1964, *Dokumente zur Außenpolitik,* 12:144–62. On the Wall's impact, see A. James McAdams, *East Germany and Detente: Building Authority after the Wall* (Cambridge: Cambridge University Press, 1985).

GDR, East Berlin had to respond to Bonn's diplomatic offensive. Willy Brandt's new departure in 1969, summed up in his phrase "two states in Germany," offered SED leaders some recognition but upheld the unity of the German nation. The chancellor's offer to recognize the GDR as a sovereign state in exchange for greater contacts between Germans, East and West, provoked an anxious response in East Berlin. Ulbricht, insistent on full diplomatic recognition, blocked bilateral accords and obstructed Four-Power efforts to normalize the situation in Berlin. Only when Erich Honecker replaced him in May 1971—with Soviet backing—did the GDR leadership embrace inter-German detente. The core result was the Basic Treaty of December 1972, which set out a framework for bilateral ties in a variety of policy areas. Different views of the national issue persisted. While the Federal Republic remained committed to the goal of reunification, the GDR under Honecker propounded the existence of a separate *socialist* German nation. The upshot of the Basic Treaty, however, was a further shift, in both Bonn and East Berlin, away from concern with national unity toward the pursuit of economic and political cooperation on the basis of the status quo of the German division.[5]

During the 1970s East Germany became further embedded within international institutions and committed to the cause of detente. The normalization of inter-German ties cleared the way for both German states' membership in the United Nations in 1973. More important in the European context, both the FRG and the GDR became founding members of the Conference on Security and Cooperation in Europe that same year. The Western powers and the Federal Republic considered the CSCE, which culminated in the Helsinki Final Act in 1975, first and foremost an institutional framework for the pursuit of human rights in Warsaw Pact states. For the Soviet and GDR leaderships, by contrast, Helsinki signified Western ratification of the status quo of the German and European division. As Honecker insisted in August 1975, the Final Act marked "the finalization [*Fixierung*] of the territorial and political results of World War II and of postwar development in Europe."[6] From the late 1940s onward GDR leaders had highlighted their commitment to peace and a complete break with German militarism. But the struggle for international recognition had consumed most of their foreign policy energies. Only after the diplomatic breakthrough of the 1970s did they make questions of peace, security, and detente their avowed priorities.

---

5. For a programmatic statement of Honecker's views, see his address at the eighth SED party conference, May 3, 1971, *Dokumente zur Außenpolitik,* vol. 19 (East Berlin: Staatsverlag der Deutschen Demokraischen Republik, 1974), 44–56.

6. Honecker interview of August 5, 1975, *Dokumente zur Außenpolitik,* vol. 23 (1979), 751.

This shift in focus persisted amid the downturn in detente of the late 1970s and early 1980s. In the context of the new cold war East Berlin remained Moscow's loyal ally. The GDR leadership supported the Soviet invasion of Afghanistan and reacted nervously to the emergence of Solidarity in Poland, tightening its policy of limiting contacts between East Germans and the West [*Abgrenzung*]. As the INF crisis accelerated, however, Honecker remained an outspoken advocate of detente, underscoring what he considered the "international responsibility of the GDR on the dividing line between socialism and imperialism, the Warsaw Pact and NATO."[7] Like the Federal Republic, but with much less freedom of action, the GDR moved to shield inter-German detente from the new cold war. Economic links between both German states flourished during the early 1980s, most dramatically with Bonn's two DM 1 billion credits to East Berlin in 1983–84. And when NATO deployed first U.S. missiles in the FRG in late 1983, GDR leaders did not join fully in the Soviet denunciation of West German militarism. The persistence of inter-German detente, part of what Honecker referred to as a "coalition of reason" amid a difficult East-West climate, did not signal a revival of the issue of German national unity. Bonn played down the reunification issue, and East Berlin dismissed its relevance altogether. Instead, both German states emphasized their joint commitment to the preservation of peace and cooperation in Europe.[8]

The years that followed saw a continued emphasis on both German states' shared commitment to detente. During a brief encounter in Moscow in March 1985, on the eve of the fortieth anniversary of the end of World War II, Honecker and Helmut Kohl jointly underscored that "war must never again originate on German soil."[9] And during Honecker's first visit to the Federal Republic, in September 1987, both leaders underlined their support for further arms control and economic and political cooperation between the blocs. Although Kohl continued to articulate the goal of national unity, his policies reflected a pragmatic acceptance of the German division. And although the GDR leadership encouraged national themes in the historical scholarship of the 1980s, it

---

7. Address before the tenth SED party conference, April 11, 1981, *Dokumente zur Außenpolitik,* vol. 29 (1985), 34.

8. On inter-German relations in the mid-1980s, see A. James McAdams, *Germany Divided: From the Wall to Reunification* (Princeton: Princeton University Press, 1993), 158–64; Timothy Garton Ash, *In Europe's Name: Germany and the Divided Continent* (New York: Random House, 1993), chap. 3.

9. Joint statement on the occasion of Konstantin Chernenko's funeral, March 12, 1985, in *Innerdeutsche Beziehungen. Die Entwicklung der Beziehungen zwischen der Bundesrepublik Deutschland und der Deutschen Demokratischen Republik 1980–1986. Eine Dokumentation* (Bonn: Bundesministerium für innerdeutsche Beziehungen, 1986), 212.

did so in order to promote a GDR identity, not an all-German one. Toward the end of the decade ideas about the German role in Europe and the lessons of German history articulated in Bonn and East Berlin were more similar than at any previous juncture.[10]

The unexpected revolution in the GDR and subsequent rush to reunification swept away the SED regime. Contrary to the concerns of some observers, the transition from a democratic to a democratic and national revolution in East Germany—evident in the weeks after the fall of the Berlin Wall in November 1989—did not presage a national foreign policy turn. Controversies abounded in the new Germany around economic, social, and cultural issues. The integration of sixteen million new citizens into the Federal Republic did not, however, produce any significant new foreign policy accents. No political pressure emerged for a more national foreign policy orientation or a more unilateral Ostpolitik. A preoccupation with the economic reconstruction of the new federal states—and the low salience of foreign policy issues in general—can explain much of this continuity. But the postwar convergence between official German foreign policy discourse, East and West, also made a contribution. While East and West Germans disagreed on many things, they remained jointly committed to a break with the nationalist, militarist past.

---

10. On new trends in the GDR historiography of the 1980s, see Jan Herman Brinks, *Die DDR-Geschichtswissenschaft auf dem Weg zur deutschen Einheit: Luther, Friedrich II und Bismarck als Paradigmen politischen Wandels* (Frankfurt am Main: Campus 1992), chaps. 7–9.

Bibliography

Interviews by Author

Albrecht, Ernst. Governor of Lower Saxony, 1976–90. Bonn, June 23, 1992.
Bahr, Egon. Deputy Minister in the Federal Chancellory, 1969–72. Bonn, July 31, 1992.
Biedenkopf, Kurt. CDU General-Secretary, 1973–77. Bonn, May 11, 1992.
Genscher, Hans-Dietrich. German Foreign Minister, 1974–92. Bonn, August 24, 1992.
Geiger, Michaela. Chairwoman, Foreign Policy Working Group, CDU/CSU Parliamentary Group, 1987–90. Bonn, July 8, 1992.
Hupka, Herbert. Chairman, Expellee Group of the CDU/CSU, 1977–89. Bonn, January 22, 1992.
Kastl, Jörg. German Ambassador to the USSR, 1983–87. Cologne, March 30, 1992.
Schäuble, Wolfgang. Chairman, CDU/CSU Parliamentary Group, 1991–. Bonn, July 15, 1992.
Teltschik, Horst. Director, Foreign and Security Policy Department, Federal Chancellory, 1982–90. Gütersloh, July 16, 1992.
Vogel, Hans-Jochen. SPD Chairman, 1987–91, SPD Chancellor Candidate, 1983. Bonn, June 3, 1992.

Archives

Archiv für Christlich-Demokratische Politik
    Werner Marx papers (I-356)
    Alois Mertes papers (I-403)

Archiv für Christlich-Soziale Politik
    Franz Josef Strauß papers (RA 72, 87)

Archiv der sozialen Demokratie
    Willy Brandt papers (Depositum Willy Brandt)
    -Bundeskanzler und Bundesregierung, 1969–74 (BK)

Media Sources Cited

Bild
Bundespresseamt Nachtrichten
CDU Dokumentation
CDU Pressemitteilungen
Deutsche–Presse Agentur
Financial Times
Frankfurter Allgemeine Zeitung
Frankfurter Rundschau
Le Monde
Presseservice der SPD
Süddeutsche Zeitung
Neues Deutschland
Newsweek
New York Times
Der Spiegel
Der Stern
Washington Post
Die Woche

Documents, Document Collections, and Works by Political Figures

Acheson, Dean. *Present at the Creation: My Years in the State Department.* New York: Norton, 1969.

Adenauer, Konrad. *Erinnerungen.* 4 vols. Stuttgart: Deutsche Verlags-Anstalt, 1965–68.

———. *Reden, 1917–1967: Eine Auswahl.* Stuttgart: Deutsche Verlags-Anstalt, 1975.

Apel, Hans. *Der Abstieg: Politisches Tagebuch, 1978–1988.* Stuttgart: Deutsche Verlags-Anstalt, 1990.

Außenpolitik der Bundesrepublik Deutschland: Dokumente von 1949 bis 1994. Cologne: Verlag Wissenschaft und Politik, 1995.

Bahr, Egon. *Zu meiner Zeit.* Munich: Karl Blessing Verlag, 1996.

Ball, George W. *Diplomacy for a Crowded World: An American Foreign Policy.* Boston: Little, Brown, 1976.

Barzel, Rainer. *Auf dem Drahtseil.* Munich: Droemer-Knauer, 1978.

Birrenbach, Kurt. *Meine Sondermissionen: Rückblick auf zwei Jahrzehnte bundesdeutscher Außenpolitik.* Düsseldorf: Econ-Verlag, 1984.

Bölling, Klaus. *Die letzten 30 Tage des Kanzlers Helmut Schmidt. Ein Tagebuch.* Hamburg: Spiegel-Verlag, 1982.

Brandt, Willy. *A Peace Policy for Europe.* New York: Holt, Rinehart and Winston, 1969.

———. *Peace: Writings and Speeches of the Nobel Prize Peace Winner.* Bonn: Verlag Neue Gesellschaft, 1971.

————. *Der Wille zum Frieden: Perspektiven der Politik.* Frankfurt am Main: Hoffmann and Campe, 1971.

————. "Konrad Adenauer—Ein schwieriges Erbe für die deutsche Politik." In *Konrad Adenauer und Seine Zeit: Politik und Persönlichkeit des ersten Bundeskanzlers.* Ed. Dieter Blumenwitz et al., 99–107. Stuttgart: Deutsche Verlags-Anstalt, 1976.

————. *People and Politics: The Years 1960–1975.* Boston: Little, Brown, 1978.

————. *My Life in Politics.* London: Hamish Hamilton, 1992.

Buchstab, Günther, ed. *Adenauer: "Es mußte alles neu gemacht werden": Die Protokolle des CDU-Bundesvorstandes, 1950–1953.* Stuttgart: Klett-Cotta, 1986.

————, ed. *Adenauer: "Wir haben wirklich etwas geschaffen": Die Protokolle des CDU-Bundesvorstands, 1953–1957.* Düsseldorf: Droste, 1990.

Bulletin des Presse- und Informationsamtes der Bundesregierung. Bonn.

Carter, Jimmy. *Keeping Faith: Memoirs of a President.* New York: Bantam, 1982.

CDU. *Dritter Parteitag der Christlich-Demokratischen Union Deutschlands.* Bonn: CDU, 1952.

————. *18. CDU Bundesparteitag.* Bonn: CDU, 1971.

————. *32. Parteitag der CDU Deutschlands. Niederschrift.* Bonn: CDU, 1983.

————. *37. Parteitag der CDU Deutschlands. Niederschrift.* Bonn: CDU, 1989.

————. *Freiheit in Verantwortung: Grundsatzprogramm der Christlich Demokratischen Union Deutschlands.* Bonn: CDU, 1994.

Documents on Germany, 1944–1985. Washington, D.C.: U.S. Department of State, 1985.

Dokumente zur Außenpolitik der Regierung der Deutschen Demokratischen Republik. Vols. 1, 7. East Berlin: Rütten and Loening, 1954, 1960; Vols. 19, 23, 29. East Berlin: Staatsverlag der Deutschen Demokratischen Republik, 1974, 1979, 1985.

Fischer, Joschka. *Risiko Deutschland: Krise und Zukunft der deutschen Politik.* Cologne: Kiepenheuer and Witsch, 1994.

Foreign Relations of the United States, 1952–1954. Vol. 4. Washington, D.C.: U.S. Government Printing Office, 1980.

Foreign Relations of the United States, 1952–1954. Vol. 7. Washington, D.C.: U.S. Government Printing Office, 1986.

Friedmann, Bernhard. *Einheit statt Raketen: Thesen zur Wiedervereinigung als Sicherheitskonzept.* Herford: Busse Seewald, 1987.

Gaus, Günther. *Wo Deutschland liegt: Eine Ortsbestimmung.* Hamburg: Hamburg and Campe, 1983.

Genscher, Hans-Dietrich. *Rebuilding a House Divided: A Memoir by the Architect of Germany's Reunification.* New York: Broadway Books, 1998.

Gorbachev, Mikhail. *Perestroika. New Thinking for Our Country and the World.* New York: Harper and Row, 1987.

Grewe, Wilhelm G. *Rückblenden, 1976–1951.* Frankfurt am Main: Propylaen, 1979.

Hanrieder, Wolfram F., ed. *Helmut Schmidt: Perspectives on Politics.* Boulder: Westview, 1982.

Hintze, Peter, ed. *Die CDU-Parteiprogramme: Eine Dokumentation der Ziele und Aufgaben.* Bonn: Bouvier, 1995.

Innerdeutsche Beziehungen. Die Entwicklung der Beziehungen zwischen der Bundesrepublik Deutschland und der Deutschen Demokratischen Republik, 1980–1986. Eine Dokumentation. Bonn: Bundesministerium für innerdeutsche Beziehungen, 1986.

Kaiser, Jakob. *Wir haben Brücke zu sein: Reden, Äußerungen, und Aufsätze zur Deutschlandpolitik.* Cologne: Verlag Wissenschaft und Politik, 1988.

Kiesinger, Kurt Georg. *Stationen, 1949–1969.* Tübingen: Wunderlich, 1969.

———. *Die Große Koalition, 1966–1969: Reden und Erklärungen des Bundeskanzlers.* Stuttgart: Deutsche Verlags-Anstalt, 1979.

———. *Dunkle und helle Jahre: Erinnerungen, 1904–1958.* Stuttgart: Deutsche Verlags-Anstalt, 1989.

Kissinger, Henry. *The White House Years.* Boston: Little, Brown, 1979.

Klein, Hans. *Es begann im Kaukasus: Der entscheidende Schritt in die Einheit Deutschlands.* Berlin: Ullstein, 1991.

Knowlton, James, and Truett Cates, eds. *Forever in the Shadow of Hitler: Original Documents of the Historikerstreit, the Controversy Concerning the Singularity of the Holocaust.* Atlantic Highlands, N.J.: Humanities Press, 1993.

Kohl, Helmut, ed. *Der Kurs der CDU: Reden und Beiträge des Bundesvorsitzenden, 1973–1993.* Stuttgart: Deutsche Verlags-Anstalt, 1993.

———. *Wir setzen auf Sieg.* Bonn: CDU, 1994.

———. *"Ich wollte Deutschlands Einheit."* Berlin: Ullstein, 1996.

McGhee, George. *At the Creation of a New Germany: From Adenauer to Brandt.* New Haven: Yale University Press, 1989.

Mensing, Hans Peter, ed. *Adenauer: Briefe, 1945–1947.* Berlin: Siedler, 1983.

Oberndörfer, Dieter, ed. *Begegnungen mit Kurt Georg Kiesinger: Festgabe zum 80. Geburtstag.* Stuttgart: Deutsche Verlags-Anstalt, 1984.

Osterheld, Horst. *Außenpolitik unter Bundeskanzler Ludwig Erhard, 1963–1966: Ein dokumentarischer Bericht aus dem Kanzleramt.* Düsseldorf: Droste, 1992.

Pfleiderer, Karl Georg. *Politik für Deutschland: Reden und Aufsätze, 1948–1956.* Stuttgart: Deutsche Verlags-Anstalt, 1961.

Pflüger, Friedbert. *Deutschland driftet: Die konservative Revolution entdeckt ihre Kinder.* Düsseldorf: Econ-Verlag, 1994.

Rühe, Volker. *Deutschlands Verantwortung: Perspektiven für das neue Europa.* Frankfurt am Main: Ullstein, 1994.

Schabowski, Günter. *Das Politbüro: Ende eines Mythos.* Hamburg: Rowohlt, 1990.

Scharping, Rudolf. *Was jetzt zu tun ist.* Munich: Piper, 1994.

Schäuble, Wolfgang. *Der Vertrag: Wie ich über die deutsche Einheit verhandelte.* Stuttgart: Deutsche Verlags-Anstalt, 1991.

———. *Und der Zukunft zugewandt.* Berlin: Siedler, 1994.

Schäuble, Wolfgang, and Rudolf Seiters, eds. *Außenpolitik im 21. Jahrhundert: Die Thesen der jungen Außenpolitiker.* Bonn: Bouvier, 1996.

Schmidt, Helmut. *The Balance of Power: Germany's Peace Policy and the Super Powers.* London: William Kimber, 1971.

————. *Men and Powers: A Political Retrospective.* New York: Random House, 1989.

Schumacher, Kurt. *Kurt Schumacher: Reden—Schriften—Korrespondenzen, 1945–1952.* Berlin: Dietz, 1985.

SPD. *Protokoll der Verhandlungen und Anträge vom Parteitag der Sozialdemokratischen Partei Deutschlands vom 23.–27. November 1964 in Karlsruhe.* Bonn: Vorstand der SPD, 1964.

————. *Protokoll der Verhandlungen und Anträge vom Parteitag der Sozialdemokratischen Partei Deutschlands vom 1.–5. Juni in Dortmund.* Bonn: Vorstand der SPD, 1966.

————. *Protokoll der Verhandlungen und Anträge vom Parteitag der Sozialdemokratischen Partei Deutschlands vom März 1968 in Nürnberg.* Bonn: Vorstand der SPD, 1968.

————. *Grundsatzprogramm der Sozialdemokratischen Partei Deutschlands.* Bonn: Vorstand der SPD, 1990.

————. *Perspektiven einer neuen Außen-und Sicherheitspolitik.* Bonn: Vorstand der SPD, 1993.

————. *Protokoll vom außerordentlichen Parteitag Essen 25 Juni 1993.* Bonn: Vorstand der SPD, 1993.

Strauss, Franz Josef. *The Grand Design: A European Solution to German Reunification.* London: Weidenfeld and Nicolson, 1965.

————. *Die Erinnerungen.* Berlin: Siedler, 1989.

Teltschik, Horst. *329 Tage: Innenansichten der Einigung.* Berlin: Siedler, 1991.

Todenhöfer, Jürgen. *Ich denke deutsch: Abrechnung mit dem Zeitgeist.* Erlangen: Straube, 1989.

Verhandlungen des deutschen Bundestags. Stenographische Berichte. Bonn, 1949–.

Zimmermann, Friedrich. *Kabinettstücke: Politik mit Strauß und Kohl 1976–91.* Munich: Herbig, 1991.

Books and Journal Articles

Altenhof, Ralf, and Eckhard Jesse, eds. *Das wiedervereinigte Deutschland: Zwischenbilanz und Perspektiven.* Düsseldorf: Droste, 1995.

Anderson, Jeffrey J., and John B. Goodman. "Mars or Minerva? A United Germany in a Post–Cold War Europe." In *After the Cold War: International Institutions and State Strategies in Europe, 1989–1991.* Ed. Robert O. Keohane, Joseph S. Nye and Stanley Hoffmann, 23–62. Cambridge: Harvard University Press, 1993.

————. "Hard Interests, Soft Power, and Germany's Changing Role in Europe." In *Tamed Power: Germany in Europe.* Ed. Peter J. Katzenstein, 80–107. Ithaca: Cornell University Press, 1997.

Anderson, Jeffrey J., and Celeste A. Wallander. "Interests and the Wall of Ideas: Germany's Eastern Trade Policy after Unification." *Comparative Political Studies* 30, no. 6 (December 1997): 675–98.

Arend, Peter. *Die innerparteiliche Entwicklung der SPD, 1966–75.* Bonn: Eichholz, 1975.

Ashkenasi, Abraham. *Reformpartei und Außenpolitik: Die Außenpolitik der SPD Berlin-Bonn.* Cologne: Westdeutscher Verlag, 1968.

Banchoff, Thomas. "Historical Memory and German Foreign Policy: The Cases of Adenauer and Brandt." *German Politics and Society* 14, no. 2 (summer 1996): 36–53.

———. "German Policy towards the European Union: The Effects of Historical Memory." *German Politics* 6, no. 1 (April 1997): 60–76.

Baring, Arnulf. *Machtwechsel. Die Ära Brandt-Scheel.* Stuttgart: Deutsche Verlags-Anstalt, 1982.

———, ed. *Germany's New Position in Europe: Problems and Perspectives.* Oxford: Berg, 1994.

Baring, Arnulf, and Rupert Scholz, eds. *Eine neue deutsche Interessenlage? Koordinaten deutscher Politik jenseits von Nationalismus und Moralismus.* Cologne: Bachem, 1994.

Baun, Michael J. "The SPD and EMU: An End to Germany's All-Party Consensus on European Integration?" *German Politics and Society* 15, no. 3 (autumn 1997): 1–23.

Becker, Josef von, and Andreas Hillgruber, eds. *Die deutsche Frage im 19. und 20. Jahrhundert.* Munich: Vögel, 1983.

Bender, Peter. *Zehn Gründe für eine Anerkennung der DDR.* Frankfurt am Main: Fischer, 1968.

———. *Neue Ostpolitik: Vom Mauerbau bis zum Moskauer Vertrag.* Munich: Deutscher Taschenbuch Verlag, 1986.

———. "Der goldene Angelhaken: Entspannungspolitik und Systemwandel." *Aus Politik und Zeitgeschichte,* no. 14 (April 8, 1994): 11–15.

Berger, Stefan. *The Search for Normality: National Identity and Historical Consciousness in Germany since 1800.* Providence: Berghahn, 1997.

Bertram, Christoph. "The Power and the Past: Germany's New International Loneliness." In *Germany's New Position in Europe: Problems and Perspectives.* Ed. Arnulf Baring, 91–105. Oxford: Berg, 1994.

Besson, Waldemar. *Die Außenpolitik der Bundesrepublik: Erfahrungen und Maßstäbe.* Munich: Piper, 1970.

Blackbourn, David, and Geoff Eley. *The Peculiarities of German History: Bourgeois Society and Politics in Nineteenth-Century Germany.* Oxford: Oxford University Press, 1984.

Booz, Rüdiger Marco. *"Hallsteinzeit": Deutsche Außenpolitik, 1955–1972.* Bonn: Bouvier, 1995.

Boutwell, Jeffrey. *The German Nuclear Dilemma.* Ithaca: Cornell University Press, 1990.

Bracher, Karl Dietrich, Wolfgang Jäger, and Werner Link. *Republik im Wandel, 1969–1974: Die Ära Brandt.* Stuttgart: Deutsche Verlags-Anstalt, 1986.

Brand, Christoph-Matthias. *Souveränität für Deutschland.* Cologne: Verlag Wissenschaft und Politik, 1993.

Brauers, Christof. *Liberale Deutschlandpolitik, 1949–1969: Positionen der F.D.P. zwischen nationaler und europäischer Orientierung.* Hamburg: Lit, 1992.

Braunthal, Gerard. *The German Social Democrats since 1969: A Party in Power and Opposition.* Boulder: Westview, 1994.

Bredow, Wilfried von, and Rudolf H. Brocke. *Krise und Protest: Ursprünge und Elemente der Friedensbewegung in Westeuropa.* Opladen: Westdeutscher Verlag, 1987.

Bredow, Wilfried von, and Thomas Jäger, eds. *Neue deutsche Außenpolitik: Nationale Interessen in den internationalen Beziehungen.* Opladen: Leske and Budrich, 1993.

Brill, Heinz. *Geopolitik heute. Deutschlands Chance?* Frankfurt am Main: Ullstein, 1994.

Brinks, Jan Herman. *Die DDR-Geschichtswissenschaft auf dem Weg zur deutschen Einheit: Luther, Friedrich II und Bismarck als Paradigmen politischen Wandels.* Frankfurt am Main: Campus, 1992.

Brochhagen, Ulrich. *Nach Nürnberg: Vergangenheitsbewältigung und Westintegration in der Ära Adenauer.* Hamburg: Junius Verlag, 1994.

Bruns, Wilhelm. *Deutsch-deutsche Beziehungen: Prämisse, Probleme, Perspektiven.* Opladen: Leske and Budrich, 1984.

Buchheim, Hans. *Deutschlandpolitik, 1949–1972: Der politisch-diplomatische Prozeß.* Stuttgart: Deutsche Verlags-Anstalt, 1984.

Buczylowski, Ulrich. *Kurt Schumacher und die deutsche Frage.* Stuttgart: Seewald, 1973.

Bulmer, Simon. *The Domestic Structure of European Community Policy-Making in Germany.* New York: Garland, 1986.

Bulmer, Simon, and William Paterson. *The Federal Republic of Germany and the European Community.* London: Allen and Unwin, 1987.

———. "West Germany's Role in Europe: 'Man-Mountain' or 'Semi-Gulliver'?" *Journal of Common Market Studies* 28, no. 2 (December 1989): 95–117.

———. "Germany in the European Union: Gentle Giant or Emergent Leader?" *International Affairs* (London) 72, no. 1 (1996): 9–32.

Calleo, David. *The German Problem Reconsidered: Germany and the World Order, 1870 to the Present.* Cambridge: Cambridge University Press, 1978.

Carr, Jonathan. *Helmut Schmidt: Helmsman of Germany.* New York: St. Martin's Press, 1985.

Catudal, Honore M., Jr. *The Diplomacy of the Quadripartite Agreement on Berlin: A New Era in East-West Politics.* Berlin: Berlin Verlag, 1977.

Chickering, Roger. "The Quest for a Usable Kaisserreich." In *Imperial Germany: A Historiographical Companion.* Ed. Roger Chickering, 1–12. Westport, Conn.: Greenwood Press, 1996.

Cioc, Mark. *Pax Atomica: The Nuclear Defense Debate in West Germany during the Adenauer Era.* New York: Columbia University Press, 1988.

Clemens, Clay. "Beyond INF: West Germany's Centre-Right Party and Arms Control in the 1990s." *International Affairs* (London) 65, no. 1 (winter 1988–89): 55–74.

———. *Reluctant Realists: The Christian Democrats and West German Ostpolitik.* Durham: Duke University Press, 1989.

Conze, Werner. *Jakob Kaiser: Politiker zwischen Ost und West, 1945–1949.* Stuttgart: W. Kohlhammer, 1969.

Cooper, Alice Holmes. *Paradoxes of Peace: German Peace Movements since 1945.* Ann Arbor: University of Michigan Press, 1996.

Crawford, Beverly. "Germany's Unilateral Recognition of Croatia and Slovenia: A Case of Defection from Multilateral Cooperation." *World Politics* 48, no. 4 (July 1996): 482–521.

Czempiel, Ernst Otto. "SDI and NATO: The Case of the Federal Republic of Germany." In *Strategic Defense and the Western Alliance.* Ed. Sanford Lakoff and Randy Willoughby, 147–64. Lexington, Mass.: D. C. Heath, 1987.

Dahrendorf, Ralf. *Society and Democracy in Germany.* Garden City, N.J.: Doubleday, 1967.

Dedring, Klaus-Heinrich. *Adenauer—Erhard—Kiesinger: Die CDU als Regierungspartei 1961–69.* Pfaffenweiler: Centaurus, 1989.

Dehio, Ludwig. *Germany and World Politics in the Twentieth Century.* New York: Knopf, 1959.

———. *The Precarious Balance: Four Centuries of European Power Struggle.* New York: Knopf, 1962.

Deubner, Christian. *Deutsche Europapolitik: Von Maastricht nach Kerneuropa?* Baden-Baden: Nomos, 1995.

Deutsch, Karl W., and Lewis J. Edinger. *Germany Rejoins the Powers: Mass Opinion, Interest Groups, and Elites in Contemporary German Foreign Policy.* Stanford: Stanford University Press, 1959.

Diwald, Hellmut. *Geschichte der Deutschen.* Frankfurt am Main: Ullstein, 1978.

Doering-Manteuffel. *Die Bundesrepublik Deutschland in der Ära Adenauer: Außenpolitik und innere Entwicklung.* Darmstadt: Wissenschaftliche Buchgesellschaft, 1983.

———. "Konrad Adenauer—Jakob Kaiser—Gustav Heinemann: Deutschlandpolitische Positionen in der CDU." In *Die Republik der fünziger Jahre: Adenauers Deutschlandpolitik auf dem Prüfstand.* Ed. Jürgen Weber, 18–46. Munich: Olzog, 1989.

———, ed. *Adenauerzeit: Stand, Perspektiven und methodische Aufgaben der Zeitgeschichtsforschung (1945–1967).* Bonn: Bouvier, 1993.

Drummond, Gordon D. *The German Social Democrats in Opposition, 1949–1960: The Case against Rearmament.* Norman: University of Oklahoma Press, 1982.

Edinger, Lewis J. *Kurt Schumacher: A Study in Personality and Political Behavior.* Stanford: Stanford University Press, 1965.

Eley, Geoff. "Nazism, Politics and the Image of the Past: Thoughts on the West German *Historikerstreit.*" *Past and Present,* no. 121 (November 1988): 171–208.

Ely, John. "The *Frankfurter Allgemeiner Zeitung* and Contemporary National-Conservatism." *German Politics and Society* 13, no. 2 (summer 1995): 81–121.

Erdmenger, Klaus. *Das folgenschwere Mißverständis: Bonn und die sowjetische Deutschlandpolitik, 1949–1955.* Freiburg: Rombach, 1967.

Eschenburg, Theodor. *Jahre der Besatzung, 1945–1949.* Stuttgart: Deutsche Verlags-Anstalt, 1983.

Evans, Peter B., Harold K. Jacobson, and Robert D. Putnam, eds. *Double-Edged Diplomacy: International Bargaining and Domestic Politics.* Berkeley and Los Angeles: University of California Press, 1993.

Feld, Werner J. *West Germany and the European Community: Changing Interests and Competing Policy Objectives.* New York: Praeger, 1981.

Feldman, Lily Gardner. *The Special Relationship between West Germany and Israel.* Boston: Allen and Unwin, 1984.

————. "Germany and the EC: Realism and Responsibility." *Annals of the American Academy of Political and Social Science* 531 (January 1994): 25–43.

Fischer, Fritz. *Germany's Aims in the First World War.* New York: Norton, 1967.

————. *The War of Illusions: German Policies from 1911 to 1914.* New York: Norton, 1975.

————. "Twenty-Five Years Later: Looking Back at the 'Fischer Controversy' and Its Consequences." *Central European History* 21, no. 3 (September 1988): 207–23.

Foerster, Roland G., et al., eds. *Anfänge westdeutscher Sicherheitspolitik: 1945–1956.* 4 vols. Munich: R. Oldenbourg, 1982–97.

Foschepoth, Josef, ed. *Adenauer und die deutsche Frage.* Göttingen: Vandenhoeck and Ruprecht, 1988.

Frei, Norbert. *Vergangenheitspolitik: Die Anfänge der Bundesrepublik und die NS-Vergangenheit.* Munich: Beck, 1996.

Freymond, Jacques. *The Saar Conflict, 1945–1955.* New York: Praeger, 1960.

Friend, Julius W. *The Linchpin: French-German Relations, 1950–1990.* New York: Praeger, 1991.

Fritsch-Bournazel, Renata. "The French View." In *Germany between East and West.* Ed. Edwina Moreton, 64–82. Cambridge: Cambridge University Press, 1987.

————. *Confronting the German Question: Germans on the East-West Divide.* Oxford: Berg, 1988.

Garthoff, Raymond L. *Detente and Confrontation: American-Soviet Relations from Nixon to Reagan.* Washington, D.C.: Brookings Institution, 1985.

Garton Ash, Timothy. *In Europe's Name: Germany and the Divided Continent.* New York: Random House, 1994.

Gelman, Harry. *The Brezhnev Politburo and the Decline of Detente.* Ithaca: Cornell University Press, 1984.

Gillingham, John. *Coal, Steel, and the Rebirth of Europe, 1945–1955: The Germans and French from Ruhr Conflict to Economic Community.* Cambridge: Cambridge University Press, 1991.

Gillis, John R., ed. *Commemorations: The Politics of National Identity.* Princeton: Princeton University Press, 1994.

Goldstein, Judith, and Robert O. Keohane, eds. *Ideas and Foreign Policy: Beliefs, Institutions, and Political Change.* Ithaca: Cornell University Press, 1993.

Gordon, Phillip H. "The Normalization of German Foreign Policy." *Orbis* 38, no. 2 (spring 1994): 225–43.

————. *France, Germany, and the Western Alliance.* Boulder: Westview, 1995.

Gourevitch, Peter. "The Second Image Reversed: The International Sources of

Domestic Politics." *International Organization* 32, no. 4 (autumn 1978): 881–912.

Grabbe, Hans-Jürgen. *Unionsparteien, Sozialdemokratie und Vereinigte Staaten von Amerika, 1945–1966.* Düsseldorf: Droste, 1983.

Griffith, William E. *The Ostpolitik of the Federal Republic of Germany.* Cambridge: MIT Press, 1978.

Groeben, Hans von der. *Aufbaujahre der Europäischen Gemeinschaft: Das Ringen um den Gemeinsamen Markt und die Politische Union (1958–1966).* Baden-Baden: Nomos, 1982.

Gutjahr, Lothar. *German Foreign and Defence Policy after Unification.* London: Pinter, 1994.

Gutscher, Jörg Michael. *Die Entwicklung der FDP von ihren Anfängen bis 1961.* Königstein: Hain, 1984.

Haas, Ernst B. *The Uniting of Europe: Political, Social, and Economic Forces, 1950–1957.* Stanford: Stanford University Press, 1958.

Habermas, Jürgen. *Vergangenheit als Zukunft.* Zürich: Pendo-Verlag, 1991.

Hacke, Christian. *Die Ost-und Deutschlandpolitik der CDU/CSU: Wege und Irrwege der Opposition seit 1969.* Cologne: Verlag Wissenschaft und Politik, 1975.

―――. *Weltmacht wider Willen: Die Außenpolitik der Bundesrepublik Deutschland.* Frankfurt am Main: Ullstein, 1993.

―――. "Nationales Interesse als Handlungsmaxime für die Außenpolitik Deutschlands." In *Deutschlands neue Außenpolitik.* Ed. Karl Kaiser and Hanns W. Maull, 3–13. Munich: R. Oldenbourg, 1994.

Hacker, Jens. *Deutsche Irrtümer. Schönfärber und Helfershelfer der SED-Diktatur im Westen.* Berlin: Ullstein, 1992.

Haftendorn, Helga. *Security and Detente: Conflicting Priorities in German Foreign Policy.* New York: Praeger, 1985.

―――. "Entstehung und Bedeutung des Harmel-Berichtes der NATO von 1967." *Vierteljahreshefte für Zeitgeschichte* 40, no. 2 (April 1992): 169–221.

―――. "Gulliver in der Mitte Europas. Internationale Verflechtung und nationale Handlungsmöglichkeiten." In *Deutschlands neue Außenpolitik.* Vol. 1. Ed. Karl Kaiser and Hanns W. Maull, 129–52. Munich: R. Oldenbourg, 1994.

Hanrieder, Wolfram F. *West German Foreign Policy, 1949–1963: International Pressure and Domestic Response.* Stanford: Stanford University Press, 1967.

―――. *Germany, America, Europe: Forty Years of German Foreign Policy.* New Haven: Yale University Press, 1989.

―――, ed. *Arms Control, the FRG and the Future of East-West Relations.* Boulder: Westview, 1987.

Hartman, Geoffrey H., ed. *Bitburg in Moral and Political Perspective.* Bloomington: Indiana University Press, 1986.

Heep, Barbara D. *Helmut Schmidt und Amerika: Eine schwierige Partnerschaft.* Bonn: Bouvier, 1990.

Heidenheimer, Arnold J. *Adenauer and the CDU: The Rise of the Leader and the Integration of the Party.* The Hague: Nijhof, 1960.

Heitmann, Clemens. *FDP und neue Ostpolitik. Zur Bedeutung der deutschlandpoli-

tischen Vorstellungen der FDP von 1966 bis 1972. Sankt Augustin: COM-DOK, 1989.

Hellmann, Gunther. "Eine Flucht nach vorn ohne Ende? Die deutsch-französische Achse und die Vertiefung der europäischen Integration." *Aus Politik und Zeitgeschichte,* no. 3 (July 21, 1995): 19–27.

———. "Goodbye Bismarck? The Foreign Policy of Contemporary Germany." *Mershon International Studies Review* 40 (1996): 1–39.

———. "The Sirens of Power and German Foreign Policy: Who Is Listening?" *German Politics* 6, no. 2 (August 1997): 29–57.

Herf, Jeffrey. *War by Other Means: Soviet Power, West German Resistance, and the Battle of the Euromissiles.* New York: Free Press, 1991.

———. *Divided Memory: The Nazi Past in the Two Germanys.* Cambridge: Harvard University Press, 1997.

Heurlin, Bertel, ed. *Germany in Europe in the Nineties.* New York: St. Martin's Press, 1996.

Hildebrand, Klaus. *Von Erhard zur Grossen Koalition, 1963–1969.* Stuttgart: Deutsche Verlags-Anstalt, 1984.

———. *Das vergangene Reich: Deutsche Außenpolitik von Bismarck bis Hitler, 1871–1945.* Stuttgart: Deutsche Verlags-Anstalt, 1995.

Hillgruber, Andreas. *Deutsche Großmacht und Weltpolitik im 19. und 20. Jahrhundert.* Düsseldorf: Droste, 1977.

———. *Die Last der Nation: Fünf Beiträge über Deutschland und die Deutschen.* Düsseldorf: Droste, 1984.

———. *Zweierlei Untergang: Die Zerschlagung des Deutschen Reiches und das Ende des europäischen Judentums.* Berlin: Siedler, 1986.

Hirsch, Herbert. *Genocide and the Politics of Memory: Studying Death to Preserve Life.* Chapel Hill: University of North Carolina Press, 1995.

Hoffmann, Stanley. *The European Sisyphus: Essays on Europe, 1964–1994.* Boulder: Westview, 1995.

Hubel, Helmut, and Bernhard May. *Ein "normales Deutschland"? Die souveräne Bundesrepublik in der ausländischen Wahrnehmung.* Bonn: Europa Union Verlag, 1995.

Hubert, Peter, ed. *Grüne Außenpolitik: Aspekte einer Debatte.* Göttingen: Die Werkstatt, 1993.

Huelshoff, Michael G., Andrei S. Markovits, and Simon Reich, eds. *From Bundesrepublik to Deutschland: German Politics after Unification.* Ann Arbor: University of Michigan Press, 1993.

Huyn, Hans Graf. *Die Sackgasse: Deutschlands Weg in die Isolierung.* Stuttgart: Seewald, 1966.

Iggers, Georg G. *The German Conception of History: The National Tradition of Historical Thought from Herder to the Present.* Middletown, Conn.: Wesleyan University Press, 1983.

Ikenberry, G. John. "Constitutional Politics and International Relations." *European Journal of International Relations* 4, no. 2 (June 1998): 147–77.

Jachtenfuchs, Markus. "Ideen und internationale Beziehungen." *Zeitschrift für internationale Beziehungen* 2, no. 2 (1995): 417–43.

Jahn, Egbert, and Volker Rittberger, eds. *Die Ostpolitik der BRD: Triebkräfte, Widerstände, Konsequenzen.* Westdeutscher Verlag, 1984.

Jarausch, Konrad H. *The Rush to German Unity.* New York: Oxford University Press, 1994.

―――. "Normalisierung oder Re-Nationalisierung. Zur Umdeutung der deutschen Vergangenheit." *Geschichte und Gesellschaft* 21, no. 4 (1995): 571–84.

Jaspers, Karl. *Freiheit und Wiedervereinigung: Über Aufgaben deutscher Politik.* Munich: Piper, 1960.

Jäger, Wolfgang, and Werner Link. *Republik im Wandel, 1974–1982: Die Ära Schmidt.* Stuttgart: Deutsche Verlags-Anstalt, 1987.

Jentleson, Bruce W. *Pipeline Politics: The Complex Political Economy of East-West Energy Trade.* Ithaca: Cornell University Press, 1986.

Joffe, Josef. *The Limited Partnership: Europe, the United States, and the Burdens of Alliance.* Cambridge, Mass.: Ballinger, 1987.

Kaiser, Karl. *German Foreign Policy in Transition: Bonn between East and West.* London: Oxford University Press, 1968.

Kaiser, Karl, and Hanns W. Maull, eds. *Deutschlands neue Außenpolitik.* 3 vols. Munich: R. Oldenbourg, 1994–96.

Katzenstein, Peter J. *Policy and Politics in West Germany: The Growth of a Semisovereign State.* Philadelphia: Temple University Press, 1987.

―――. "United Germany in an Integrating Europe." In *Tamed Power: Germany in Europe.* Ed. Peter J. Katzenstein, 1–48. Ithaca: Cornell University Press, 1997.

―――, ed. *Tamed Power: Germany in Europe.* Ithaca: Cornell University Press, 1997.

Kehr, Eckart. *Der Primat der Innenpolitik: Gesammelte Aufsätze zur preussisch-deutschen Sozialgeschichte im 19. und 20. Jahrhundert.* Berlin: Walter de Gruyter, 1965.

Keithly, David M. *Breakthrough in the Ostpolitik: The 1971 Quadripartite Agreement.* Boulder: Westview, 1986.

Kelleher, Cathleen McArdle. *Germany and the Politics of Nuclear Weapons.* New York: Columbia University Press, 1975.

Keohane, Robert O. *International Institutions and State Power: Essays in International Relations Theory.* Boulder: Westview, 1989.

―――., ed. *Neorealism and Its Critics.* New York: Columbia University Press, 1986.

Keohane, Robert O., and Lisa L. Martin. "The Promise of Institutionalist Theory." *International Security* 20, no. 1 (summer 1995): 39–51.

Keohane, Robert O., Joseph S. Nye, and Stanley Hoffmann, eds. *After the Cold War: International Institutions and State Strategies in Europe, 1989–1991.* Cambridge: Harvard University Press, 1993.

Khong, Yuen Foong. *Analogies at War: Korea, Munich, Dien Bien Phu, and the Vietnam Decisions of 1965.* Princeton: Princeton University Press, 1992.

Kirchner, Emil J. "Genscher and What Lies Behind 'Genscherism.'" *West European Politics* 13, no. 2 (April 1990): 159–77.

Kitschelt, Herbert. "The 1990 German Federal Election and the National Unification: A Watershed in German Electoral History?" *West European Politics* 14, no. 4 (October 1991): 121–48.

Kleinmann, Hans-Otto. *Geschichte der CDU, 1945–1982.* Stuttgart: Deutsche Verlags-Anstalt, 1993.

Klönne, Arno. *Zurück zur Nation? Kontroversen zu deutschen Fragen.* Cologne: Diedrichs, 1984.

Kolinsky, Eva, ed. *The Greens in West Germany: Organisation and Policy Making.* Oxford: Berg, 1989.

Köhler, Henning. *Adenauer: Eine politische Biographie.* Frankfurt am Main: Ullstein, 1994.

Kramer, Jane. *The Politics of Memory: Looking for Germany in the New Germany.* New York: Random House, 1996.

Kreile, Michael. *Osthandel und Ostpolitik.* Baden-Baden: Nomos, 1978.

Küntzel, Matthias. *Bonn und die Bombe: Deutsche Atomwaffenpolitik von Adenauer bis Brandt.* Frankfurt am Main: Campus, 1992.

Küsters, Hans-Jürgen. *Die Gründung der europäischen Wirtschaftsgemeinschaft.* Baden-Baden: Nomos, 1982.

Lankowski, Carl F., ed. *Germany and the European Community: Beyond Hegemony and Containment?* New York: St. Martin's Press, 1993.

Lantis, Jeffrey S. "Rising to the Challenge: German Security Policy in the Post–Cold War Era." *German Politics and Society* 14, no. 2 (summer 1996): 19–35.

Lehmann, Hans Georg. *Der Oder-Neiße Konflikt.* Munich: Beck, 1979.

Leonhard, Wolfgang. *Child of the Revolution.* Chicago: Regnery, 1958.

Lindemann, Helmut. *Gustav Heinemann: Ein Leben für die Demokratie.* Munich: Kösel, 1978.

Little, Richard, and Steve Smith, eds. *Belief Systems and International Relations.* Oxford: Basil Blackwell, 1988.

Longerich, Michael. *Die SPD als "Friedenspartei"—mehr als nur Wahltaktik?* Frankfurt am Main: Lang, 1990.

Lösche, Peter, and Franz Walter. *Die FDP: Richtungsstreit und Zukunftszweifel.* Darmstadt: Wissenschaftliche Buchgesellschaft, 1996.

Loth, Wilfried, ed. *Die deutsche Frage in der Nachkriegszeit.* Berlin: Akademie Verlag, 1994.

Löwenthal, Richard. *Vom Kalten Krieg zur Ostpolitik.* Stuttgart: Seewald, 1974.

Löwke, Udo F. *Die SPD und die Wehrfrage: 1949 bis 1955.* Bonn: Verlag Neue Gesellschaft, 1976.

Lübbe, Hermann. *Abschied vom Superstaat. Vereinigte Staaten von Europa wird es nicht geben.* Berlin: Siedler, 1994.

Lucas, Michael R., ed. *The CSCE in the 1990s: Constructing European Security and Cooperation.* Baden-Baden: Nomos, 1993.

Maier, Charles S. *The Unmasterable Past: History, Holocaust, and German National Identity.* Cambridge: Harvard University Press, 1988.

———. *Dissolution: The Crisis of Communism and the End of East Germany.* Princeton: Princeton University Press, 1997.

Maier, Klaus A., and Bruno Thoss, eds. *Westintegration, Sicherheit und deutsche Frage: Quellen zur Außenpolitik in der Ära Adenauer.* Darmstadt: Wissenschaftliche Buchgesellschaft, 1994.

Markovits, Andrei S., and Philip S. Gorski. *The German Left: Red, Green and Beyond.* New York: Oxford University Press, 1993.

Markovits, Andrei S., and Simon Reich. *The German Predicament: Memory and Power in the New Europe.* Ithaca: Cornell University Press, 1997.

———, ed. *The Political Economy of West Germany: Modell Deutschland.* New York: Praeger, 1982.

Marshall, Barbara. *Willy Brandt: Eine politische Biographie.* Bonn: Bouvier, 1993.

Maser, Werner. *Helmut Kohl: Der deutsche Kanzler.* Frankfurt am Main: Ullstein, 1990.

Mastny, Vojtech. *Helsinki, Human Rights, and European Security: Analysis and Documentation.* Durham: Duke University Press, 1986.

———. *The Helsinki Process and the Reintegration of Europe, 1986–1991: Analysis and Documentation.* New York: New York University Press, 1992.

McAdams, A. James. *East Germany and Detente: Building Authority after the Wall.* Cambridge: Cambridge University Press, 1985.

———. *Germany Divided: From the Wall to Reunification.* Princeton: Princeton University Press, 1993.

McAdams, A. James, and John Torpey, eds. "The Past as Arsenal: Debating German Unification." *German Politics and Society* no. 30 (fall 1993).

Mead, Walter Russell. "The Once and Future Reich." *World Policy Journal* 7, no. 4 (autumn 1990): 593–638.

Mearsheimer, John J. "Back to the Future: Instability in Europe after the Cold War." *International Security* 15, no. 1 (summer 1990): 5–56.

———. "The False Promise of International Institutions." *International Security* 19, no. 3 (winter 1994–95): 5–49.

Meinecke, Friedrich. *The German Catastrophe: Reflections and Recollections.* Cambridge: Harvard University Press, 1950.

———. *Die Idee der Staatsräson in der neueren Geschichte.* Munich: R. Oldenbourg, 1957.

Merkl, Peter H. *German Unification in the European Context.* University Park: Pennsylvania State University Press, 1993.

Merseburger, Peter. *Der schwierige Deutsche: Kurt Schumacher.* Stuttgart: Deutsche Verlags-Anstalt, 1995.

Miller, Susanne, and Heinrich Potthoff. *Kleine Geschichte der SPD: Darstellung und Dokumentation, 1848–1983.* Bonn: Verlag Neue Gesellschaft, 1983.

Mintzel, Alf. *Die CSU: Anatomie einer konservativen Partei, 1945–1972.* Opladen: Westdeutscher Verlag, 1975.

Mommsen, Wolfgang J. "Gegenwärtige Tendenzen in der Geschichtsschreibung der Bundesrepublik." *Geschichte und Gesellschaft* 7, no. 2 (1981): 149–88.

Moravcsik, Andrew. "Negotiating the Single European Act: National Interests and Conventional Statecraft in the European Community." *International Organization* 45, no. 1 (winter 1991): 19–56.

————. "Taking Preferences Seriously: A Liberal Theory of International Politics." *International Organization* 51, no. 4 (autumn 1997): 513–53.

Morgan, Roger. *The United States and West Germany, 1945–1973: A Study in Alliance Politics.* London: Oxford University Press, 1974.

Morgenthau, Hans J. *Politics among Nations: The Struggle for Power and Peace.* New York: Knopf, 1948.

Morris, David B. "Bitburg Revisited: Germany's Search for Normalcy." *German Politics and Society* 13, no. 4 (winter 1995): 92–109.

Morsey, Rudolf, and Konrad Repgen, eds. *Adenauer-Studien III.* Mainz: Matthias-Grünewald-Verlag, 1974.

————. *Die Deutschlandpolitik Adenauers: Alte Thesen und neue Fakten.* Opladen: Westdeutscher Verlag, 1991.

Moses, John A. *The Politics of Illusion: The Fischer Controversy in German Historiography.* London: George Prior Publishers, 1975.

Müller, Harald, "German Foreign Policy after Reunification." In *The New Germany and the New Europe.* Ed. Paul B. Stares, 126–73. Washington, D.C.: Brookings Institution.

Nagle, John David. *The National Democratic Party: Right Radicalism in the Federal Republic of Germany.* Berkeley and Los Angeles: University of California Press, 1970.

Naimark, Norman M. *The Russians in Germany: A History of the Soviet Zone of Occupation, 1945–1949.* Cambridge: Harvard University Press, 1995.

Newhouse, John. *Cold Dawn: The Story of SALT.* New York: Holt, Rinehart and Winston, 1973.

Niclauß, Karlheinz. *Kanzlerdemokratie: Bonner Regierungspraxis von Konrad Adenauer bis Helmut Kohl.* Stuttgart: W. Kohlhammer, 1988.

Ninkovich, Frank A. *Germany and the United States: The Transformation of the German Question since 1945.* New York: Twayne Publishers, 1995.

Nipperdey, Thomas. *Nachdenken über die deutsche Geschichte: Essays.* Munich: Beck, 1986.

Noelle-Neumann, Elisabeth. "Öffentliche Meinung und Außenpolitik. Die fehlende Debatte in Deutschland." *Internationale Politik* 50, no. 8 (August 1995): 3–12.

Oldenbourg, Fred. *Sowjetische Deutschland-Politik nach den Treffen von Moskau und Bonn 1988–89.* Cologne: Bundesinstitut für ostwissenschaftliche und internationale Studien, 1989.

Oye, Kenneth A., Robert J. Lieber, and Donald Rothchild, eds. *Eagle Resurgent? The Reagan Era in American Foreign Policy.* Boston: Little, Brown, 1987.

Padgett, Stephen, ed. *Adenauer to Kohl: The Development of the German Chancellorship.* London: Hurst, 1994.

Paterson, William E. *The SPD and European Integration.* Lexington, Mass.: Lexington Books, 1974.

Pierson, Paul. "The Path to European Integration: A Historical Institutionalist Analysis." *Comparative Political Studies* 29, no. 2 (April 1996): 123–63.

————. "Path Dependence, Increasing Returns, and the Study of Politics." *Center for European Studies Working Paper Series,* no. 7.7 (1997).

Pittman, Avril. *From Ostpolitik to Reunification: West German–Soviet Political Relations since 1974.* Cambridge: Cambridge University Press, 1992.

Plock, Ernest D. *The Basic Treaty and the Evolution of East-West German Relations.* Boulder: Westview, 1986.

Plum, Werner, ed. *Ungewöhnliche Normalisierung: Beziehungen der Bundesrepublik Deutschland zu Polen.* Bonn: Verlag Neue Gesellschaft, 1984.

Polkinghorne, Donald E. *Narrative Knowing and the Human Sciences.* New York: State University of New York Press, 1988.

Pond, Elizabeth. *Beyond the Wall: Germany's Road to Unification.* Washington, D.C.: Brookings Institution, 1993.

Poppinga, Anneliese. *Konrad Adenauer. Geschichtsverständnis, Weltanschauung und politische Praxis.* Stuttgart: Deutsche Verlags-Anstalt, 1975.

Potthoff, Heinrich. *Die "Koalition der Vernunft": Deutschlandpolitik in den 80er Jahren.* Munich: Deutscher Taschenbuch Verlag, 1995.

Pridham, Geoffrey. *Christian Democracy in Western Germany: The CDU/CSU in Government and Opposition, 1945–1976.* London: Croom Helm, 1977.

Puhle, Hans-Jürgen. "Die neue Ruhelosigkeit: Michael Stürmers nationalpolitischer Revisionismus." *Geschichte und Gesellschaft* 13, no. 3 (1987): 382–99.

Putnam, Robert D. "Diplomacy and Domestic Politics: The Logic of Two-Level Games." *International Organization* 42, no. 3 (summer 1988): 427–60.

Rattinger, Hans. "Public Attitudes to European Integration in Germany after Maastricht: Inventory and Typology." *Journal of Common Market Studies* 32, no. 4 (December 1994): 525–40.

Ready, Brian. *The Fourth Reich.* London: Weidenfeld and Nicolson, 1995.

Regelsberger, Elfriede, Phillippe de Schoutheete de Tervarent, and Wolfgang Wessels, eds. *Foreign Policy of the European Union: From EPC to CFSP and Beyond.* Boulder: Lynne Rienner, 1997.

Ricoeur, Paul. *Time and Narrative.* Vol. 1. Chicago: University of Chicago Press, 1984.

Risse-Kappen, Thomas. *The Zero Option: INF, West Germany, and Arms Control.* Boulder: Westview, 1988.

Rittberger, Volker, and Frank Schimmelfennig. "Deutsche Außenpolitik nach der Vereinigung: Realistische Prognosen auf dem Prüfstand." *Tübinger Arbeitspapiere zur internationalen Politik und Friedensforschung,* no. 28 (1997).

Ritter, Gerhard. *Staatskunst und Kriegshandwerk: Das Problem des "Militarismus" in Deutschland.* Vol. 1. Munich: R. Oldenbourg, 1954.

———. *The German Problem: Basic Questions of German Political Life, Past and Present.* Columbus: Ohio State University Press, 1965.

Rosenau, James N., ed. *Domestic Sources of Foreign Policy.* New York: Free Press, 1967.

Rosenbaum, Ulrich. *Rudolf Scharping.* Berlin: Ullstein, 1993.

Röpke, Wilhelm. *The Solution of the German Problem.* New York: G. P. Putnam's Sons, 1947.

Ruggie, John Gerard, ed. *Multilateralism Matters: The Theory and Praxis of an Institutional Form.* New York: Columbia University Press, 1993.

Rummel, Reinhardt, ed. *Toward Political Union: Planning a Common Foreign and Security Policy in the European Community.* Baden-Baden: Nomos, 1992.

Rupieper, Hermann-Josef. *Der besetzte Verbündete: Die amerikanische Deutschlandpolitik, 1949–1955.* Opladen: Westdeutscher Verlag, 1991.

Rühl, Lothar. *Mittelstreckenwaffen in Europa: Ihre Bedeutung in Strategie, Rüstungskontrolle und Bündnispolitik.* Baden-Baden: Nomos, 1987.

Schmid, Günther. *Entscheidung in Bonn: Die Entstehung der Ost- und Deutschlandpolitik, 1969–1970.* Cologne: Verlag Wissenschaft und Politik, 1979.

Schmoeckel, Reinhard, and Bruno Kaiser. *Die vergessene Regierung: Die Große Koalition 1966–1969 und ihre langfristigen Wirkungen.* Bonn: Bouvier, 1991.

Schoenbaum, David, and Elizabeth Pond. *The German Question and Other German Questions.* New York: St. Martin's Press, 1996.

Schöllgen, Gregor. *Die Macht in der Mitte Europas: Stationen deutscher Außenpolitik von Friedrich dem Großen bis zur Gegenwart.* Munich: Beck, 1992.

———. *Angst vor der Macht: Die Deutschen und ihre Außenpolitik.* Berlin: Ullstein, 1992.

———. "National Interest and International Responsibility: Germany's Role in World Affairs." In *Germany's New Position in Europe: Problems and Perspectives.* Ed. Arnulf Baring, 35–49. Oxford: Berg, 1994.

Schulz, Eberhard. *An Ulbricht führt kein Weg mehr vorbei: Provozierende Thesen zur deutschen Frage.* Hamburg: Hoffmann and Campe, 1967.

Schulz, Eberhard, and Peter Danylow. *Bewegung in der deutschen Frage? Die ausländischen Besorgnisse über die Entwicklung in den beiden deutschen Staaten.* Bonn: Europa Union Verlag, 1984.

Schwabe, Klaus, ed. *Die Anfänge des Schuman-Plans, 1950–51.* Baden-Baden: Nomos, 1988.

Schwartz, Thomas Alan. *America's Germany: John J. McCloy and the Federal Republic of Germany.* Cambridge: Harvard University Press, 1991.

Schwarz, Hans-Peter. *Vom Reich zur Bundesrepublik: Deutschland im Widerstreit der außenpolitischen Konzeptionen in den Jahren der Bestatzungsherrschaft, 1945–1949.* Neuwied: Lucherhand, 1980.

———. *Die Ära Adenauer: Gründerjahre der Republik, 1949–57.* Stuttgart: Deutsche Verlags-Anstalt, 1981.

———. *Die gezähmten Deutschen: Von der Machtbessessenheit zur Machtvergessenheit.* Stuttgart: Deutsche Verlags-Anstalt, 1985.

———. *Adenauer: Der Aufstieg, 1876–1952.* Stuttgart: Deutsche Verlags-Anstalt, 1986.

———. "Das Deutsche Dilemma." In *Deutschlands neue Außenpolitik.* Vol. 1. Ed. Karl Kaiser and Hanns W. Maull, 81–97. Munich: R. Oldenbourg, 1994.

———. *Die Zentralmacht Europas. Deutschlands Rückkehr auf die Weltbühne.* Berlin: Siedler, 1994.

———, ed. *Die Legende von der verpaßten Gelegenheit: Die Stalin Note vom 10. März 1952.* Stuttgart: Belser, 1982.

Schweigler, Gebhard. *West German Foreign Policy: The Domestic Setting.* New York: Praeger, 1984.

Schwilk, Heimo, and Ulrich Schacht, eds. *Die selbstbewußte Nation.* Frankfurt am Main: Ullstein, 1995.

Senghaas, Dieter. "Was sind deutsche Interessen?" In *Politik ohne Projekt? Nach-*

denken über Deutschland. Ed. Siegfried Unseld, 463–91. Frankfurt am Main: Suhrkamp, 1993.

———. "Deutschlands verflochtene Interessen." *Internationale Politik* 50, no. 8 (August 1995): 31–37.

Sethe, Paul. *Zwischen Bonn und Moskau.* Frankfurt am Main: Scheffler, 1956.

Siebenmorgen, Peter. *Gezeitenwechsel: Aufbruch zur Entspannungspolitik.* Bonn: Bouvier, 1990.

Simonian, Haig. *The Privileged Partnership: Franco-German Relations in the European Community, 1969–84.* Oxford: Clarendon Press, 1984.

Skocpol, Theda. *Protecting Soldiers and Mothers: The Political Origins of Social Policy in the United States.* Cambridge: Harvard University Press, 1992.

Sodaro, Michael J. *Moscow, Germany and the West from Khrushchev to Gorbachev.* Ithaca: Cornell University Press, 1990.

Soell, Hartmut. *Fritz Erler: Eine politische Biographie.* Vol. 1. Berlin: Dietz, 1976.

Sontheimer, Kurt. *Die verunsicherte Republik: Die Bundesrepublik nach 30 Jahren.* Munich: Piper, 1979.

———. *Zeitenwende? Die Bundesrepublik zwischen alter und alternativer Politik.* Hamburg: Hoffmann and Campe, 1983.

Steininger, Rolf. *Wiederbewaffnung: Die Entscheidung für einen westdeutschen Verteidigungsbeitrag.* Erlangen: Straube, 1989.

———. *The German Question: The Stalin Note of 1952 and the Problem of Reunification.* New York: Columbia University Press, 1990.

———. "John Foster Dulles, the European Defense Community, and the German Question." In *John Foster Dulles and the Diplomacy of the Cold War.* Ed. Richard H. Immerman, 79–108. Princeton: Princeton University Press, 1990.

Steinmo, Sven, Kathleen Thelen, and Frank Longstreth, eds. *Structuring Politics: Historical Institutionalism in Comparative Analysis.* Cambridge: Cambridge University Press, 1992.

Stent, Angela. *From Embargo to Ostpolitik: The Political Economy of West German-Soviet Relations.* Cambridge: Cambridge University Press, 1981.

Stürmer, Michael. *Das ruhelose Reich: Deutschland 1866–1918.* Berlin: Severin and Siedler, 1983.

———. *Die Grenzen der Macht: Begegnung der Deutschen mit der Geschichte.* Berlin: Siedler, 1992.

———. "Deutsche Interessen." In *Deutschlands neue Außenpolitik.* Ed. Karl Kaiser and Hanns W. Maull, 1:39–61. Munich: R. Oldenbourg, 1994.

Szabo, Stephen F. *The Diplomacy of German Unification.* New York: St. Martin's Press, 1992.

Talbott, Strobe. *Deadly Gambits: The Reagan Administration and the Stalemate in Nuclear Arms Control.* New York: Knopf, 1984.

Taylor, A. J. P. *The Course of German History.* London: Hamilton, 1945.

Treverton, Gregory F. *The Dollar Drain and American Forces in Germany: Managing the Political Economics of Alliance.* Athens: Ohio University Press, 1978.

Tucker, Robert W., and Linda Wrigley, eds. *The Atlantic Alliance and Its Critics.* New York: Praeger, 1983.

Ulam, Adam B. *Dangerous Relations: The Soviet Union in World Politics, 1970–1982.* New York: Oxford University Press, 1983.

Ullman, Richard H. *Securing Europe.* Princeton: Princeton University Press, 1991.

Van Oudenaren, John. *Detente in Europe: The Soviet Union and the West since 1953.* Durham: Duke University Press, 1991.

Veen, Hans-Joachim, Norbert Lepszy, and Peter Mnich. *The Republikaner Party in Germany: Right-Wing Menace or Protest Catchall?* Westport, Conn.: Praeger, 1993.

Venrohr, Wolfgang, ed. *Die deutsche Einheit kommt bestimmt.* Bergisch Gladbach: Gustav Lübbe Verlag, 1982.

Walker, Martin. "Overstretching Teutonia: Making the Best of the Fourth Reich." *World Policy Journal* 12, no. 1 (spring 1995): 1–18.

Waltz, Kenneth N. *Theory of International Politics.* Reading, Mass.: Addison-Wesley, 1979.

———. "The Emerging Structure of International Politics." *International Security* 18, no. 2 (autumn 1993): 44–79.

Wassermann, Sherri L. *The Neutron Bomb Controversy: A Study in Alliance Politics.* New York: Praeger, 1983.

Wehler, Hans-Ulrich. *Die Gegenwart als Geschichte: Essays.* Munich: Beck, 1995.

Weidenfeld, Werner. *Konrad Adenauer und Europa. Die geistigen Grundlagen der westeuropäischen Integrationspolitik des ersten Bonner Bundeskanzlers.* Bonn: Europa Union Verlag, 1976.

Whetten, Lawrence L. *Germany East and West: Conflicts, Collaboration, and Confrontation.* New York: New York University Press, 1980.

White, Hayden. *The Content of the Form: Narrative Discourse and Historical Representation.* Baltimore: Johns Hopkins University Press, 1987.

Wiegandt, Manfred H. "Germany's International Integration: The Rulings of the German Federal Constitutional Court on the Maastricht Treaty and the Out-of-Area Deployment of German Troops." *American University Journal of International Law and Policy* 10 (winter 1995): 889–916.

Wilker, Lothar. *Die Sicherheitspolitik der SPD, 1956–1966: Zwischen Wiedervereinigungs- und Bündnisorientierung.* Bonn: Verlag Neue Gesellschaft, 1977.

Yee, Albert S. "The Causal Effects of Ideas on Policies." *International Organization* 50, no. 1 (winter 1996): 69–108.

Zelikow, Philip, and Condoleezza Rice. *Germany Unified and Europe Transformed: A Study in Statecraft.* Cambridge: Harvard University Press, 1995.

Zerubavel, Yael. *Recovered Roots: Collective Memory and the Making of Israeli National Tradition.* Chicago: University of Chicago Press, 1995.

Zimmer, Matthias. *Nationales Interesse und Staatsräson: Zur Deutschlandpolitik der Regierung Kohl, 1982–1989.* Paderborn: Schöningh, 1992.

Zitelmann, Rainer, ed. *Adenauers Gegner. Streiter für die Einheit.* Erlangen: Straube, 1991.

Zitelmann, Rainer, Michael Großheim, and Karlheinz Weißmann, eds. *Westbindung: Chancen und Risiken für Deutschland.* Frankfurt am Main: Ullstein, 1993.

Index